MW00980993

Sinews of War and Trade

Sinews of War and Trade

Shipping and Capitalism in the Arabian Peninsula

Laleh Khalili

London • New York

First published by Verso 2020

1 3 5 7 9 10 8 6 4 2

Verso
UK: 6 Meard Street, London W1F 0EG
US: 20 Jay Street, Suite 1010, Brooklyn, NY 11201
versobooks.com

Verso is the imprint of New Left Books

ISBN-13: 978-1-78663-481-8
ISBN-13: 978-1-78663-483-2 (UK EBK)
ISBN-13: 978-1-78663-484-9 (US EBK)

British Library Cataloguing in Publication Data
A catalogue record for this book is available from the British Library

Library of Congress Cataloging-in-Publication Data
Names: Khalili, Laleh, author.
Title: Sinews of war and trade : shipping and capitalism in the Arabian Peninsula / Laleh Khalili.
Description: London ; New York : Verso, 2020. | Includes bibliographical references and index. | Summary: "On the map of global trade, China is now the factory of the world. A parade of ships full of raw commodities-iron ore, coal, oil-arrive in its ports, and fleets of container ships leave with manufactured goods in all directions. The oil that fuels China's manufacturing comes primarily from the Arabian peninsula. Much of the material shipped from China are transported through the ports of Arabian peninsula, Dubai's Jabal Ali port foremost among them. China's 'maritime silk road' flanks the peninsula on all sides. Sinews of War and Trade is the story of what the making of new ports and shipping infrastructure has meant not only for the Arabian peninsula itself, but for the region and the world beyond. The book is an account of how maritime transportation is not simply an enabling companion of trade, but central to the very fabric of global capitalism. The ports that serve maritime trade, logistics, and hydrocarbon transport create racialised hierarchies of labour, engineer the lived environment, aid the accumulation of capital regionally and globally, and carry forward colonial regimes of profit, law and administration"-- Provided by publisher.
Identifiers: LCCN 2019052101 (print) | LCCN 2019052102 (ebook) | ISBN 9781786634818 (hardback) | ISBN 9781786634849 (ebook)
Subjects: LCSH: Shipping--Arabian Peninsula. | Capitalism--Arabian Peninsula. | Arabian Peninsula--Commerce. | Arabian Peninsula--Economic conditions.
Classification: LCC HE559.A73 K43 2020 (print) | LCC HE559.A73 (ebook) | DDC 387.5/440953--dc23
LC record available at https://lccn.loc.gov/2019052101
LC ebook record available at https://lccn.loc.gov/2019052102

Typeset in Sabon LT by Hewer Text UK Ltd, Edinburgh
Printed and bound by CPI Group (UK) Ltd, Croydon CR0 4YY

For Clare Hemmings and Kris Muhlner
for the sustenance of love, pleasure and friendship
over the years

. . . whatever is given
Can always be reimagined

Seamus Heaney, 'The Settle Bed'

Where are your monuments, your battles, martyrs?
Where is your tribal memory? Sirs,
in that grey vault. The sea. The sea
has locked them up. The sea is History.

Derek Walcott, 'The Sea Is History'

Contents

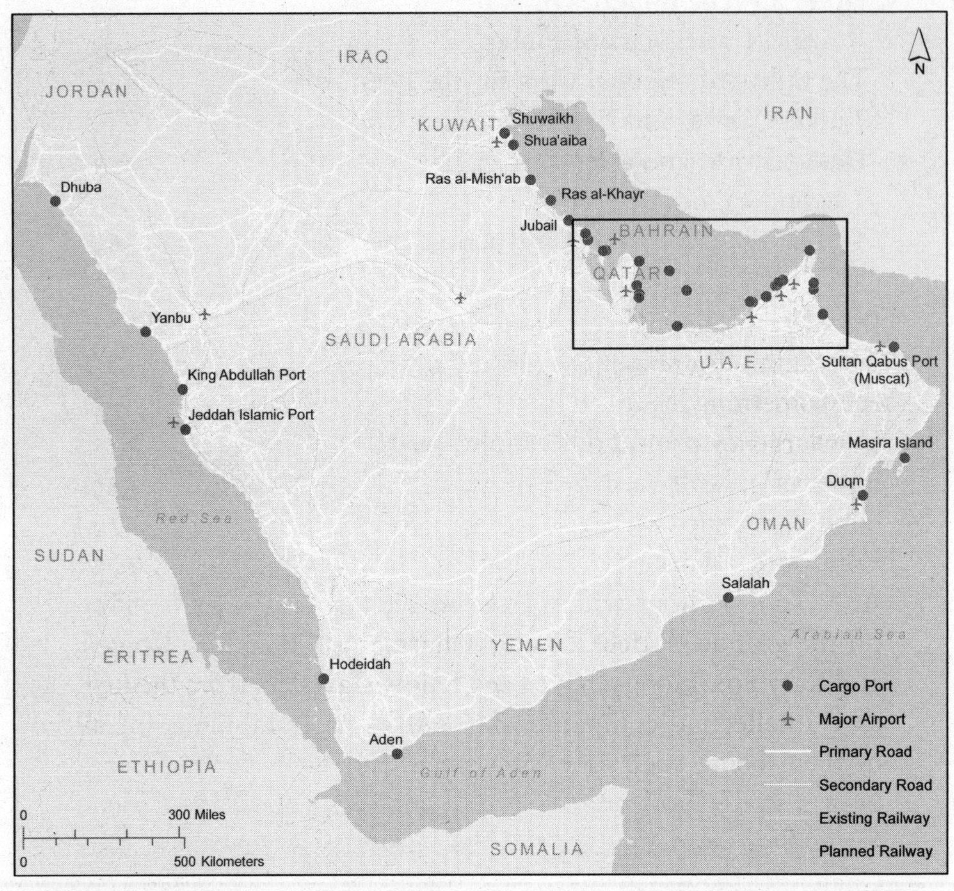
IRAQ
JORDAN
KUWAIT
Shuwaikh
Shua'aiba
IRAN
Ras al-Mish'ab
Ras al-Khayr
Dhuba
Jubail
BAHRAIN
QATAR
Yanbu
SAUDI ARABIA
U.A.E.
Sultan Qabus Port (Muscat)
King Abdullah Port
Jeddah Islamic Port
Masira Island
Duqm
Red Sea
OMAN
SUDAN
Salalah
YEMEN
Arabian Sea
ERITREA
Hodeidah
Cargo Port
Major Airport
Aden
Primary Road
ETHIOPIA
Gulf of Aden
Secondary Road
Existing Railway
SOMALIA
Planned Railway
0
300 Miles
0
500 Kilometers
N

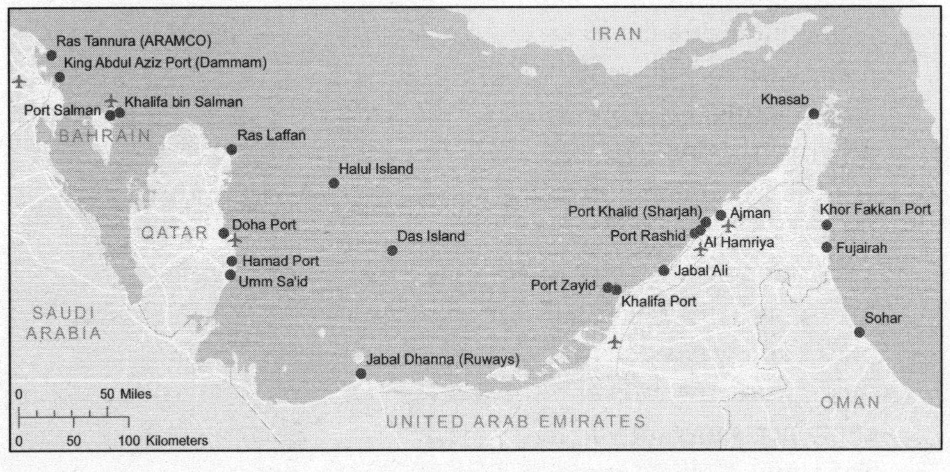
Ras Tannura (ARAMCO)
IRAN
King Abdul Aziz Port (Dammam)
Khalifa bin Salman
Port Salman
Khasab
BAHRAIN
Ras Laffan
Halul Island
Port Khalid (Sharjah)
Ajman
Khor Fakkan Port
QATAR
Doha Port
Port Rashid
Das Island
Al Hamriya
Fujairah
Hamad Port
Jabal Ali
Umm Sa'id
Port Zayid
Khalifa Port
SAUDI ARABIA
Sohar
Jabal Dhanna (Ruways)
0
50 Miles
OMAN
UNITED ARAB EMIRATES
0
50
100 Kilometers

Acknowledgements

David Hansen-Miller planted the seeds of this project when I was flailing for something totally new, something really different, something less bloody and grim to research after my counterinsurgency project had wound down (and 'beaches and bars in Beirut' wasn't cutting it as a long-term proposition). He also hooked me up with the lovely people at the International Transport Workers' Federation, and especially Jeremy Anderson, without whom this project would not have gotten off the ground. Rafeef Ziadah, Charmaine Chua, Deb Cowen, and Katy Fox-Hodess have been fellow travellers from the first, their intellectual companionship all the more fabulous for all of them being such kickass women. Rafeef in particular has been a marvellous colleague and sounding board and friend throughout. I am grateful to Fahad Bishara, Rosie Bsheer, John Chalcraft, Neve Gordon, Toby Craig Jones, Johan Mathew, Catherine Rottenberg, and Al Withrow for reading the whole manuscript or substantial portions thereof and for giving exact and exacting, lucid, constructive feedback. John Gall made me re-write the introduction to appeal to an audience beyond academia. I am humbled by their patience, their generosity and their friendship.

In the glorious three years I set aside to be a student in a field I initially knew so little about, I visited a great many places and was aided by a great many people. Foremost among them were the officers and crew of the two CMA CGM container ships on which I travelled, *Corte Real* in February 2015 and *Callisto* in August 2016. The seafarers were, to a person, open, thoughtful, astute, patient, and immensely helpful in answering all my random questions and explaining the details of shipping work. Their insights about the ports we visited, about work aboard ships, about their lives and feelings at sea and at home, all flow through the veins of this book, even if I have not named them here, even in places where the subject or the time period seemingly doesn't have anything to do with them. I also want to thank Horatio Clare, whose *Financial Times* piece published in advance of his beautiful *Down to the Sea in Ships*, made me realise I could travel on freighters as a passenger.

On shore, numerous lovely people gave of their time for interviews or port tours or introduced me to people they knew far away from London. Some of these interviews and visits were foundational or transformative for my thinking and this project. I especially want to thank Jairus Banaji (for perspicacious conversations and very useful introductions in Mumbai); Fahad Bishara (for sharing his Arabic language sources and scanning books and chapters and sending them along with the kind of generosity with one's precious research materials I have rarely seen in the academy, and also for his stern corrections of immensely embarrassing errors in the first draft of the manuscript); Captain Roy Faccy (who taught me many things about Aden and about the business of shipping); Lamya Harub (for introducing me to so many crucial people in Oman); Antony Joseph (of the Forward Seamen's Union of India for an unforgettable introduction to and hospitality in Kerala); Simeon Kerr (for imparting his incisive insights in Dubai); Ryan Kim (for enlightening conversations about migrants' rights in Manila); Bilal Malkawi (of ITF Middle East, for sharing his ideas and stories); Munzir Naqvi (for being such a great tour guide in Mumbai); Keith Nutall (then of Gulftainer, for a foundational visit to the port of Khor Fakkan); Vicente Rafael (for brilliant introductions in Manila); and Maria Rashid (for setting up such a productive interview for me in Karachi).

Thank you to Sebastian Budgen for his terse emails, endless (and endlessly useful) references, and for wanting this book in the first place. Thanks are due to Eseld Imms for the amazing maps she has created for this book and for the website named after it. I am so impressed with the care and scrupulousness of my amazing copyeditor, Sarah Grey, and the rest of the wonderful Verso staff – especially Duncan Ranslem – for their efficiency and professionalism (and sense of humour).

Also thanks to the archivists at American University of Beirut, the British Petroleum archives, Durham University Archives, Georgetown University Archives, Imperial War Museum, the India Office Records, Liverpool Maritime Museum, London Metropolitan Archives, National Maritime Museum in Greenwich, the UK and US National Archives, the Trades Union Congress Archives at Warwick University; and the librarians and archivists at the American University of Beirut and the British Library. I could not quite believe it when the Economic and Social Research Council of Britain decided to fund this project and the delightful and enlightening fieldtrips, container ship journeys, and archival visits it entailed (ES/L002833/1). For that, I thank them. My immense gratitude to colleagues at my former employer, SOAS University of London, and especially Charles Tripp, for their generosity in allowing me such a long time away from the quotidian business of the Department. I have been generously invited to give talks at many places and hosted by many brilliant colleagues and friends. Your questioning, prodding, suggestions, criticisms, and conversations over wine or coffee or meals have sharpened my arguments here. I hope you recognise your intellectual contributions.

Finally, I want to acknowledge the people who make my extra-academic life a feast and therefore hospitable to teaching, research and writing, which, no matter how pleasurable, are after all *work*. Love and gratitude to Clare, Catherine and Neve, Katharine (and the B&M posse) in London, Kris in Washington,

DC and Bret in Atlanta, Lisa Hajjar, Sonya Knox and the whole of the Beirut gang (in Lebanon and in exile), and last and definitely not least the original NYC gang – Leslie and Akiva, Jessica and Colin, Geoff and Alex, Jason and Nikki, Tanisha, and Heather – for the habits of friendship, conviviality, and commensality all through the decades. May and Pablo only get more hilarious, creative, brilliant, engaged and engaging, and a joy to be around the older they get. They have nothing to do with this project and that is just as it should be. And thank you Al, my 'F1', for your immense love and affection, magical companionship and fabulous storytelling, restorative breakfasts and salades niçoise, goofy jokes and terrible singing, and especially for the ridiculous amounts of fun we have.

Introduction

Shipping statistics illuminate the contours of an astonishing story about contemporary capitalism and trade. Ninety per cent of the world's goods travel by ship. Crude oil, carried in tankers, constitutes nearly 30 per cent of all maritime cargo; almost 60 per cent of world trade in oil is transported by sea. While containerised cargo accounts for some 23 per cent of all dry cargo by volume, it constitutes 70 per cent of all world cargo by value. But despite the aesthetic and political prominence of container shipping, 44 per cent of all dry-cargo shipping by volume is still bulk commodities (coal, grain, iron ore, bauxite, and phosphate rock).[1] But these numbers do not give a sense of the scale of the ports exporting or receiving these cargoes. Nor do they give a sense of the tremendous transformations in maritime transportation that have remade the seas and the shores and the port cities. Today, working cargo harbours are no longer central to the lives of port cities. They are often far away, behind layers of barbed wire and security – invisible, even forgotten. As ports and ships become ever more distended, they have also aspired to automation, with fewer and fewer seafarers and stevedores.

On the map of global trade, China is now the factory of the world. A parade of ships full of raw commodities – iron ore, coal, oil – arrive in its ports, and fleets of container ships leave with manufactured goods in all directions. The oil that fuels China's manufacturing comes primarily from the Arabian Peninsula. Much of the material shipped from China is transhipped through the ports of the Arabian Peninsula, Dubai's Jabal Ali foremost among them. China's 'maritime silk road' flanks the Peninsula on all sides. The Peninsula has long been a node of trade between Europe and Asia, and in the nineteenth century it became an irreplaceable British command post and anchorage on the route to India. But the transformations that the internationalisation of capital and the commodification of oil have wrought, including creating titanic maritime infrastructures, are something else altogether. This book is the story of these maritime infrastructures and how they work, then and now.

Cities of Salt is a magisterial novel about the coming of oil to Arabia. No other Arabic-language text chronicles the cataclysm of capital on the coasts of Arabia in such coruscating detail as Abdulrahman Munif – himself a petroleum engineer – did. In a scene recounted from the viewpoint of sceptical Arab observers standing on the shore of Qatif in Eastern Arabia, he describes the arrival of the petroleum-extraction equipment:

> The traffic of ships never slowed or stopped. Some were small and others were as huge as mountains, and from these ships came endless new things – no one could imagine what they were or what they were for. With the cargoes that mounted and piled up came men from no one knew where, to do God only knew what. All day they unloaded the heavy cargoes, tied them with strong ropes and hoisted them higher than the ships themselves. Who was pulling them up? How were they raised? Everyone was possessed by numb fear as they watched the huge crates rising in the sky, with no one pulling them up. Even the man on the deck of the ship who pushed the tremendous crates with one hand, moving them from one side to the other, seemed to the watchers on shore more a demon than a man.[2]

In writing this story of demonic upheavals, Munif was supremely alive to what was needed to make oil companies sovereigns in Arabia. Not only did lives have to be undone and redone, but spaces and places had to be redrawn. Munif records the banal details that most accounts elide: new, large ports were needed to facilitate unearthing petroleum in some places and turning the wheels of commerce in others. Between 1933, when oil was discovered in Bahrain, and the late 1960s, when it was feverishly exploited in the United Arab Emirates (UAE) and Oman, the shores of the Arabian Peninsula were monumentally reshaped. This redrawing of maps and the rapid construction of harbours epitomise the stupendous changes in global capital. New ports, new harbours, new coastal conurbations, new industrial megalopolises, new oil terminals and breakwaters and jetties and piers arose out of the mudflats of the Gulf, the jagged coral-reef coasts of the Red Sea. The pearling, fishing, and dhow trades, for which many of the Peninsula havens had long been known, were overshadowed by ports hosting cargo boats, very large crude carriers (VLCCs), and roll-on/roll-off (ro/ro) ships carrying thousands of automobiles. Harbours and warehouses shifted out of city centres to far-flung suburbs. So much of the machinery of capital has been made inaccessible, invisible, hidden behind the veils of security and bureaucracy and distance.

This book is the story of what the making of these new ports and shipping infrastructures has meant for the Peninsula, the region, and the world beyond. Reflected 'in the murky mirrors of distant waters'[3] is that maritime transportation is not simply an enabling adjunct of trade but is central to the very fabric of global capitalism. Maritime trade, logistics, and hydrocarbon transport are the clearest distillation of how global capitalism operates today. The maritime transport enterprise displays this tendency through its engineering of the lived environment: transforming 'natural' features of the world into juridical ones, creating new spaces, structures, and infrastructures that aim at (though rarely achieve) frictionless accumulation and circulation of capital; creating fictive commodities, financial fetishes, and ever more innovative forms of speculation; and creating racialised hierarchies of labour.

Think of a port as a bundle of routes and berths, of roads and rails leading away, of free zones and warehouses and the people who make and populate them. The sea routes are evanescent – whether they are ephemeral foam in the wake of a ship or digital fragments flowing through wires. When harbours are built, the material that goes into the concrete comes not only from this land but from the sea and from other places. Sometimes the roads and rail are built long after the ports, as if in an afterthought. Sometimes the free zones are built before the ports, as if in a fond wish. Geographical features near ports and harbours are remade into legal categories to facilitate their exploitation. Commercial rules; the law, in its multilayered, multivalent complexity; and transnational tribunals all reinforce some version of maritime economic and political relations. All are meant to magic into being the intercourse of commerce.

This is a book about the landside labourers who build the ports and work in them: their collective struggles, their migrations, and their gains and losses. It is also about shipboard workers, their racialisation over the centuries, and the work they do today, with eyes trained to gaze far to sea. I write about the colonial continuities of capital, and about finance and insurance and subterfuge and paternalism and pressure that are the hallmarks of these ports; about kings and bureaucrats, advisers and courtiers, and merchants and industrialists, and middlemen and brokers. And, of course, war – and the mutually constitutive relationship between violence and maritime commerce.

But this book is also specifically about the Arabian Peninsula, written from the sea, gazing at the shores. The historical accounts of the Peninsula are often radically bifurcated – a great deal of excellent works tell the story of the Peninsula as a node in historical Indian Ocean trade; many more modern accounts recount the story of a world undone and redone by oil. If maritime trade is spoken of, it is often in the context of the former, not the latter. No matter that the ports in the Peninsula are some of the biggest and highest-volume in the world. Or that there are more of them, and more people working in them, than ever in history. Or that the connections they forge – not just to destinations for petroleum and petroleum products – are global conduits not just for cargo, but for migrants, capital, new financial instruments, management regimes, and legal categories. This book is what Michael Pearson has called an 'amphibious' story, 'moving between the sea and the land'[4] in telling the story of maritime transportation infrastructures in the Peninsula.

My interest in the area arose partially because of how the ports of the Peninsula seem to manifestly crystallise the confluence of military/naval interest, capital accumulation, and labour. I was also interested in the region because I have found that so much writing about the Peninsula exceptionalises the area or focusses on tired old scholarly clichés (whether around rentierism or the security role of the Persian Gulf). I have wanted to better understand a region whose fortunes are so tightly tied to not only other Arab countries of the Middle East but to South Asia, East Africa, East Asia, and the metropoles of Europe and North America.

The book draws on my research in several archives, including US and UK national archives, India Office Records, the UK Maritime Museum archives, the papers of Lloyd's of London at the Liverpool Maritime archives, those of Grey Mackenzie/P&O at the London Metropolitan Archives, the British Petroleum archives, papers related to Aramco and Oman at Georgetown University Archives, and several other university archives in the US and UK where private papers of relevant historical figures are held. Other research materials include back issues of a vast range of newspapers, trade magazines, business journals and the like (some via online databases, others from the dusty shelves of libraries); memoirs, poetry, and novels written by people in the region, in businesses related to the region, or visiting the region; and vast repositories of statistics and reports produced by transnational organisations, think tanks, and management consulting firms, and the region's governments. I also draw on landside visits to most of the main cargo ports of the region (except for those in Saudi Arabia and Yemen), interviews with a range of businessmen, government officials, workers, activists, and others with stakes in the business throughout the Peninsula, as well as my own travel on two different container ships (some of the largest on the seas today) which afforded me shipboard visits to the ports in the regions (including Jeddah in Saudi Arabia).

This is an untidy book. It is curious about everything and hungry to tell stories. Mike Davis writes about one of the sprawling chapters in his idiosyncratic, absorbing, magisterial *City of Quartz* that 'I became so attached to every sacred morsel of facts about picket fences and dog doo-doos that I failed to edit the chapter down to a reasonable length. I soon came to fear that I had made a suicidal mistake. "No one", I told myself, "will ever read this".'[5]

I also became obsessed with everything maritime: ports and ships and the routes that led to them. The strange conjunctures of capitalism and trade and migrant labour and geopolitics and oil and dirt and filth and violence that make the sector are no less fascinating because they are made so invisible.

As sprawling as the book may be, it does not aim to be comprehensive. It does not sketch out reviews of scholarly literature, nor does it mention all possible sources about a given subject (though it cites whatever it quotes or paraphrases and what ideas have influenced its arguments). I have not alluded to a huge swathe of academic scholarship not because I did not read it or because I did not deem it worthy, but because this book wanted to do something else: it wanted to tell stories. Stories about how ports and maritime transport infrastructures have emerged out of the conjuncture of so many histories, struggles, conflicts, and plans (half-formed, implemented, and failed).

The first four chapters of the book are about four factors that constitute a functioning port: routes, harbours, legal infrastructures and zones, and land transport. Chapter 1 looks at how ports anchor sea routes – whether they are mapped on the sea or in the route-pricing indices of maritime exchanges and freight derivative markets. Plans to build harbours are rarely about objective or neutral calculations of cost. Politics and geopolitics matter, as chapter 2 makes clear. But environmental considerations matter a lot less, at least to the planners. The construction of harbours transforms fragile and coastal marine ecosystems, not just where ports are built but in faraway places from which construction materials are extracted. Chapter 3 deals with the legal presences and absences that are the virtual scaffolding of maritime trade. Arbitration courts and the mapping of geophysical features to legal categories all speak to the complex legal apparatuses capitalism needs to facilitate the building of ports. But laws and regulations held in abeyance – as they are in free zones or special economic zones that so often flank ports – are also crucial in creating the pulsating economic macro-organisms that port systems are today. Chapter 4 ties the ports to their hinterlands by drawing out the variegated history of the land transport that carries goods away from or to the port on roads and rail.

The next three chapters are about the people who have played roles in the making and operating of ports. Chapter 5 is about international, regional, and local capitalists and merchants, bankers and insurance companies, and political and technical experts who had a hand in the transformation of maritime trade in the Peninsula. Chapters 6 and 7 focus on landside and shipboard workers: the racialisation of their labour; the legal, migratory, and technical systems that have been used to discipline them; and the ways they have struggled for better workplace conditions and for political causes.

The final chapter of the book is about war and the bounties it has provided for shipping in most of the Peninsula – though not Yemen. Though war stories are woven through the fabric of the book, in chapter 8 I focus on how wartime has so often been the impetus and setting for the rise of military and civilian logistics and benefitted the ports of the region that have sided with metropolitan or imperial powers.

In all, this book makes a case that mercantile histories, colonial pasts, and the stories of empires of free trade indelibly shape today's shipping practices. It insists that we gaze at invisible infrastructures, forgotten histories of struggle, and hidden and recognisable relations of power. It is a book about the sinews of capitalism and conflict.

1
Route-Making

> We think of paths as existing only on land, but the sea has its paths too, though water refuses to take and hold marks . . . Sea roads are dissolving paths whose passage leaves no trace beyond the wake, a brief turbulence astern. They survive as conventions, tradition, a sequence of coordinates, as a series of waymarks, as dotted lines on charts, and as stories and songs.
>
> Robert Macfarlane, *The Old Ways*

The first time I travelled on a freighter, I boarded *CMA CGM Corte Real* in Malta in a Mediterranean winter. Though the headquarters of CMA CGM is in a building designed by Zaha Hadid in Marseille, the company's European transport hub is in Malta. Malta's free-port designation protects shippers from taxes on transhipments (goods that are passing through Malta from the port of origin to their final destination), while its proximity to the Middle East, Africa, and Europe makes it a geographically convenient distribution centre for goods to be transhipped from there. At that time, *Corte Real* was, at 366 metres long, one of the largest CMA CGM ships, and, because of its length and width, it could not berth at all the ports that dot the company's maps of places it does business. Marsaxlokk in Malta has gantry cranes with arms broad enough to oblige *Corte Real's* width, and berths long enough to allow the ship to fit alongside, and its harbour has been dredged deep enough to accommodate laden ships easily.

The village of Marsaxlokk teems with international seafarers, and buses full of crew members and officers arriving to board ships or leaving to go home ferry between its modest hotels and the sun-drenched airport. The day I came aboard, the officers of *Corte Real* were ashen-faced with hangovers, though warmly welcoming. The city of Valletta, some ten kilometres away, is known for its bars and nightclubs, and its proximity and ebullient atmosphere make it a welcoming port of call for the seafarers. The sailors were also relieved to be in the Mediterranean, after having come from Bremerhaven and Antwerp through the Bay of Biscay, where, predictably, the sea had been unsettled. The other two passengers on the ship told me awed stories of the ship listing forty-five degrees in the storm. They'd had to tie down all furniture in their cabins to prevent it from flying around when the ship hit the trough of a gigantic wave.

I travelled on *Corte Real* in February 2015, just before a dramatic collapse in global trade. Marseille ordered the ship to steam at speed to its next port of call, Khor Fakkan on the Gulf of Oman, a newish port in the Emirate of Sharjah, one of CMA CGM's hubs and at the time one of *Journal of Commerce*'s top fifty ports in the world. As we arrived near Khor Fakkan, we saw dozens of tankers at anchor near the port of Fujairah, one of the busiest petrochemical terminals in the Middle East. After Khor Fakkan, our ship was to head to Jabal Ali, then and now the biggest port in the Middle East and the ninth busiest container port in the world, where I was to disembark and fly home. Because of congestion at Jabal Ali, *Corte Real* slowed down considerably after Khor Fakkan and spent a day or so at anchor while a berth became free at the port. Because the world trade in goods was still at full throttle, the containers transporting cargo from the industrial ports of northern Europe to the Middle East and onwards to China were all full and the arrangement of containers both below and above deck was dense, with boxes stacked high and blocking the view out of my cabin's porthole.

By contrast, in August 2016, the containers were placed much less densely on the deck of *CMA CGM Callisto*. All the way to

Jeddah (the penultimate destination of the route segment I was taking) I had a clear view from the porthole. On that second journey, *Callisto* had scheduled stops at Damietta (Egypt), Beirut (Lebanon), and Jeddah (Saudi Arabia) before arriving in Jabal Ali. However, a day or so after leaving Malta, the ship's master was directed to also make a stop at the port of Mersin in Turkey, between Beirut and entry into the Suez Canal. This detour entailed spending half a day at Beirut, then steaming north at speed from Beirut to Mersin. The arrival in Mersin was also a bit of an adventure. The port of Mersin had only just extended its berths to accommodate the largest ships, and the quays were still half finished. What concerned the captain of *Callisto*, however, was that, despite the berths having been extended, the breakwaters for the port were far too narrow for easily manoeuvring a ship as gargantuan as *Callisto*. Throughout this trip, we did not really have to wait at anchor anywhere – surprisingly, not even at Jabal Ali – because ports were nowhere as congested as they had been the previous year. The last-minute detour to Mersin was added, to the chagrin of the crew and officers of the ship, in order to make the trip profitable. The decline in oil prices which made fuel cheaper for each trip than the previous year, and therefore the *ad hoc* addition of a port of call, had a lower marginal cost and a potential to earn a bit more for the shipping company. The captain and crew did not much like these lightning stops, though, because the length of the stopover was too short to make a visit to the town practical and because arrival and departure are often the most stressful portion of any journey, requiring the attention and work of all crew members on board.

Corte Real's cargo had been loaded at the industrial harbours of northern Europe and seemed to contain basic materials for chemical manufacturing, high-tech medical equipment, and a disassembled yacht being transported to China. *Callisto* had very few full containers loaded at those industrial ports, and a great deal of what it took on at Damietta, Beirut, and Mersin consisted of refrigerated containers. Presumably, given the agricultural facilities and hinterlands of those three ports, the reefers (the refrigerated containers) were laden with fruits and vegetables and other farm products. I say 'presumably' because I could not view the bills of lading, but the hazardous goods documents indicated that not many of the reefers contained toxic materials (which are often shipped in refrigerated containers in order to ensure their stability).

Aboard both ships, we had to convoy on several occasions. Ships form convoys for safety or to follow prescribed routes. As expected, we had to form a cortège through the Suez Canal. A significant proportion of the canal is still one-way and either the southbound or northbound convoys must remain in bypass bays in the Great Bitter Lake until the other convoy has completely passed it and gone through the other one-way portion of the canal. But our ship also had to convoy with other ships upon arrival at Jabal Ali, because the approach channel from the anchorage to the port is surprisingly narrow; ships run aground far more often than one would imagine for such a significant port. In the Red Sea, ships are required to keep to their own lanes, with northbound ships closer to the coasts of Asia and southbound ships steaming along the African coast. Allowances had to be made in the ships' routes for offshore oil and gas platforms, coral islands just under the surface of the sea, and tiny volcanic islets strewn near the coast, especially near the Bab al Mandab.

Another locale for convoying was along the coast of Yemen. Companies and navies often recommend that ships convoy together when passing through the southern Red Sea and the Gulf of Aden. At the height of piracy in the mid-2000s, the convoys were escorted by EU or NATO antipiracy forces or by naval vessels of individual European or Asian countries. The antipiracy convoys kept as far as possible from the African coast. They travelled along predrawn routes, marked and updated on naval charts.

When I was travelling on *Callisto*, the ship did not have the same imperative for speed as *Corte Real* and was commanded to slow down considerably in order to preserve fuel. *Corte Real* had also been ordered to steam closer to the coasts of Yemen and Oman to shorten its route. The ship thus held very close to the coast, and we could clearly see the dramatically jagged mountains of Arabia rising from the steamy shores. CMA CGM ships only bunker (or take on fuel) in certain countries because they get better deals in some ports, but also because the bunkering fuel in some ports is reputed to be adulterated.[1] Both *Corte Real* and *Callisto* flew the British Red Ensign flag and had to follow European and British rules on sulphur emissions and other environmental regulations. Therefore, they could only take low-sulphur, untainted, uncontaminated bunkers on board. This also limited which ports were deemed appropriate for refuelling.

Port	Annual bunker sale (millions of tonnes)	Last year available
Singapore	42.4	2014
Fujairah	24.0	2013
Rotterdam	10.6	2013
Hong Kong	7.4	2012
Antwerp	6.5	2012

Table 1.1 – World's biggest bunkering ports[2]

The differences in routes indicate that the delivery of specific commodities from a port of origin to a destination does not necessarily determine the path of travel. The specific qualities of ports that become nodes of trade matter: how updated their facilities are, how deep their harbours, what bunkering services they provide. Global factors also matter: a fall in trade saw many containers being shipped to China entirely empty. The volume of cargo shipped from one site to another in turn determines freight rates on those routes. The price of oil affects bunkering rates and therefore the unit cost of transportation by sea. But a ship's route is not the outcome of a series of rational calculations. CMA CGM is, in some ways, distinct from the other European shipping firms with which it competes. The firm has Middle Eastern roots, with its founders hailing from Syria and Lebanon. A quarter of the company's shares are, at the time of this writing, held by a major Turkish shipping and mining conglomerate, the Yıldırım Group. CMA CGM has also long had shipping alliances with United Arab Shipping Company, the firm originally owned by several countries of the Arabian Peninsula. Many of CMA CGM's hubs *and* smaller feeder ports (ports that receive transhipments from the hubs) are in the Middle East, and the sinuous routes that connect its European and Asian termini often snake through North African, Arab, and Turkish ports.

The routes that shipping companies or naval guards or international antipiracy organisations devise, for everyday shipping as well as in seas designated dangerous, so often seem 'naturally' made. Unlike markings on land, which the earth holds across time and space, the crossing of ships on the deep leaves little trace but the foam that forms in the wake. Yet shipping routes – or, more accurately, their representation on charts and maps and in the myriad documents of corporate planning – have a solidity, a durability that their marine ephemerality belies.

A range of political factors (including technological changes, economic calculations, and social upheavals) can spell the end of one route and the birth of another over the course of time. In the age of steam, ships are not beholden to wind and current patterns as they were in the age of sail, and routes are determined by the ports strung along them. Some ports remain constant and important: Jeddah, as the port of Mecca, has always mattered in the making of pilgrims' sea routes and has been a crucial stop on the Red Sea, despite being flanked by perilous coral shoals. Aden was one of the earliest imperial coaling stations for Britain and for nearly a century and a half its most important strategic port in the Indian Ocean. The emergence of Jabal Ali (and its smaller cousins Khor Fakkan, Port Khalifa, Hamad, and Salalah, among others) in the Arabian Peninsula calls for an explanation: what accounts for such a proliferation of destination ports, when the population of the Peninsula is only around 60 million?

The answer is that everything from technological change – the coming of steam and the invention of telegraphs, tankers, container ships, and internet cables – to the end of empires and the emergence of new nation-states can shift the contours of these routes across the water. But this doesn't happen in a uniform way. The technological innovations that remake communication and transportation sometimes reinforce existing routes and, at other times, redraw them. In the Arabian Peninsula, especially before the coming of oil, pilgrimage and the Suez Canal were the factors that determined *where* sea routes were pinned to the land.

But routes are not only prescribed by the exigencies of travel. What cargo is carried, and from where and in what volumes, determines the rates charged for routes. Routes are not only evanescent paths through the sea or lines upon the map, but also a series of calculations about costs and freight rates. The moment routes are quantified by way of pricing, they – the routes themselves, not what travels on them – can also become commodities to be speculated upon. So many of the ingredients of route-making in the age of sail shaped the paradoxes of our permanently transient routes; today, many of those old routes are embodied in the digital pathways of market models.

Admiralty Charts and the Making of Routes

Proudly, as always, the ships will set sail
for Madras, Algeria and Singapore;
in an office bent over some nautical maps
I'll make calculations in ledger books.

Nikos Kavvadias, 'Mal du Départ'

In the wheelhouse of the freighters on which I travelled, Admiralty Charts corresponding to our coordinates were spread on a table and updated every hour with a notation in pencil tracing our sea route. The wheelhouse abounded with electronic devices, and the captain and his officers directed the ship using global positioning systems (GPS) and radar. Nevertheless, the conventions of seafaring – at least for this shipping company – required that the ship's officers regularly update these gorgeous charts. The charts recorded depths, forbidden areas, coastal zones, submarine ammunition dumping grounds, port approaches, and less frequent and often fascinating notations about whales, anomalous magnetic zones, volcanic activity, and treacherous reefs that had been sighted but not confirmed. On this route, the one legend that was repeated consistently across all charts was a warning about taking care with dragging the anchor along the seabed for fear of snagging submarine cables and pipelines.

The charts were a palimpsest of past pencilled routes, erased and replaced on every trip. The lines seemed to follow more or less the same latitudes and longitudes on every trip. Like the rhumb lines which connected ports on seventeenth-century European maps,[3] these pencilled lines showed the persistence of certain routes. Many – at least those that have not been erased by war or 'natural' disaster or a gradual decline in the importance of a port – are hundreds of years old, if not older. Some connect the harbours of the Arabian Peninsula and the Persian coast to their counterparts on East African or Indian shorelines, and further to Southeast Asian archipelagos and China. Others trace coastal connections around the Peninsula, or across narrower seas – the Red Sea, for example – and on to nearby shores.

Before the age of steam, sailing ships were largely captive to currents, winds, and especially to the monsoons of the Arabian Sea, whose winds dictated the direction of travel for ships. The 'huge sum of free energy provided by the monsoons'[4] was at once the most significant barrier to *and* the biggest advantage for determining the timing and routes of maritime trade. The monsoon systems allowed the ships to sail with the winds, and because of the predictability of the seasons, monsoon winds determined the dates for sailing to and from the facing coasts of the western Indian Ocean. The south-western monsoon blows from June through September from the Himalayas towards the Arabian coasts. The north-eastern monsoon sweeps from the Horn of Africa towards the shores of India. The winds bring 'rainwater running in rills' (in Rabindranath Tagore's evocative words). High swells vibrate through the bones of seafarers and wash over the decks of dhows. On a container ship, heavy-bottomed and cargo-laden, all one feels is a gentle sway that slightly changes the calibration of your walk. Even a ten-metre swell is dwarfed by a megaship's high freeboard: the distance of the deck from the waterline can be as far as fifteen metres above the surface of the sea.

In the age of sail, if a port's ship designers, shipwrights, and master seafarers could harness the force and energy of the wind in sailing across the ocean, that port could come to preeminence. But most deepwater ports also served coastal trade, and different merchants specialised in transhipping goods brought in from afar and their distribution to nearer harbours. Aden, Muscat, and Peninsular ports on the Indian Ocean served as such entrepôts during medieval times (and perhaps even before) precisely because of their command over the monsoon routes.

But the monsoons were not the only consideration in determining the optimal routes and their termini. Geography also mattered. As Indian Ocean historian R.N. Chaudhuri paraphrases the son of Portuguese conqueror Afonso de Albuquerque: 'There are three places in India ... which serve as markets for all the trade in merchandise in that part of the world and are the principal keys of it. The first is Malacca, the second Aden, and the third Hormuz. All three command the entrance and the exit in narrow sea passages.'[5] Beyond their mastery of monsoons and straits, ports in the age of sail could flourish because they provided safe – or 'noble' – havens. Aden had a naturally deep harbour that sheltered from the winds and a hard enough seafloor complementing its depth to host oceangoing ships. The wondrous account of Sulayman, the ninth-century itinerant merchant, similarly indicates the reasons Siraf, on the Persian shores of the Gulf, became the early medieval entrepôt for the western Indian Ocean:

> Most of the Chinese boats are loaded at Siraf and the goods are carried to Siraf from al-Basra, Uman and other [ports], and then they are loaded on the Chinese boats at Siraf. This is because the waves are abundant in this sea and the water is at a low [level] in some places ... So when the goods are loaded at Siraf, they store sweet water from there and set sail.[6]

Aden and Siraf, however, languished from the sixteenth to nineteenth centuries, and while Aden became a major port after being colonised, Siraf never regained its early prominence. Politics and social relations were often more important than geographic felicity. So many of the ports of the Red Sea and the coasts of the Persian Gulf were placed there *despite* their location. Mudflats, treacherous coral reefs, and access only to brackish water supplies and meagre ships' stores did not prevent the emergence of ports in inhospitable locales. Access to hinterlands, credit, networks of trade, and seafaring skills all played a role.

Long before Europeans found the maritime route to the Indian Ocean, Arabs and the archipelago peoples of the eastern Indian Ocean before them had already developed sophisticated navigational methods for travel across the unruly waters. In his beautiful manual of navigation, the fifteenth-century Arab seafarer Ahmad ibn Majid al-Najdi writes about the knowledge required to traverse the perilous deeps that lay between the Arabian Peninsula and the far shores of Asia and Africa:

> Know oh reader, that sailing the sea has many principles. Understand them: the first is the knowledge of lunar mansions and rhumbs and routes, distances, latitude measuring, signs (of land), the courses of the sun and moon, the winds and their reasons, and the seasons of the sea, the instruments of the ship . . . It is desirable that you should know about risings and 'southings' and the methods of taking latitude measurements and their variations and graduations, the risings and settings of the stars, their latitudes, longitudes and distances and their passing the meridian . . . It is also desirable that you should know all the coasts and their landfalls and their various guides such as mud, or grass, animals or fish, sea-snakes and winds. You should consider the tides, and the sea currents and the islands on every route.[7]

The accumulated corpus of navigation knowledge came not only from a panoply of navigation manuals written by seasoned seafarers over the course of centuries, but also from the quotidian experience of *nakhodas* (captains) aboard both oceangoing and coastal ships. This vast archive of experience and memory also served to make ephemeral sea routes more concrete.

But, beyond geophysical accident and the congealed skills of seafarers in great ports, what mattered greatly to the making of routes in the Indian Ocean was relations of trade and pilgrimage that made sea routes so much more than imagined lines on maps. If port cities were designated neutral or free ports, they attracted these transoceanic networks of trade more readily. As trade relations flourished, so did credit, exchange, and trade. Merchants and other traders could borrow money in one port for the purchase of goods and repay in another port. When ports flourished, taxes and fees for the rulers followed.

We know a great deal about transoceanic networks of merchants throughout the Indian Ocean's history, where ties of kinship and community lubricated the machinery of exchange. But kinship and trust alone did not suffice; trade networks also depended on legal frameworks and mechanisms for enforcement of contracts.[8] The routes of exchange were many-cornered[9] and goods and people – merchants, slaves, soldiers, adventurers, imperial officers, seafarers, immigrants and pilgrims – were transported between the coasts of East Africa, Arabia, India and the Southeast Asian archipelagos. Long before the Portuguese, Dutch, French, and British East India Companies forcefully inserted themselves into these pre-existing trade networks,[10] precious metals, spices, timber, aromatics, and other goods travelled aboard cargo ships across the waters and along the coasts. Many of these routes and ports of trade became objects of European conquest precisely because of their abundance, the sophistication of their mechanisms of exchange, the depth of their infrastructures of trade, and their extensive and longstanding connections to their hinterlands, to their coastal neighbours, and across the seas.

The Portuguese entry into Indian Ocean commerce formalised some existing relations and rivalries of trade and force, and transformed others.[11] The coercion used to police trading ports and routes was embodied in the Portuguese forts and citadels overshadowing harbour entrances. Many still survive. Conflict between the Portuguese and local merchants and rulers, and later between the Portuguese and the Dutch, reshaped the volumes of trade for cargoes traversing the sea. Spice became more important than other commodities and the routes that incorporated spice-producing lands became more profitable.

Imperial monopoly restrictions on particular commodities encouraged new routes but also spelled the decline of many shorter, more local or coastal routes for products manufactured in India and Southeast Asia.

Under European control of trade in the Indian Ocean, and especially with British colonialism, ports were forced to specialise. Some primarily exported raw materials, while others became adept at producing specific manufactured goods. This process of specialisation affected what sorts of ships these ports could host and how well they were incorporated into imperial networks. New legal systems differentiated ports within the same imperium, allowing European powers to take advantage of variegations in sovereignty and a version of legal arbitrage. New monetary and credit regimes were introduced. Racialised hierarchies and various forms of exploitation of labour – from wage labour to corvée (or forced) labour, to indentured labour – were institutionalised by law.[12] Sea routes, emporia of trade, and colonial bases were now affected by new modes of production. Colonial expansion ruthlessly decimated some ports and founded new nodes of trade in the region.

The production of knowledge about the empire was, from the first, a fiercely urgent need of the colonisers. Mapping both the sea and the land, oceanography, subsea topography, familiarity with the flora and fauna of the colonised ports, and ethnography all served the purpose of more effective colonisation and competition with imperial rivals. The Admiralty Charts that I had so admired were important tools for colonial powers. Long before they became a lucrative income stream for the British state through commercial sales, they were much coveted and jealously guarded sources of colonial knowledge. The men who invented new tools for navigation and the men who used them at sea became subjects of nationalist admiration.[13] Colonial charts took routes defined by accidents of geography or topography or advantageous currents and winds, transformed them through the political power of commerce, and 'naturalised' them again. The age of steam only reinforced the process.

The Emergence of Steam

Steamships changed the face of navigation and the pathways of trade. Ships were no longer bound to the seasons and winds. Even more important, the provision of fuel for oceangoing ships – first coal and, in the twentieth century, oil – spread the tentacles of empire to numerous ports around the world. The earliest steamships required vast amounts of coal and, when traversing open seas, their boilers encrusted with sedimented and corrosive salts and their inner machinery required all-too-frequent lubrication.[14] But the navigability and power of steamships made them an irresistible weapon in the strategic and commercial contestation between European empires. The French colonisation of Algeria in 1830 stoked British fears that the Mediterranean was becoming a French lake in the same way the Black Sea had become a Russian lake. British imperial officials thought the consolidation of their control in South Asia could prove advantageous against France and Russia.[15] But to reach South Asia profitably, more powerful, faster ships were needed.

The British East India Company's conversion of its fleet to steamships in the 1830s marked the ascendance of steam, though it took decades before all the oceangoing ships rounding the Cape of Good Hope to India were converted. The East India Company's turn to steam spurred the Government of Bombay to find a coaling station on the route from Bombay to Suez (and from there overland to Alexandria), resulting in the occupation of the island of Soqotra in the Indian Ocean in 1835. Soqotra's harbours, however, did not provide good shelter, and the islands did not have the necessary infrastructure to support a coaling station. This led to the British abandoning Soqotra and bloodily conquering Aden in 1839. As a historian of the Suez Canal writes, Aden was 'the first territorial acquisition of the Red Sea route and the first coaling station annexed to any empire'.[16] The governor of Bombay, Sir Robert Grant, justified the conquest of Aden thus:

> The establishment of a monthly communication by steam with the Red Sea, and the formation of a flotilla of armed steamers, renders it absolutely necessary that we should have a station of our own on the coast of Arabia, as we have in the Persian Gulf . . . As a coal depot, no place on the coast is so advantageous; it divides the distance between Bombay and Suez, and steamers may run into Back Bay during the night and unload at all seasons in perfect security.[17]

Distance and suitability as a halfway house went hand in hand with the possibilities both of trade and strategic access. Aden remained a fuelling outpost for the British Empire in the Indian Ocean even after petroleum displaced coal, until the British were driven out of Aden in 1967 by the anticolonial struggles there.

By the 1840s, the British Admiralty had also begun converting its naval vessels to steam, further intensifying the need for imperial coal depots. Between 1850 and 1869 alone, the net tonnage of British goods transported by steamships had increased from 168,474 to 948,367.[18] Steamship technologies and imperial expansion were mutually reinforcing. The imperial steamships trading around, policing, and fighting upon the Indian Ocean required frequent and high-volume replenishment of their fuel coal. This, in turn, led to the conquest of new colonial beachheads along trade routes. These strategic outposts themselves generated additional trade, required a great deal more administrative information and communication, and necessitated more capital investment, more intensive exploitation of labour, and ever-expanding knowledge and intelligence about local conditions. In his account of the age of coal, On Barak explains the prevalence of British coal by the fact that products mined in Wales or Northern England could be exported to the colonies in ships that would otherwise have been in ballast (or not carrying cargo). The vast trade in British coal overseas encouraged industrialisation at home, while the rise of mass democracy in Europe resulting from the materialities of coal mining was accompanied by the projection of authoritarian power over colonies overseas.[19]

British control over much of the coastal areas in West, South, and East Africa translated into British supremacy over the Cape route to India. Britain also controlled the coal supplies, since 'coal from Bengal was being used in steamers in the 1830s, from Borneo in the 1840s, and from Natal in the 1860s. Though not as good as Welsh coal, they gave Britain a near-monopoly of the world's steamer coal supplies'.[20] The opening of the Suez Canal in 1869 made Britain's imperial coaling stations – and the routes that were strung between them – still more significant to Britain's dominion over the oceans. Even as the British feared the French mastery in the Mediterranean and controlling shares in the Suez Canal, British primacy over the sea routes of the Red Sea, the Persian Gulf, and the Cape were never in doubt. And that was owed to coal.

But steam was not the only technology that reinforced the mapping of routes and the importance of ports as landing stations.

'The Seas Inlaid with Eloquent, Gentle Wires'[21]

The handsomely moustachioed Syrian American writer Ameen Rihani was an ardent supporter of Arab reform and an observer of the region. A 1931 review in *The Geographical Journal* lamented his 'malevolence towards British policy and British officials' in the Arab world, just as they commended the 'charming' and 'vivid and attractive' ethnographic accounts of 'mysterious Arabia'. Rihani visited the Arabian Peninsula in the 1920s and became friendly with Abdulaziz ibn Saud, who shortly thereafter became the king of Arabia. In his travels in the Peninsula, Rihani was particularly impressed with Aden Colony, which was a central hub in the global network of colonial communication that ran on the 'modern magic' of the telegraph:

> There are certainly bigger telegraph offices in the world than this of Aden, but they are not more important. Abolish the colony on that height, silence the hundred instruments which buzz and click night and day, cut the cable which connects the Orient and the antipodes with Europe and America, and lo, the oceans will be plunged again in gloom, distance will revert to its ancient tyranny, and the continents will become insular with nothing to connect them but steam and the sail. That colony of telegraph operators, therefore, is one of the living centres of the intelligence and progress of the world.[22]

Before the advent of the telegraph and for a long time after, packet-ships carrying postal cargo were necessary for the transmission of information across the oceans. Merchant vessels and specialised ships carried the post from Europe to Asia and back; postal contracts given by governments were the best conduit for state subsidies to shipping companies. Then telegraphic communication came about. The first telegraph lines were laid across the Atlantic, but the next two were planted between France and Algeria and between Britain and India. The technology was crucial to the control of the colonies. Historian Douglas Farnie goes so far as to argue that in India, communication by cable was more pivotal to the maintenance of British economic and political power than railways or steamships because it stitched the internal Indian information-gathering systems onto overseas networks and thus centralised the state's ability to collect strategic intelligence and expanded its capacity to project state power.[23] Telegraph consolidated British control over the interiors of the places they colonised in the nineteenth century. They also facilitated the creation of world markets by rapidly transmitting commodity prices and market information from port to port.[24] The telegraph also directly affected the shape of the shipping market, encouraging tramp shipping (shipping between ports without a fixed schedule or itinerary) over established charters or routes: because it expedited transmission of up-to-date information about the availability of commodities to be shipped, the telegraph allowed more flexibility in shipping routes and vitalised 'ship to order'. Laying telegraph cables bound ports across the sea to one another ever more closely, while at the same time bringing the ports closer to their hinterlands.

It is no surprise then that the British attempted – and succeeded in – monopolising the most extensive communication networks between Asia and Europe. These undersea networks closely followed the shipping routes that had become such standard cartographic imaginaries. The cables' landfall sites were often major ports and their routes traced the journeys of ships, since they were inevitably laid by ships that were themselves subject to vagaries of wind, waves, and weather. These cables also added a concrete weight to the British Empire's claims to rule the waves and transformed the less visible pathways of its dominion into materially substantial subsea passages.

But the process was not all smooth sailing. The first set of cables laid down the length of the Red Sea were catastrophically faulty: the sea floor had not been sufficiently or effectively surveyed and, in places, the profundity of its depths meant that cables could not effectively follow safer topographic contours. In those early days, the cable-laying machinery was also crude and incapable of regularising the tension of the cable. In some places, where the cable lacked slack, it snapped. But, perhaps most importantly, the cable itself – a thin copper wire laminated with gutta-percha and swathed in hemp – proved vulnerable to the warm salty water of the Red Sea, to the naval shipworms who found the covering irresistible, and to the scabrous layer of barnacles that weighed it down and sometimes made it split. It took several tries before a line was laid from Constantinople to Alexandria and from Suez onwards to Aden and Karachi. These networks could not have been completed without lavish subsidies from the British government.[25]

The routes that the telegraph cables of old mapped at the bottom of the sea were, in the twentieth century, followed by copper telephone cables, and now map closely to the pathways of fibreoptic internet cables. Like undersea telegraph and telephone cables, internet cables require landing stations and amplification points (power repeaters under the sea).[26] The location of such intervening points is determined as much by geopolitical calculations as they are by geographic or commercial ones. Whoever rules the seas and the coastal areas flanking it always has more access to such landing stations and the subsea cables themselves. The expanse and reach of British and later the US mastery over a great many islands in the Pacific and Caribbean transformed ports there into landing points and nodes of imperial communication networks. Where whaling ships had gone in the eighteenth and nineteenth centuries, cable-laying vessels followed.

What is most striking about the maps that chart the routes of internet cables is the extent to which the density of cable internet corresponds to the weight and volume of shipping in a given geographic area.[27] The Arabian Peninsula is flanked by a rainbow of colourfully mapped cable networks. Some are owned by consortia of national telecommunication companies along a route from Hong Kong to the ports of the Mediterranean. Others are owned by private firms headquartered in Mumbai or Hong Kong, or the famously powerful and astronomically rich Tata and Ambani families of India *inter alia*. One such network, the Falcon, is a subsidiary of the Ambani-owned Indian conglomerate Reliance. Falcon has Suez as one terminus and Mumbai as another, but it weaves all around the Arabian Peninsula and lands at Jeddah, Saudi Arabia; Hodeidah and Al Ghaydah in Yemen; Manama, Bahrain; Doha, Qatar; Dubai in the UAE; Al-Safat in Kuwait; Iraq's Al-Faw Peninsula; Khasab and Seeb in Oman, and two ports on the Iranian shore. The cable goes 'from port to port around the Gulf like a packet ship'.[28]

Cable networks are heavily subsidised just as imperial mail ships were, protected by their national states and crucial in determining the significance of the ports along their routes. I shall only mention Al Ghaydah here. A small port deep in the Mahra governorate of eastern Yemen, it has, since December 2017, become a base for the Saudi-led coalition that has waged war on Yemen since 2015. The port can accommodate dhows and other boats with smaller draughts, but not larger freighters or tankers. Yet its location on the Indian Ocean, and its hosting the landing station for Falcon, have given the port an importance incommensurate with the volume of the goods traded through its harbour.

Pilgrimage

While steam and subsea cables were crucial to the designation of sea routes, pilgrimage was pivotal in transforming Jeddah into a major Red Sea port, especially from the nineteenth century onwards. Jeddah has long been the main port of Mecca, which is a little under a hundred kilometres inland. Many pilgrims bought and sold goods in Mecca in order to secure their passage home from Arabia; others used hajj as an occasion for profit-making trade. Braudel has described the hajj pilgrimage as one of the richest trade fairs in early modern times, but others have disputed its significance, given that the lunar calendar to which the hajj conforms cannot be made to agree with the monsoon schedules, which follow a solar calendar.[29]

The age of steam, which unshackled travel from the regularity of the monsoon winds, made the sea routes as important as land routes for pilgrimage. The expansion of maritime pilgrimage routes, in turn, proved a lucrative source of income for

European shipping businesses. As early as the 1850s, European companies based in Asia (including the British India Steam Navigation Company) were chartering ships for pilgrims. The opening of the Suez Canal accelerated the trend of Europe-based firms getting into the business.[30] For the vast majority of the period after the opening of the canal, and until aeroplanes overtook ships as the primary transport for pilgrimage, European shipping firms controlled the most profitable pilgrimage routes from India, Southeast Asia, and Egypt to Jeddah. This focus on hajj transportation intensified following World War I, when the US instituted quotas on the number of migrants, thus truncating the business of transatlantic shipping. European shipping companies thereafter focused on expanding (or creating from scratch) their Asian and Middle Eastern markets.[31] Their success far outstripped that of local firms, not only because most state officials regulating the process were Europeans themselves but also because these shipping firms received major mail subsidies from governments and had far easier access to finance. Because of the regularity of the hajj pilgrimage and its vast scale, the logistics of pilgrimage travel on the sea was a microcosm of the global relations and local considerations that shaped the business, including the viability and transformations of sea routes over time.

Travelling to the hajj by sea was a matter of trial and tribulation. As one eighteenth-century pilgrim from India wrote, 'During travel on sea, one is faced with shortage of space, problems of food and drink, stores which can only be obtained at distant ports, and the fear of drowning.'[32] The ships were often dangerously and claustrophobically overcrowded.[33] Disasters could easily result in hundreds of passenger deaths. If the sea routes were treacherous, arrival in Jeddah was not very pleasant either, all the way through the early decades of the twentieth century. This major port which had once been controlled by the Ottomans, came under the control of the British-sponsored Sharif Hussein after World War I. After the ascendance of Ibn

Saud to the throne, Jeddah was eventually side-lined in favour of Riyadh, from which the Saud family hailed. Throughout this turbulent history, the rulers of Jeddah spent just as much as necessary – and no more – on dredging the harbour. A 1923 account by a pilgrim lamented the inadequacy of the port:

> Jeddah Harbour is not like other seaports. Generally, the water is very shallow all along the coast. But the port authorities keep removing the sand (by dredging) so as to make the channel deep enough for passage of boats; this allows easy loading and unloading of passengers and cargo possible, if not at all times then at least at high tide. The Turkish rulers did not consider it essential to make a deep-water jetty by straightening out the beaches, as they probably did not have the required force for defending the harbour. They only made a channel for small boats that is marked off by pillars placed at many places. Since this channel is not too wide, boats also get struck up on the sand bars.[34]

Despite all this, until the early years of the 1950s, 75 per cent of pilgrims still travelled to Jeddah by ship. Several factors led to a dwindling of maritime hajj pilgrimage only twenty years later: new modes of transport and better infrastructures, paved roads and aeroplanes among them.[35] Throughout the 1950s and 1960s, as anticolonial struggles forced European powers to abandon their colonies, European shipping firms also discontinued their pilgrimage services. The closure of the Suez Canal in 1956 was particularly significant as it put a stop to maritime journeys of pilgrims from the Mediterranean. Jeddah's proximity to Mecca, however, encouraged its growth as a port of arrival and departure – by air or sea – for pilgrims, while its location in the vicinity of the Suez Canal guaranteed its significance as a commercial seaport for decades to come.

The Suez Canal

> . . . the Suez canal initiated, open'd,
> I see the procession of steamships, the Empress Eugenie's leading the van;
> I mark, from on deck, the strange landscape, the pure sky, the level sand in the distance;
> I pass swiftly the picturesque groups, the workmen gather'd,
> The gigantic dredging machines.
>
> Walt Whitman, 'Passage to India'

Though the Suez Canal was not regularly incorporated in the journey from Europe to Asia until at least a decade after it opened, one cannot overestimate its subsequent effects on global trade. The opening of the canal encouraged the expansion of Aden and Jeddah, helped Britain consolidate its imperial power, facilitated the transformation of the petroleum industry (via opening markets in the East to Azeri oil), and accelerated the expansion of extractive industries in Asia and Africa.

The canal was a site of technological experimentation and innovation and an exemplar of capitalist infrastructural power and colonial expansion. Its construction followed hard on the heels of an Egyptian cotton boom in the early 1860s that spurred breakneck imperial investment in transport and extraction. The business device used for the construction and management of the canal had been the joint stock company, so crucial a form in the emergence and maintenance of capital-intensive infrastructures (such as railroads and ports). Joint stock companies had also been central to both maritime trade and the mercantilist colonisation of Asia and Africa. The canal was constructed with French capital and Khedival acquiescence, by Egyptian peasants pressed into corvée labour.[36]

The canal's inauguration proved seismic in shaping routes of trade and facilitating the European powers' strategic projection of naval force into Asia. An Admiralty warship, *HMS Newport*, was the first ship to pass surreptitiously through the canal on the eve of its official opening in 1869. On the ceremonial opening day, it was followed by the French royal yacht, the pleasure-boats of European royalty and industrialists, British gunboats, telegraph ships, and steamers owned by European shipping companies.[37] Canal fees were extremely high, and the canal was fully operational only in 1871; therefore, its early years saw it primarily utilised by naval vessels and only a decade later by European packet-ships.[38] In other words, the newly built canal was subsidised by European navies and, later still, indirectly by European states. The canal became the preferred route for Europeans regularly travelling to India, among them British colonial officials and military officers.

From the very start, the infrastructural effects of the Suez Canal on maritime trade were far-reaching. The canal allowed Britain to consolidate state power over its Asian colonies. It certainly worked to the detriment of Egypt itself. Rosa Luxemburg pointed out that the canal 'deflect[ed] the entire trade between Europe and Asia from Egypt and would painfully affect her part in this trade'.[39] When the loans borrowed to finance its construction became due, the British used the Egyptian debt along with the 'threat' of the Urabi revolt to occupy the country militarily. In so doing, Britain secured its hold over the entirety of the route to India. The British were not the only power to gain strategic advantage from the canal. European powers with colonies in Asia, East Africa, and the Pacific found the canal route most expedient. Even the Sublime Porte shipped its troops through the canal in order to reinforce its power along the Red Sea coast of the Peninsula, in Asir and Yemen.

The Suez Canal route, like so many other technological marvels of the nineteenth century invented to lubricate the machinery of empire, reproduced the empire itself through feedback loops and self-perpetuation mechanisms – popular revolts or starving labourers and peasants or indebted nations be damned. Because winds blew east–west across the Sinai – transversal to the canal's north–south route – sailing ships could not navigate the canal. This meant that they were limited to the Cape route, and eventually the canal entailed the decline of oceangoing sailing ships in intercontinental trade.[40] Like the railways crisscrossing colonies in Asia and Africa, the canal became an infrastructure constructed in service of further colonial extraction of commodities and capitalisation of global economies. The movement of capital in the era after the inauguration of the Suez Canal is stunningly instructive. In the period between the opening of the canal and the start of World War I, capital investment outside country of origin surged from US$9 billion to $44 billion. The vast majority of this capital was invested in mineral extraction in Asia and Africa.[41]

Suez Canal policies also influenced the spread of petroleum tanker ships. Perhaps the single most important ingredient in the transformation of oil into a globally tradeable commodity has been the invention of tankers to convey this liquid cargo more easily in bulk. Before tankers, oil was carried in barrels packed in regular sailing freighters (this explains the use of 'barrels' as the standard unit of measurement for petroleum). The Nobels of Sweden, who had major investments in Russia, and whose oil business was among the most powerful and influential in Azerbaijan, perfected the use of tanker ship steamers fuelled by oil itself (rather than the then-dominant coal) on the inland waterways Russia and the Caspian Sea. But for the tanker ship to become a global carrier, a different alliance was needed: that between a British mercantile house, Shell Transport and Trading Company, and a French oil firm based in Azerbaijan, the Rothschilds' Bnito.

Marcus Samuel (1853–1972), the founder of Shell, is credited with showing that a tanker ship steamer was the most efficient mode of transport for petroleum. Samuel was an Iraqi Jew born in Whitechapel, London. Samuel, who in later life became the

Lord Mayor of London, had worked in his father's export and import business, which began by trading mollusc shells, used for interior decoration, as well as antiques imported from the Dutch East Indies, among other things. Samuel's familiarity with the markets in Southeast Asia (after having lived there for a time) and a keen sense of which commodities were becoming more desirable directed him to oil. His decision to transport petroleum by ship dramatically changed the purpose and character of the family's trading house. In 1898, Samuel decided to transport Bnito's oil (extracted in Azerbaijan and piped to Batumi in Georgia) from the Black Sea coast to Southeast Asia. Instead of using the standard barrels, Samuel commissioned ships that could move the liquid in bulk, taking advantage of economies of scale in transport but also ease of loading and unloading via pumps and hoses.

Establishing the route of the first such ship, the *Murex*, required much backroom negotiation as well as the support of the British government. The latter hoped that, by helping a British business gain a head-start on transport companies carrying Standard Oil's products, it could secure strategic advantage against the world's largest petroleum producer. Suez Canal authorities – now more or less an extension of British imperial interests abroad – were wary of letting ships carrying US oil through. The fear was that Standard Oil would bring oil to the East and monopolise the markets there, then use this monopoly to import petroleum from the West Coast of the US, shutting out British firms. The canal authorities' fealty to Britain and concern about the Pacific trade in oil bypassing the canal led them to grant Shell permission to steam *Murex* through the canal. For the canal officers, 'to allow the passage of British tankers, carrying Russian oil with the object of building up, instead of destroying, the oil trade between Batumi and the Orient, was obviously to the advantage of the Canal's finances. The Authorities would naturally be sympathetic to any such proposition.'[42] The plan was a success for Shell, which eventually merged with Royal Dutch (an oil-production firm operating in Southeast Asia) to become Royal Dutch Shell.

Within a few short years, tankers became the standard vehicle for petroleum transport and their widespread adoption enormously increased canal traffic. The ease of transporting petroleum by tanker was one factor in the eventual displacement of coal as the fuel of global economies.[43] A drop in the southbound transportation of coal through the canal was eventually balanced by a massive increase in the northbound traffic of petroleum. While in 1910 crude oil constituted only 1 per cent of the total northbound tonnage of oil through the canal, by 1960, petroleum's share of tonnage travelling northbound through the canal had increased to nearly 82 per cent.[44] This was two-thirds of all the petroleum transported from the Middle East to Europe.[45] The surge in extraction and trade of oil in this fifty-year period also had seismic effects in the making of the politics and social relations of the Arabian Peninsula and the world.

The closure of the canal – first for eight months after the 1956 tripartite invasion of Egypt by Britain, France, and Israel, and again for eight years after the 1967 War – had its own extraordinary effect on global shipping. The closure of the canal proved a boon in the construction of very large crude carriers (VLCCs) and ultra-large crude carriers (ULCCs) that could round the Cape of Good Hope with notable economies of scale. In 1971, 80 per cent of all tanker orders were for such supertankers.[46] After the canal was cleaned of the debris of the 1967 and 1973 wars, dredged, deepened, and reopened in 1975, it saw the return of much of the freight it had lost – but not the VLCCs and ULCCs, which were now too large to pass through. The additional flow of traffic, along with the post-1973 surge in construction in the oil-producing countries of the region, saw a deluge of building goods and consumer products imported into the ports of the Arabian Peninsula via the canal.

In the intervening years, the business of the canal has flourished or diminished not only in accordance with volumes of cargo passing through it but also as refracted through political calculations near and afar. Most recently, in 2015, the canal saw the opening of a bypass channel along its middle third. The project has in part been General Abdel Fattah el-Sisi's attempt to replicate the glories of early postcolonial mega-infrastructure construction. It involved excavating a parallel canal for thirty-five kilometres and dredging the already operational channel. It was said to have cost US$8.2 billion and, although the regime claimed that public subscriptions had financed the construction, there were always rumours that the Saudi state had poured money into the canal as a means of encouraging trade for its Red Sea ports.[47]

The captain of *Callisto* told me that the expansion of the canal was the fastest maritime construction project he had ever seen. When I first steamed through the canal in February 2015, one could see bulldozers and earth-movers on the Sinai shore of the canal. By August 2016, the second channel of the canal had opened between the top of the Great Bitter Lake, all the way up to Qantara, thirty kilometres short of Port Said at the northern end. Though the top and bottom thirds of the canal are still one-way, the newly dug bypass allows for a shorter travel time, as a convoy can make it halfway through the canal and await the passage of the convoy coming from the opposite direction before proceeding apace. The new channel reduces the passage time through the canal; dredging and deepening mean that tankers heading north along the canal need not be in ballast.

Although many economists in Egypt are sceptical about the wisdom of expanding the canal, the success of the expansion will be judged by shipping speeds. Cyclical collapses in the price of oil slow down tramp tankers, which await small increases in oil prices before delivering their cargo. More recently, shipping companies have been commissioning ships designed for slow-steaming and are even reverting to using a high-tech form of sail to deploy wind power for their ships and save on fuelling costs.[48] Whether companies that deliberately slow down their ships in order to secure small savings will be willing to pay the exorbitant – and mushrooming – fees for crossing the canal remains to be seen.

Port Management of Routes

> They are the conquerors of the world
> Seeking a personal chemical fortune;
> Sports and comfort travel with them;
> They take the education
> Of races, classes, and animals, on this Boat.
>
> Arthur Rimbaud, 'Motion'

In the summer of 2017, only one day after Saudi Arabia, the UAE, and their allies declared a blockade against Qatar, the largest shipping company in the world, Copenhagen-based Maersk, announced that it was rerouting containers intended for Qatar, delivering them via a new feeder service from the port of Salalah in Oman instead of the original transhipment port, Jabal Ali in Dubai.[49] Eventually, Qatar shifted its transhipment hub from Jabal Ali to the Omani port of Sohar, which is much closer than Salalah. Maersk could accomplish this nimble manoeuvre because, like many of the world's major shipping companies, it has close relations with a terminal-management company. Maersk and APM Terminals are both owned by AP Moller-Maersk. APM Terminals (APMT), the third-largest terminal operator in the world, manages the container terminals at the Salalah port. Sohar's container terminals are managed by Hong Kong–based Hutchison, which is the second-largest in the world (after Singapore-based PSA International). Jabal Ali is managed by Dubai Ports World (DP World), the fourth-largest terminal operator in the world.[50]

These terminal-management arrangements can be crucial in deciding shipping routes, since a Maersk ship is more likely to unload its goods at an APMT-managed terminal close to its cargo's final destination. Special arrangements between other large shipping companies and specific terminal operators that are not co-subsidiaries can also similarly influence shipping routes and destinations.

The world's third-largest shipping company, CMA CGM, is based in Marseille, France; I travelled on its freighters between Malta and Dubai. The company is owned by the Lebanese-French Saadé family, who hail from Latakia in Syria. Escaping the Lebanese civil war in 1977, Jacques Saadé and his brother Johnny (who later left the firm) founded Compagnie Maritime d'Affrètement (CMA) in Marseille in 1978 to ferry wheeled vehicles on 'ro/ro' ships between Marseille and Beirut.[51] In 1996, the French government offered to privatise the state-owned shipping firm, Compagnie Générale Maritime (CGM), which had been established in the mid-nineteenth century and whose early success had depended on the mail subsidies it had received from the government. Saadé's CMA bought CGM, and his CMA CGM was born. In the aftermath of its founding, the company aggressively acquired smaller shipping lines in Africa, Asia, and the Middle East and forged alliances with terminal operators throughout these regions.

CMA CGM today operates in an alliance with two other shipping companies, China Shipping Container Lines (headquartered in Shanghai, China) and United Arab Shipping Company (based in the UAE, though partially owned by investment vehicles of the governments of Qatar and Saudi Arabia).[52] The alliance gives the companies access to one another's ports, shipping arrangements, and routes and has changed each company's steaming schedules, their destination ports, and the frequency of travel along some routes. CMA CGM's dominance in the Middle Eastern and African markets also means that it has longstanding arrangements with terminal operators there, foremost among them DP World. CMA CGM ships are therefore more likely to take on or unload cargo at terminals operated by DP World (rather than, say, APMT).

These alliances between shipping companies and agreements between them and terminal operators translate into discounted port fees, preferential treatment at arrival and loading or unloading, and lower freight costs for the shipping companies. Should they be able to secure such agreements with shipping companies, some ports or terminals expand at the expense of neighbouring ports. In return for these lucrative deals, the ports must accommodate the shipping companies' hunger for ever larger ships. I will write more about this effect in the next chapter.

Container terminal operator	Headquarters	Relations with shipping companies
COSCO Shipping Ports	Hong Kong	The company has become the largest container terminal operator after the merger of COSCO and China Shipping companies
Hutchison Ports	Hong Kong (but incorporated in the British Virgin Islands)	
PSA International	Singapore	Has an alliance with COSCO
DP World	Dubai	Partners with many shipping companies, including CMA CGM and UASC
China Merchant Port Holdings	Hong Kong	
APM Terminals	Netherlands	APM Terminals' parent organisation is Maersk (whose shipping company of the same name is the largest in the world)

Yılport	Turkey	Owned by the Yıldırım Group which has long had mutual investment agreements with CMA CGM
Shanghai International Port Groups	China	Has partnered with COSCO
International Container Terminal Services	Philippines	
Terminal Investment Ltd	Netherlands	MSC (based in Italy)

Table 1.2 – The world's largest container terminal operators[53]

Sea routes are constantly reimagined to accommodate geopolitical realignments, corporate alliances, and shifting calculations about ship sizes, route expediencies, and maritime power plays. Another set of ephemeral assumptions and imaginaries, often invented far from the ports themselves, also influences the making and unmaking of these oceanic highways: how routes are priced. Once they are priced, these price indices form the basis of speculations that in turn affect the underlying prices.

Freight Rates

Freight rates have historically been crucial components of how shipping routes were devised, traversed, and imagined. As they change, so do the fortunes of maritime countries. Between 1820 and 1913, freight rates plummeted by a factor of four, just as the volume of merchant shipping within and across empires quintupled.[54] The primary beneficiaries of the decline in freight rates in the nineteenth century were Great Britain and other Western European countries. Because they imported foodstuffs and raw materials – bulky materials – in very large volumes, they profited from the ever cheaper maritime freight costs. Further, the ships that had imported such goods backhauled manufactured goods rather than travelling back in ballast, and therefore encouraged the expansion of markets for European goods.[55] Freight rates fell in part due to technological innovations in shipbuilding and navigation, as well as improvements in port facilities over the course of the nineteenth century. But freight rates were also significantly influenced by such factors as 'monopoly or collusion, navigation laws, the relationship between inward and outward cargoes on a route, and so forth'.[56]

Around the Indian Ocean, for the vast majority of its history and until the introduction of European corporate shipping in the nineteenth century, freight rates were negotiable and fluctuated with the level of demand (both for particular goods and destinations), seasons, and the kind of ship that carried them.[57] Coastal trade, tramp shipping (maritime transportation that does not have a fixed schedule or predetermined ports of call), and feeders (where goods are transported from a hub port to a smaller port) all commanded different rates. Price-setting for freight rates in the area was influenced by the forms of trade European firms engaged in. As Johan Mathew has written in his engaging account of illicit shipping in the Indian Ocean,

> British firms considered cartel arrangements more ethical than competition on price, which might deprive other [British] companies of their business. This form of business ethics derived from the idea that market competition was feasible only when a market was sufficiently developed. In this view, the Arabian Sea was too undeveloped an area to justify capitalist competition. To build up business and develop local economies, profits had to be secured by the coercion and collaboration of firms. This ensured that British companies would receive 'handsome' profit margins on a smaller but more secure amount of business.[58]

Another effect was that, while the British firms monopolised more profitable oceangoing routes, local shippers were pushed into providing services on coastal or feeder routes where profit margins were smaller. This meant that among these smaller or more local shippers, more productive technologies (including steam) were adopted later because of their costs. In his account of travel in the Arabian Peninsula, Ameen Rihani describes Kuwaiti dockyards 'from which are launched the dhows and baggalas that sail across the Gulf and beyond it, perpetuating trade between India and Iraq, as well as between the towns along the Persian and the Arabian coasts, which are beyond the reach of steam. *For another reason, the low rate of freight, the sail is still indispensable.*'[59] Oral histories show the clever calculations that went into trading from port to port. One old sailor from Ras al-Khaimah recounted how at the beginning of the monsoon season,

> we picked up dried dates from Basra . . . We took these to India on the monsoon. Then we got a bulk cargo of roof tiles from Mangalore near Calicut on the Malabar coast. We waited until the monsoon changed and sailed to east Africa where we sold the roof tiles and bought building wood, especially roof beams, *chandal*, and big carved wooden doors. These were bulk cargo for the Gulf, and we sailed back here on the southwest monsoon.[60]

This division of labour has continued with dhows – which began to be motorised from the 1940s onwards – traversing the Indian Ocean, the Red Sea, and the gulfs around the Arabian Peninsula on both longer and shorter coastal routes, responding to demand for specific goods in ports large shipping companies could not or would not serve.[61] Their trade flourishes even if they are more vulnerable to piracy, their rates of profit are marginal, and the labour required to operate them is backbreaking and poorly paid. They draw on their longstanding relations of trust, extant legal frameworks for trade, and fine-grained knowledge of local conditions to offer everything from parcelled goods (like bulk packaged foods or notebooks) to electronics and household appliances to livestock, used cars, and sometimes contraband.

Meanwhile, global shipping companies order increasingly larger ships, attempting to keep their costs down all the while. Until 2008, the larger shipping companies based in Europe benefitted from an antitrust immunity conferred on them by European Council Regulation No. 4056/86.[62] The 1986 regulation allowed these shipping firms to act as cartels and coordinate in setting prices, polling cargoes, and harmonising schedules for trade. The repeal of the regulation in 2008 was likely in response to China and other rising Asian economies threatening to pass reciprocal protectionist shipping regulations. The effect of the repeal was a precipitous drop in freight rates, exacerbated by the global financial and economic crash that saw a 20 per cent decline in global trade.[63] The boom years of 2002 to 2008 and the subsequent crash were pivotal in making new financial devices that better facilitated the financialisation of shipping routes.

Speculative Routes

Thus far, I have insisted on the interplay between the ephemerality of sea routes upon water and the historical, political, and socioeconomic mechanisms that congeal them into more durable forms. These routes traverse the seas between ports. But, in recent decades, these maritime routes have been joined by freight routes that constitute derivative markets, pulsing through wires and cables. Some of the more significant are the Baltic Dry Index and various containerised freight indices.

The setting of price of goods depends on spot and forward contracts, among other things. Spot transactions follow the price of a good at the moment of purchase. Forward commodity prices, by contrast, are a calculation of the expected price of the desired good at a future date. Forward contracts, when first invented, were intended to mitigate the effect of possible price fluctuations in the future by guaranteeing exchange prices at the time the contract of sale was being drawn up. Forward contracts have long been a feature of most market transactions, as they are often applied to commodities which are subject to speculative pricing but require lead time for production and export.[64] Futures and options, 'derivative' financial products invented in the nineteenth and late twentieth centuries, respectively, became speculative market instruments that played on the differences between spot and forward prices.

Imagine an index of possible forward prices for a commodity. This index includes that commodity's prices at different future dates. In a futures contract, a buyer and a seller agree to an exchange on an underlying product at a future price on a given date. In financial futures, that underlying product is not the commodity itself but the value of the market index. In other words, in a futures contract, a bet is made on whether the forward price will fall or rise at a given future time. An options contract gives an investor the right (but not the obligation) to buy ('call') or sell ('put') an underlying good (again, a set of price indices).[65] In both futures and options, the buyer and sellers are speculating on the rise or fall of a price index rather than entering a contract for the sale of a good. What makes derivatives, or futures and options, particularly desirable as speculative products is that they allow investors to make money from a *falling* market by buying put options or selling forward contracts.[66] This ability to hedge against a possible loss is a kind of insurance for future transactions. There are futures indices on oil, on grains, even on weather; they are essentially wagers on whether the price of oil or grain will fall or rise, or on whether the weather will improve or deteriorate.

It is also possible to speculate on the future price of sea routes. The underlying object of trade in freight futures is an index tracking the cost of freight on a given route. Such an index, the Baltic Dry Index, was first devised in the Baltic

Exchange in the 1980s. The Baltic Dry Index tracks the freight rates for bulk goods (such as iron ore or grain), and is produced by the Baltic Exchange, a maritime exchange established in mid-eighteenth-century London and purchased by the Singapore Exchange (SGX) in 2016.[67] The exchange chooses from among its members and subscribers a number of major shipbrokers (or shipping companies) who provide on a daily basis an assessment of the spot and forward prices on a given route for a range of different dry bulk cargoes on ships of specified sizes.[68] The information is weighted and aggregated by the model-builders at the Baltic Exchange, who then publish a single price quote representing an average of cargoes, routes, and ship sizes.[69] It is important to point out that these prices are not some objective, singular, 'scientifically determined' number but a convergence by a number of different vested actors on a set of estimated current and future prices. Freight futures contracts based on this index emerged in 1985, while freight options were invented in 2007, at the height of the boom in global trade. Freight futures were to be used to 'hedge' (or protect) against price volatility on a given route by speculating on the future of the index. For a buyer of a futures contract, if future freight rates rise, any loss on spot prices can be offset by future gains.[70]

While derivatives were ostensibly invented as a risk management scheme for buyers and sellers to protect themselves (or 'hedge') against price fluctuations, from the very first they had two major effects. First, they allowed for speculation, in ways that made the underlying goods or products immaterial to the process of exchange. It did not matter what commodity was exchanged. The wagers were placed on the price going up or down rather than on the commodity itself. In effect, financial derivatives encouraged 'the greatest gambling game on earth' by placing bets on stock markets.[71] Second, the derivatives could – and did – directly affect prices through a feedback loop. In Donald MacKenzie's words, the mathematical models that underlay options pricing were 'an engine not a camera' – producing the effect they claimed to represent. And, as MacKenzie's meticulous account shows, the model 'provided an economic justification for what might otherwise have seemed dangerously unrigorous mathematics'.[72] Though MacKenzie's language is circumspect, 'dangerously unrigorous mathematics' is essentially a euphemism for wild gambling on a completely imaginary future.

While the Baltic Dry Index is now the prevalent index for bulk goods and WorldScale (established in 1952) is used for tracking tanker cargo, no single index exists for tracking prices of containerised freight. Shipbrokers' associations and freight consulting firms can provide such indices based on pricing data provided by their members or subscribers. For example, Drewry Shipping Consultants started producing the World Container Index (on eight major container routes) in 2006; Harper Petersen & Co. has offered HARPEX (also on eight time-charter routes for various container ship sizes) since 2004.[73] The Chinese government has also created its own indices. The China Containerised Freight Index and the Shanghai Containerised Freight Index were first devised in 1998 and 2005, respectively. The former is an amalgam of both spot and futures prices on containerised export routes from ten Chinese ports on twelve international routes (calculated by twenty-two domestic and international shipping firms). The latter tracks only spot prices on containers exported from Shanghai (whose freight market is characterised by high fluctuations).[74] The Shanghai Index was invented very specifically because the Chinese government hoped to create a freight derivatives market to benefit from the volatility – and rising prices – of freight rates.[75]

As is clear from this account, the price-setting processes are determined not only by empirically measurable factors but also by subjective measures determined by panellists – the very profitability of whose businesses depends on the prices their data constructs. This tautological magic has animated the financialisation of the shipping routes. The 'science' at the heart of financial route-making is as much about the affective attachments, political landscapes, and financial interests of the participants as it is about supposedly 'objective' market factors. Something of the traces of the political relations that created trade routes survives in these electronic models.

2

Harbour-Making

> By the time residents woke from their stupor, their patch of sea was already buried under hundreds of thousands of tonnes of earth and divided up into valuable plots of real estate and housing developments. None of their carefully preserved deeds confirming their ownership could help them recover the lands of their ancestors.
>
> Abdo Khal, *Throwing Sparks*

Curzon's 'Prancing in the Persian Puddle'[1]

In the left side of this photograph from the India Office Records, a tall man wearing a heavy striped robe and kufiya is standing next to his horse. On the far right, a canopied raft carries a blurry load of berobed and kufiya-wearing Arab men. But the gaze inevitably lands at the centre of the photograph, where three men – one half-naked with sun-darkened skin and two clothed in white robes – carry two other men in full British imperial regalia and pith helmets across the wet sand. Another pith-helmeted colonial officer seems to be directing the raft on the right, his back to the camera. The robed man on the left is thought to be Shaikh Mubarak al Sabah, the ruler of Kuwait. One of the men carried on the back of the Arab porters is the Viceroy of India, Lord Curzon of Kedleston.

In November 1903, Curzon arrived on a viceregal tour of the Persian Gulf so that he could claim the much-contested body of water and its littorals for Britain. The tour took in Muscat, Bandar Abbas, Bahrain, Kuwait, and Sharjah. Curzon's authorised biographer Earl Ronaldshay wrote,

Lord Curzon arriving in Kuwait[2]

> The presence of the ships gave to the prestige of the Viceroy the spectacular reinforcement which appealed so directly to the oriental mind. 'The small harbour', he wrote when describing his visit to Muscat, 'with our big white ship and the *Lawrence* in the foreground, and behind them the dark hulls of no less than six British men-o-war, presented a spectacle such as the Muscatis never before have witnessed'.[3]

Curzon landed at Shuwaikh, a small anchorage about three miles from Kuwait City (and today a thriving cargo port), rather than at the burgeoning dhow harbour at the centre of the town. Curzon was to ride into town, so that he could enact 'a ceremonial entry ... with becoming display'.[4] The becoming display, however, was belied by Curzon's arrival on the shore in Kuwait. This was 'less dignified than he could have wished, for, the water being shallow, he was faced with the alternative of being carried ashore, or of arriving on the back of a donkey without bridle or stirrup'.[5] Charles Belgrave, the much-hated, domineering British colonial adviser imposed on the ruler of Bahrain, described such ceremonial arrivals in Bahrain thus:

> Even when the pier was built official arrivals were not very dignified proceedings. When the tide was low, distinguished visitors, with their swords swinging round their legs, had to leap, nervously, from a bobbing skiff on the slippery pier steps, watched by the anxious reception committee waiting above them ... Now [in 1960], most people travel by air and visitors arriving by ship can come alongside in launches, for the pier extends a quarter of a mile into the sea. But until the deep-water pier, which is under construction, is built, steamers still anchor about three miles from the shore.[6]

Long before the modern dredging projects that created those deepwater piers, a *Times* reporter reflected on Curzon's visit to the Gulf, lamented the condition of the infrastructure there, and claimed that with 'a moderate expenditure of money and engineering skill' Britain could 'improve the existing harbours and perhaps open up new ones' to encourage commerce.[7] But, of course, at that stage, long before the discovery of petroleum around the Gulf, the British were not interested in investing in infrastructures that could have given the Gulf emirates a modicum of independence or financial autonomy. The excuse often given was the inhospitable geography.

Not only Kuwait and Bahrain but all the other port cities on the shores of the Gulf sit on a coast known for its mudflats, *sabkhas* (salt flats), mangroves, and shallow waters. Before the age of oil, some had harbours in town centres, where wooden dhows berthed while loading and unloading or preparing for their pearling trips to sea. Some of those dhow harbours still survive. The aesthetically pleasing dhow harbour of Kuwait City hosts a mix of museum pieces and working fishing and cargo vessels. The functioning dhow harbours of Dubai, Sharjah, and other Gulf cities house metal-hulled dhows, plying their trade

– licit and illicit – to Iran and other ports of the Peninsula, South Asia, and East Africa. It is a mistake to imagine these dhows as remnants or residues of 'traditional' trade; their business has flourished alongside, in the interstices of, and because of the more global, large-scale, and mechanised trade of container ships and modern bulk carriers. The dhows serve regional ports efficiently, and the flexibility and eclecticism of their cargo makes them ideal for smaller volumes of trade and nearer distances.

But although the dhow harbours survive – many in their original historical locales – many more ports, gargantuan and mechanised, have sprung up along these shallow, muddy, ecologically rich coasts. The ever-expanding number of competing ports raises the question: why go through the vast expenditure, investment and effort of creating so many deepwater harbours in these shallow seas? What was the impetus behind the upsurge of oceangoing ports on the Peninsula in the middle of the twentieth century?

The response to these questions lies in part in the importance of technological transformations – innovations in dredging and land reclamation – in the construction of harbours and ports of the Arabian Peninsula. Still more important are the political calculations that went into dredging some harbours and not others, and the colonial and nationalist policies that led to the development of some ports and the gradual waning of others. In this story, Dammam and Dubai matter a great deal. Created to serve the cargo needs of the Arabian American Oil Company (Aramco), Dammam has become one of the most important ports on the Arabian Peninsula. The decision to expand the harbour on the Dubai Creek in the 1950s was crucial for providing the emirate the funding to construct Port Rashid and Jabal Ali. The decline of the port of Aden demonstrates that despite natural advantages, a deep harbour, and a strategically fortuitous location, a port can be made to wither and fade away. In all these harbours, geopolitical and political decisions – rather than geographic advantage or 'neutral' economic calculations – created the conditions for the work of commerce and maritime transport. All these transformations ripple globally. The construction of new harbours requires landscapes to be dramatically reshaped not only where harbours are being built, but also in distant locales where the raw materials of construction are extracted.

Dammam

> Since the completion of the deep-water pier on the mainland at Dammam much trade has by-passed Bahrein. Most of the cotton goods, foodstuffs, lumber, hardware, and other products destined for eastern Arabia now land at this pier, instead of being unloaded at Bahrein and repacked for shipment to the coast by small dhows.
>
> Richard Sanger, *Arabian Peninsula*

At the beginning of the twentieth century, Arabia was an assemblage of different forms of rule, with the Ottoman Empire holding sway on the Red Sea coast, tribal leaders in the interior, and the Sharif of Mecca ruling Hijaz. The end of the Ottoman rule and the interference of British government agents like T.E. Lawrence ('of Arabia') precipitated a power struggle that ended with Abdulaziz ibn Saud of Najd declaring himself the king of Hijaz in 1926. He was immediately recognised by the Soviet Union. The Kingdom of Hijaz and Najd changed its name to Saudi Arabia in 1932. Ibn Saud's hold over much of the Arabian Peninsula was consolidated in the coming decades and was aided by the discovery of oil in the eastern provinces in 1938.

When oil was discovered and exploited in Bahrain, then in Saudi Arabia, and – after the Second World War – in rapid succession in other Gulf countries, new ports were needed not only to export crude oil via tankers but also to import heavy goods, equipment, and cement for building oil-extraction facilities, labour camps, and new urban conurbations to serve the oil fields. Saudi Arabia's Dammam was such a port.

In a striking scene in his magnificent petro-novel about Saudi Arabia, *Cities of Salt*, Abdulrahman Munif writes about the arrival of the cargo ships that brought with them the tools and equipment required for drilling oil. As more and more ships came to Saudi Arabia, more and more infrastructure was required to cope with the arriving cargo. The volume of goods was now far too large for offshore lighterage (offloading cargo onto barges whose shallower draughts were better accommodated by the coastal shoals). Munif tells the story of how the port area was built.

> The ships docked one after the other, and no sooner were the huge crates mounted up in ever higher hills with every new ship, than another large plot of land was sealed off behind barbed wire. This land began in the middle of the gulf coastline and stretched northward and eastward as far as the far-off hills . . . Soon after the arrival of a new group of foreign men in a ship different from the others, a phase of work began that never slowed or stopped. It was like madness or magic. Men raced back and forth with the raging yellow machines that created new hills racing behind them. They filled the sea and levelled the land, they did all this without pausing and without reflection.[8]

If ships are to berth at the shore, rather than out to sea, harbours have to be dredged. The Gulf coastline, as I have already written, is quite shallow, subject to underwater *shamal* currents and thus, without interference, it is not amenable to the close berthing of ships with deeper draughts. To make these new ports, the existing rhythm of life and spaces of work on the sea had to be changed. Fishermen were no longer welcome where the large cargo ships and tankers steamed. Seaside villages, if not razed, were overshadowed by the great ports and the refineries disgorging fire and smoke.

Until the Ras Tanura and Al-Khobar piers were built to load crude and bring in imports, shallow barges to and from Bahrain managed all trade with Saudi Arabia's Gulf coast. In Saudi Arabia, California Arabian Standard Oil Company (CASOC) soon changed its name to Arabian American Oil Company (Aramco). Bahrain Petroleum Company (BAPCO) was operated by a subsidiary of California Standard Oil Company. The intimacy of the geographies of Saudi Arabia and Bahrain, not to mention corporate relations between the two companies, facilitated the collaboration in construction, refining and sale of crude.

The first tanker to take up oil at Ras Tanura was celebrated with a fanfare that indicated the significance of the oil port. *DG Scofield* was almost 140 metres long and could carry 81,224 barrels of crude and 10,676 barrels of fuel.[9] As Robert Vitalis recounts, King Abdulaziz was there to turn the valve to fill the ship, sending off 'the first tanker full of Saudi crude to pay for all the roads, railways, ministries, prisons, pipelines, and palaces that the new California construction company Bechtel Brothers ultimately built for the Al Saud'.[10]

During World War II, Aramco was forced to halt production due to shortages of personnel and equipment. In his commissioned hagiography of Aramco, Wallace Stegner describes the momentary silence of the oil terminals:

> At Ras Tanura the crude oil tank farm stood idle, the pumps were still, the port facilities were unused ... No crude coursed through the pipeline from Dammam, no tanker followed the course of the *D.G. Scofield* to the moorings ... Any tankers plying the Gulf, and any naval vessels in need of refuelling, were headed for Bahrain or Abadan, where they could obtain refined products.[11]

By 1944, production had begun again. In that year, 60,000 tonnes of equipment arrived at the rudimentary Al-Khobar pier and the Ras Tanura cargo wharves, intended for repairing the oil fields left idle during the war. Ras Tanura's harbour was so busy with tankers loading crude, as well as with unloading nearly 260,000 tonnes of cargo in one year, that plans were made in 1946 to relieve the pressure on the oil terminal by building a new port exclusively to receive cargo.[12] Only five years later, Dammam had been transformed from a small village into a major port, connected to Riyadh by a newly built railway.

In the 1950s, Aramco's maritime operations required an outpost at Jeddah on the Red Sea, where both crude and bunkering fuel were sold to its customers. Archival records show bout after bout of expansion of piers at Dammam, Ras Tanura, and Jeddah, including a major dredging programme in 1967 to address the silting of all three harbours and deepen the draughts to accommodate VLCCs and ULCCs. The Aramco report for 1970 described the process of deepening as drilling holes into 'rocky knolls' in the seabed and dredging away a vast section of the seabed to a depth of nearly thirty metres. The new oil terminal of Ju'ayma was built in 1974 on the Gulf coast and is today the largest crude-loading port of Saudi Arabia. The late 1970s saw nothing but the expansion of tank farms and the addition of new berths and offshore technologies, including sea islands to facilitate loading ULCCs at some distance from the shore.[13]

The effect of such traffic in both crude and cargo was not only to expand ports and offshore loading islands and buoys in Saudi Arabia, but also to expand Aramco's procurement and distribution activities in the US and Europe. Trucking fleets, pipelines, and barge ports were all mustered. The network of trade in petroleum, refined products, and goods and equipment needed for the oil business extended worldwide.[14] Only the Tanker Wars of the 1980s between Iran and Iraq brought a temporary abatement in the business both of Ras Tanura and Dammam. Both ports continue to be – along with others on the Gulf coast of Saudi Arabia – operated by Aramco and, as such, are far less transparent to outside scrutiny than ports managed by cargo port authorities.

As in Bahrain before Saudi Arabia, and Kuwait after, the development of these new harbours was facilitated through the work of petroleum corporations that did *not* originally specialise in harbour construction, transport engineering, or infrastructure management. The early financing for these ports and harbours came not from the public purse or through fiscal allocations, but from investments by foreign petroleum companies. The private ownership structures of these cargo ports limited the extent to which local merchants and traders could access them; such shared use was only secured through negotiation or force.

Of course, this was a pattern familiar from the corporate sovereigns of the colonial era, foremost among them the myriad East India Companies. In the Gulf, British and American petroleum companies forged a vertical integration of infrastructure construction and commodity extraction that facilitated the emergence of this new and rapacious form of commodity capitalism. They did so for a long time with total carte blanche, their 'developmental' programmes blurring into the work of states, their officers and officials playing musical chairs in the consultancies or diplomatic corps of their home countries. The histories of Mina Ahmadi and Shuwaikh in Kuwait, Dammam and Ras Tanura in Saudi Arabia, and others in the upper Gulf are intimately tied to the history of extraction of oil there.

Creeks and Harbours of the Trucial Coast

> Most of the Dubai shore line is a flat and barren waste traversed by small creeks and with little vegetation beyond coarse grass, clumps of mangroves, and an occasional small garden or palm grove around a well. In fact, this stretch of coast is so flat that the little hill of Jebel Ali is the chief landmark. A long reef running parallel to the shore has been the graveyard of many vessels, including the British East India Company's sloop *Elphinstone* which struck there in 1837.
>
> Richard Sanger, *Arabian Peninsula*

Dubai's history differs from that of the ports of the upper Gulf. Although some petroleum was discovered there in the early 1960s, it was never considered to be enough for commercial exploitation; and in any case the port was already being developed as a hub of trade. The city of Dubai, like the other coastal emirates that formed the UAE in the early 1970s, was situated on sand spits with protected lagoons or creeks that allowed for safe anchorage, but which could not accommodate ships with deep draughts. These creeks and lagoons were also vulnerable to silting.[15] The emirates were distinct in governance and economic specialisation, and if they had any relationship with one another, it was via maritime connections and trade.[16] Dubai was a special case among them, as it had already been designated a free port in 1904.[17] This and its tax-free, customs-free entrepôt status distinguished Dubai from other emirates on the coast. Further, its location and overseas ties (especially to Iran and India) developed through trade and smuggling proved durable and influential, shaping the patterns of commerce and parameters of rule. But what also differentiated Dubai from the other emirates was its ruling family's always friendly relations with the British. By contrast, though Sharjah had provided an air outpost for Imperial Airways (a precursor to British Airways) since 1932 and an airbase for the Royal Air Force during World War II, its rulers were considered to have historically had 'a general attitude of obstruction and opposition' to Britain in ways the Al Maktum of Dubai had not.[18]

In the 1950s, as anticolonial movements unravelled the empire and nationalist sentiments roiled the tricontinents, the British began to consider a programme of economic development as a bulwark against the possibility of revolution. Given that the Gulf region was no longer simply a transit or trade outpost but the hub of oil production in the Eastern Hemisphere, colonial officials began to look to infrastructure projects that could encourage commerce and industry in the places where the British still held sway. There was also pressure from local rulers for means to enrich their purse and give their treasuries leverage over an increasingly vocal merchant class. As part of this push for development, in the early 1950s, the British political officers commissioned a British engineering firm, Halcrow, to conduct a study of the Sharjah and Dubai Creeks to gauge their suitability to house a new harbour. Halcrow issued two reports, one for each emirate. The reports, at around twenty pages each, briefly described the economic significance of the two harbours and the prevailing marine conditions that could affect their design (tides, winds, currents, and the like), and considered the difficulties and costs of their engineering and construction.

Halcrow's report on Dubai described its commerce as 'entrepôt trade in European and Far Eastern commodities which are imported by oceangoing vessels and distributed over a wide area by local craft'. However, the harbour itself was silting, and the

> ships anchor about a mile offshore and transfer cargo to lighters having a loaded draught of five feet, which are consequently able to enter the harbour only during periods of relative high tide. Storms are liable to arise suddenly and the risk of damage to lighters and cargoes is reflected in the high insurance rates operating.[19]

The report added that fully laden ships of draughts deeper than six feet (two metres) were unable to leave the harbour, over the sandbar at its mouth.

Their report on Sharjah recognised the commercial significance of the town, which 'was for many centuries the most prosperous centre of maritime activity in the region', and acknowledged that unsuccessful attempts had been made in the past to 'build a harbour in the shelter of the rocky point at Layya'.[20] The report also pointed out that the silting of the Sharjah Creek had gone so far that most of Sharjah's everyday supplies were now imported through Dubai. Halcrow's report emphasised not only the degradation of Sharjah Creek but also its transport infrastructures, and indicated the other options the ruling family of the emirate was considering:

> The Customs Wharf at Sharjah was built some twenty years ago to facilitate the landing of heavy materials when the airport was being constructed but because of the deterioration in the condition of the harbour referred to above, practically all the stores and plant required now for both service and civilian stations are imported through Dubai ... The recent acquisition of new possessions on the Muscat coast is likely to give a new impetus to this [entrepôt] trade and efforts are being made to open up a trading centre based on the fine natural harbour of Khor Fakkan.[21]

Both reports contained a long litany of the problems that a construction project of this magnitude would face. These included

> (a) Lack of raw materials. Only sand and stone are available naturally. Cement, timber, oil, fuel and fresh water in any quantity would have to be imported. (b) Lack of skilled labour. (c) Lack of adequate housing for the necessary [European] supervisory staff and cost of providing special housing. (d) All plant would have to be imported and freight charges would be heavy. (e) A comparatively small job of this nature would not be attractive to first class contracting firms unless they happened to be working within a reasonable distance from Dubai. Competition would therefore be limited and tendering would consequently not be keen.[22]

The report then indicated that these factors could increase the cost of construction of these harbours by several factors beyond the cost of similar projects in the UK. The reports estimated the cost of dredging the creek and construction of a harbour for Dubai at £388,000 (approximately £9.6 million in today's value) and for Sharjah at a range between £250,000 and £825,000 (or between £6.2 and £20 million today).

Upon receiving Halcrow's 1955 reports on the development of Sharjah and Dubai Harbours, the commercial secretary at the political residency in Bahrain, W.H. Adams, wrote in a memo that Sharjah's 'harbour facilities must continue to decline and in due course it will cease to exist as a "deep sea" port'. Commercially, however, Dubai would be encouraged to 'survive and probably develop'. Financing options for dredging the Dubai Creek included a possible loan from the UK government 'secured by a lien on Customs revenues' or loans from construction companies or banks. Adams added that he preferred the first option, 'as we could then dictate terms and the dictation of terms would seem to be most necessary'. The dictation of terms was deemed crucial for the British to create a 'free-port' facility for Sharjah in Dubai and allow Sharjah to decline as a port.[23]

In the event, Shaikh Rashid of Dubai attempted to raise some part of the necessary financing for the dredging project through a bond issue. The issue was taken up by both Dubai merchants (whose purchase of the bond secured a third of the necessary budget at £200,000). The rest of the cost was covered by a loan from the government of Kuwait. The Kuwaiti loan was guaranteed with the anticipated incomes from customs collection in Dubai. To improve the process of customs collection, the ruler of Bahrain seconded businessman Mahdi al-Tajir as the head of Dubai Customs.[24] Mahdi al-Tajir went on to become the most powerful man in Dubai, after Shaikh Rashid himself, and acquired a vast estate in Scotland in 1975, becoming one of the richest men there. The Dubai Creek was eventually dredged by Overseas AST of Austria and Halcrow.[25] Dredgers then expurgated the sand bank at the mouth of the creek and the harbour was deepened to eight feet.

The effect was to provide Dubai with a deep harbour – and enrich Shaikh Rashid's own purse. The UAE historian Frauke Heard-Bey explains how the Dubai Creek dredging project

> proved to be not only a costly convenience but was turned to good advantage because the spoil was deposited in a low-lying area nearby to create new building land. The sale of this land paid for the cost of dredging. The value of reclaimed land became an integral part in the assessment of all marine projects; no amount of dredging work seemed too large when the cost of that work was already debited against expected commercial value of the new building sites. The Ruler personally became the owner of such reclaimed land. Since he also often personally guaranteed loans raised for certain projects, the money he would eventually realize from selling land was taken into consideration when negotiating such loans.[26]

Sharjah's fate – at least for the following decade – was determined not only by British reluctance to dredge its creek but also by the winds blowing from the deserts of Iran across the waters. In 1960, one particularly stormy *shamal* – which lasted several days and caused drastic changes in currents, tides, and temperatures – blustered so unrelentingly that it shifted a sandbar to the mouth of the Sharjah Creek and sealed it shut. 'Overnight the tidal creek became a saltwater lake.'[27] With the enclosure of the Sharjah Creek just as Dubai Creek was being deepened, the merchant families of Sharjah relocated their businesses down the coast to Dubai. The British rancour against Shaikh Saqr of Sharjah arose because they deemed his closer relations with the Arab League and Egypt's Gamal Abdel Nasser threatening to their interests on the Peninsula. Enclosing Sharjah Creek and dredging Dubai Creek was meant as a punishment for one and reward for the other. The transformation of Sharjah Creek into a deepwater port had to wait until the British began planning to leave the Gulf.

Dubai

Delicate aluminium girders
Project phantom aerial masts
Swaying crane and derrick
Above the sea's just surging deck.

Stephen Spender, 'Air Raid Across the Bay at Plymouth'

Dubai's next maritime transport project was an even larger mechanised port to relieve the congestion of the now-deepened creek harbour. Halcrow was again involved in the surveys for what eventually became Port Rashid at the entrance to the creek. The British projections for Dubai trade formed the basis for the 1967 port plans, even as Shaikh Rashid (and his Scottish economic adviser, Bill Duff) argued for four times as many berths as Halcrow allowed. When Port Rashid was inaugurated in 1971, it was already congested and had to be expanded to thirty-seven berths by the end of that decade.[28] The congestion of the port had everything to do with the independence of Aden from British colonial yoke. Dubai benefitted from revolution and war in Southern Arabia as shipping and bunkering businesses moved their base there from Aden. By the late 1970s, Port Rashid was the largest port in the Gulf, and typical of the ports of its time: still close to the commercial centre of the city, capable of serving large container ships, and later complemented with a drydock suitable for repairing crude carriers, liquefied natural gas (LNG) vessels, and dredgers. Shaikh Rashid had appointed the British shipping firm Gray McKenzie to manage the port, consolidating the old and powerful colonial company's reach into new Dubai's commercial life. The old Creek harbour was in turn transformed into a dhow port.

Even before the expansion of Port Rashid, however, Shaikh Rashid (or his advisers) planned for a much larger port about forty-five kilometres south of Port Rashid, very close to the border with Abu Dhabi. This border area had been contested for some time between the two emirates, with the dispute only settled in 1968. Rashid's placement of the new port there was not only an act of commercial foresight but of sovereign prerogative. The lore behind the genesis of Jabal Ali has Shaikh Rashid, a kind of hagiographic archetype of the wise and visionary ruler, standing astride a dune on the windswept and beautiful sand flats of Jabal Ali, striking his staff on the ground in 1976 and declaring that a new port would be built there. And it was. The construction of Jabal Ali consolidated Rashid's claim over the contested borderland. It was also intended to send a message to Saudi Arabia, which had just begun an ambitious maritime construction project in Jubail and Yanbu, also planned by Halcrow.[29]

Notwithstanding the Orientalist fantasy of a visionary shaikh calling infrastructures into being, there is something extravagantly modernist about making the largest artificial harbour in the world – as in Jabal Ali – without regard to the obvious unsuitability of the site, both geologically and geopolitically. It is wildly optimistic to ignore natural topographies in trying to make harbours conform to the demands of ever larger ships, especially on the shores of a sea that is so shallow and so prone to capricious undersea currents that continually shape and reshape the seabed and affect its depth. Jabal Ali was constructed in record time, and with it a free zone whose enterprise was crucial for the early growth in trade and custom at the port. A vast amount of sand and stone had to be dredged, which was then used to reclaim the port's built-up area. Shaikh Rashid gave the management contract for Jabal Ali to the US-based SeaLand company, which was originally founded by Malcom McLean, the inventor of the twenty-foot shipping container.[30] Both SeaLand and Gray McKenzie, however, gave way to the Dubai Port Authority, which took over managing Jabal Ali and Port Rashid in 1991. Dubai Port Authority merged with Dubai Ports International in 2005, forming Dubai Ports World.[31] Today, Jabal Ali is the busiest container port in the Middle East and is always included in top-ten lists of the world's container terminals.[32] It is typical of today's container ports: vast, distant from the town centre, and thoroughly and entirely secured.

Port	2016 Rank	2016 Volume (million Twenty-foot Equivalent Units or TEUs)	2017 Rank	2017 Volume (million TEUs)
Shanghai, China	1	37.13	1	40.23
Singapore	2	30.90	2	33.67
Shenzhen, China	3	23.97	3	25.21
Ningbo-Zhoushan, China	4	21.60	4	24.61
Busan, South Korea	5	19.85	6	20.49
Hong Kong, S.A.R., China	6	19.81	5	20.77
Guangzhou Harbour, China	7	18.85	7	20.35
Qingdao, China	8	18.01	8	18.31
Jabal Ali, Dubai, UAE	9	14.77	9	15.37
Tianjin, China	10	14.49	10	15.07
Port Klang, Malaysia	11	13.20	12	11.98
Rotterdam, Netherlands	12	12.38	11	13.73
Khor Fakkan, UAE	37	4.33	43 (combined with all other Sharjah ports)	3.8
			78 (ranked alone)	2.32
Jeddah, Saudi Arabia	40	3.96	36	4.15
Salalah, Oman	46	3.32	39	3.94
Port Said East, Egypt	50	3.04	56	2.97
Dammam, Saudi Arabia	86	1.78	97	1.58
King Abdullah, Saudi Arabia	100	1.40	89	1.69

Table 2.1 – World's top container ports[33]

During my research, I desperately wanted to visit Jabal Ali port, but had immense trouble getting an entry permission. Most port workers from whom I requested interviews offered to meet me outside its perimeter. I managed to visit the port eventually by travelling there twice, aboard two different container ships. The second time, arriving at midnight, the sea near Jabal Ali coruscated with the reflection of innumerable ships' lights as they awaited the call to enter the channel towards the port. When we were finally given permission to enter the channel, we were at the head of a small convoy of ships all traversing along the slightly bent route of the channel, towards the port, in the hot early-morning haze of August 2016. I was struck by the sheer scale of the port and the engineering that had made it possible: a channel deep enough to accommodate the very largest container ships, so much land reclamation, so many security fences, and beyond them the endless Jabal Ali Free Zone stretching to the murky horizon. The Admiralty Charts that mapped our approach also showed this vast port, all of it reclaimed and dredged, the roadstead wholly engineered. On the chart itself, the waters were shallow, the shorelines drawn straight as if with a ruler, the Palm Jabal Ali's artificial islands marked as incomplete while recognisable in their duplication of the contours of other Palm islands further up the coast. Unfinished terminals and breakwaters also appear on the map. The port, heaving with activity and exhaling haze and pollution, is constantly metamorphosing, expanding, convulsing with production and trade.

The material needed for all this construction and manufacture had to come from somewhere, especially as the pace of commerce, town planning, and the fashioning of infrastructures gathered in the 1960s and 1970s, raising the demand for cement and sand, aggregate and stone. The UAE did not acquire a cement factory until 1975.[34] Most of the cement was imported from Japan and other sources. Even the sand and stone required for the construction of harbours in Abu Dhabi and Dubai had to come from somewhere. Ghalilah and Khor Khwair in the poorer northern emirate of Ras al-Khaimah became the source for aggregate for construction in 1963 and thereafter.[35] The first jetties in Ras al-Khaimah were built at the behest of Abu Dhabi in 1966, to facilitate the extraction of aggregate for the construction of Abu Dhabi's Port Zayed. The proximity of Ras al-Khaimah's quarries in the mountains to the new jetty on the shore and the quality of the mountain rocks, rich in silicate and limestone, made the emirate an ideal source for construction material. Precisely because these construction materials were so precious and so necessary for the expansion of the UAE's infrastructures, extracting them was not without conflict. Local groups clashed with one another and with the ruler over rights of access and profits from their richer southern neighbour's exploitation of these coveted commodities.[36]

The building of harbours and ports in the UAE has grown apace. Today, Abu Dhabi, Dubai, Sharjah, Fujairah, and Ras al-Khaimah all have major oceangoing ports as well as a number of smaller harbours and oil terminals on and offshore. In 2012, Abu Dhabi inaugurated Port Khalifa, a mere seventy kilometres south of Dubai's Jabal Ali. Port Khalifa replaces Port Zayed, which is centrally located within the city of Abu Dhabi, and will soon be 'redeveloped'. Abu Dhabi has clearly followed the precedent set by Jabal Ali: a vast free zone (Khalifa Industrial Zone Abu Dhabi, or Kizad) benefitting from proximity to an oceangoing port with deep channels. Whether Khalifa will ever be as significant a cargo port as Jabal Ali has to do not only with economic calculations and incentives but also the push and pull between the rival emirates. Khalifa itself is built on land reclaimed from the sea and sits astride forty million cubic metres of materials dredged from the access channels and harbour area. Although its construction included a breakwater meant to protect a rare coral reef near the site, an environmental impact assessment by Halcrow produced at the start of the project indicated that there was very little environmental data available as a baseline. Nor had there been any consultation on environmental impact before the master plan was put forward. Like so many other ports in the region, it displays a gaping chasm between the discourse of preservation and the practice of port-building.

The story of Dubai is emblematic of other port-states of the British Empire. Dubai may be ridiculed as a kind of mirage in the desert and an embodiment of hubris, but neither its headlong rush to capitalisation nor its mercantile history nor even its ignominious story of exploitation of migrant workers and hierarchies of expertise and management are too dissimilar from Singapore or Hong Kong. In its constant scramble for ever-deeper harbours; in its ruthless moulding, whittling, and carving up of sea into land and land into more land; in its stories of colonial control and decision-making; even in the self-serving legends told about its visionary local leaders, Dubai is like so many other nodes in the great matrix of commerce and capital worldwide. As Jabal Ali rises, Port Rashid becomes something else – serving passengers, not cargo, while the commerce seeping from the skin of Jabal Ali's vast port and free zone keeps the engines of dhows, feeder ships, intermodal transport vehicles, and even air cargo well-lubricated.

With the transformations of Ports Rashid and Zayed in the Emirates and Port Qabus in Muscat into cruise-ship ports, as in other ports throughout the Peninsula and beyond, old ports close to the cities and embedded in the thriving life of the urban quarters begin to disappear or cease functioning in the lively way they had done at their inauguration. In his account of the decline of European ports, Allan Sekula writes:

> Harbors are now less *havens* (as they were for the Dutch) than accelerated turning basins for supertankers and containerships. The old harbour front, its links to a common culture shattered by unemployment, is now reclaimed for a bourgeois reverie on

> the mercantilist past. Heavy metals accumulate in the silt ... The backwater becomes the frontwater. Everyone wants a glimpse of the sea.[37]

The new cargo ports that replace city-centre ports are vast, securitised, and far from the heart of the city, nearly impossible to access. The transformation of the old ports into places of entertainment, consumption, and tourism resonates with the inception of semi-automated cargo ports. 'Technology, trade and tourism' (the motto of Dubai), the far port, the 'accelerated turning basins', environmental impact assessments as afterthoughts, and automation are all fundamental to the working of economies of these modern free ports, where ecological degradation and exploitation of labour are obscured in the haze of efficient commercial functioning and the technological sublime of colourful cargo boxes. So much of this history is tinged by colonial decision-making.

Aden

Aden has a different story. In 1837, the East India Company's Court of Directors agreed to convert their ships to steam to escape the directional tyranny of the monsoon winds.[38] Captain Stafford Bettesworth Haines set off to survey the coasts of Arabia and first alighted on the island of Soqotra. When, after a scant few months, Soqotra's harbour and climate proved inhospitable, Haines decided that Aden would be a useful refuelling port for steamships on their way to Suez and overland to Alexandria. A pretext was needed to conquer Aden. The grounding of a Bombay ship that was looted by locals (probably in collusion with its owner, for insurance takings) provided the excuse. Aden was occupied in 1839 by the warships of the British governorate of Bombay under the command of Haines himself, citing 'outrage against' women passengers of the stranded ship. Haines was then appointed Political Agent of

Aden by the Bombay Presidency of the East India Company, and went on to transform Aden into a coal depot and naval base to serve the Company's Indian Ocean trade. Beyond using Aden as a strategic refuelling outpost, however, successive governments of Bombay (whether ruled through a corporation or the empire) were not interested in developing the Aden harbour for commerce and even rejected a local proposal to build a new wharf there in the early twentieth century.[39]

Aden's crucial strategic value was predicated on it being one of the most important coaling stations in the world, at one point bunkering more ships than any other port besides London, Liverpool, and New York City. To protect their strategic outpost from Yemeni tribes, the British created a buffer zone, a bulwark of 'British troops, mostly Indian' around the port city.[40] The port itself had always been a multilingual place of work for lighterers and fishermen (prominent among them Somalis) and for traders from the four corners of the world.[41]

Once the Suez Canal opened in 1869, the strategic position of Aden and its fine, deep natural harbour made it even more important to the British. It was easily the empire's most indispensable strategic node east of Suez at the time. Like so many other city-states, it had been absorbed by the empire as an outpost in the ocean, in a chain of port cities from Gibraltar to Hong Kong that bolstered British trade in the Mediterranean and the Indian Ocean. In his account of visiting the Arabian Peninsula in the 1920s, Ameen Rihani described Aden's two important commercial sites:

> the one for replenishing steam-power, the other for guiding at night; the one consists of black piles rising in squares and pyramids near the water and adding a touch of realism to the inferno of Steamer Point, the other stands aloft, above all the heights, housed in a circular tower, protected with glass, and made articulate with colours. King Coal, the Harbour Light, and the Electric Wire, here is Aden's trinity of materialism.[42]

With 'King Coal' depots came inland trade. As historian On Barak writes, 'railways, tramways, telegraphs, and water pumps [all] facilitated the movement and operation of policemen, judges, inoculation officials, and irrigation inspectors' deep into Aden and the hinterland.[43] Gujarati and other Indian capitalists made Aden their base of trade,[44] as did European traders in coffee, salt, hides, and other regional products. Many famous London trading houses had offices in Aden, including Cory Brothers, who by the end of the nineteenth century were the most important coal traders in the London docks. The best-known shipping companies of Aden in the early half of the twentieth century were owned by Antonin Besse and Cowasjee Dinshaw. The French-born Besse was a ruthless businessman who treated his workers poorly and had a monopoly on Shell products in Yemen. His donations went on to found St Antony's College of Oxford. Cowasjee Dinshaw & Bros. shipping company astutely contracted with British India Steamship Navigation from early on and secured contracts with the (British) Indian Navy, thus accumulating enough capital to guarantee expansion throughout the western Indian Ocean.[45] The company's extensive network of branches in East Africa and on the Red Sea coast (including Hodeidah and Jeddah), its ownership of a fleet of steamers trading to East Africa, and a 'floating dock capable of accommodating ships of 1,400 tons' in the early twentieth century aided it in becoming a significant shipping agent for larger firms, including British P&O (Peninsular and Oriental Steam Navigation Company); an employer of vast numbers of dockers (about which more in later chapters); and an influential player in the politics of Aden.[46]

Colonial Aden was so significant an outpost that many well-known writers and poets earning a living as functionaries or merchants passed through there. The great French poet Arthur Rimbaud lived and worked as a coffee trader (or gun runner) in Aden in 1880 before shifting his trading business to Abyssinia. Some decades later, in the 1930s, another Frenchman, the communist Paul Nizan, ran away to Aden from Paris in a rebellion against the stultifying conservatism of France. In Aden, he became the tutor to Besse's son, and many of the scenes in his *Aden Arabie* are thought to take place in the offices of the French-born millionaire. By the time Nizan arrived in Aden, coal was being slowly replaced by petroleum products as ships' fuel, and the port city once known as the world's coaling station was now one of the most important oil-bunkering ports in the world. Nizan described oil throbbing through the veins of the port:

> In the great, open port between Steamer Point and Maala, there is tremendous activity. The liners of the P. and O. and the Messageries Maritimes clear a path for themselves through a tangle of peeling freighters, tankers, motor boats, and Arab [dhows] . . . The oil flows through big, jointed pipes that run just below the surface of the water, like sea serpents – the only authentic ones. The oil feeds the ships' tanks.
>
> Not so long ago, Aden was a coaling station. Oil brought with it offices, docks, the black tanks of the Anglo-Persian and Asiatic Petroleum, and intrigues that rouse the emotions of the little potentates who have become sellers of oil and buyers of gasoline for automobiles. A little war for concessions is spreading all around.[47]

After India's independence, Aden's significance as a trade hub, a bunkering port, and a strategic outpost for the British increased still further. Its location bolstered Britain's waning supremacy over trade routes that brought oil and commodities to the war-wrecked metropole. In 1954, a former diplomat's description of Aden saw it as handling

> more trade than any other city in Arabia. By virtue of a good harbour, the business acumen of its merchants, and the fact that it is a free port, Aden controls an extensive market, embracing

> the territories of Aden Protectorates, Yemen, Ethiopia, and the Somaliland. Furthermore, it is a worldwide entrepôt centre on the routes to South Africa and Singapore.[48]

But the same free-port status that made it such a good transhipment port also prevented it from developing domestic industries; much of the profit from merchant trade was repatriated to the home countries of these merchants.[49]

Events in the region only underlined the geopolitical and geoeconomic significance of Aden. When Iranian prime minister Mohammad Mosaddegh nationalised the Anglo-Iranian Oil Company (British Petroleum) in 1951, the company lost access to its largest refinery in the world in Abadan. It constructed a replacement refinery in Aden which refined Kuwaiti petroleum into marine fuel oils. The Aden Port Trust was happy to welcome the new refinery. It provided a vast tract of land to the company and promised that the 'cost of reclaiming the land would be borne by the Port Trust and rent charged at 6 per cent per annum on the cost of area required'.[50] The reclaimed land was built on 'dredging spoils' and the company dictated how much water frontage it needed.

The coming of the refinery to Aden further consolidated Aden's position as a petroleum bunkering port. Constant improvement ensured that the port's infrastructure kept up with the enlarging ships and their expanding numbers. In 1956, just before the closure of the Suez Canal in the tripartite war against Egypt, it was decided that the traffic in the harbour necessitated further expansion of the port. This massive project of engineering entailed the construction of two colossal quay walls built from concrete and connected to the Ma'alla wharf, as well as 'excavation and dumping into the sea of over half a million tons of rock to form retaining embankments' to hold the prodigious volumes of dredged materials from the harbour.[51]

All this construction required far more skilled labour than past forms of building and assembly, giving workers more leverage than ever before, which foreshadowed the coming anticolonial struggles.[52] The strikes and political mobilisation that began in the 1950s had intensified by the 1967 War. The closures of the Suez Canal in 1956 and 1967 were felt swiftly and deeply in Aden, sharpening the struggle against the British. By the end of 1967, the British had abandoned Aden and the southern Yemeni hinterland. The formation of the People's Democratic Republic of Yemen (PDRY) was accompanied by a catastrophic economic collapse in which over 80,000 workers migrated to the Gulf and to East Africa, another 20,000 Adenese became unemployed, and the port economy was shattered.[53] In the space of a year, port traffic reduced to only one-fifth of its previous volume, with Dubai's Port Rashid picking up much of Aden's trade and bunkering business.[54]

The reopening of the Suez Canal in 1975 provided some relief as the bunkering business picked up again. To acknowledge this upturn, the World Bank lent Yemen US$16.8 million that year to improve the port in Aden. Over the course of the next two decades, Aden regained some of its former business, but it was surpassed in size and significance by the ports of the Gulf. The next chapter in the development of the port brought regional capital into Aden. In 2008, Yemen signed a contract with Dubai Ports World which stipulated DP World's investment of US$220 million to improve the port and increase port capacity and throughput. When, in 2012, it became clear that DP World had not increased capacity or throughput (and had likely diverted traffic *away* from Aden to Jabal Ali), the Yemeni government paid the company off to cancel its concession.

United Arab Emirates returned to Yemeni ports in 2015, when a coalition led by Saudi Arabia and the UAE attacked Yemen. The very first act of the coalition was to shut down the ports of Aden and Hodeidah and halt all commercial activity. Port facilities throughout the country were laid to waste through repeated bombardment. The naval blockade and the destruction of the ports, particularly Hodeidah in 2017, led to starvation, a cholera epidemic, and a catastrophic shortage of medicine. The coalition prevented aid cargoes from arriving in ports, even if ports had been functioning to take delivery of food and medicine. Oblivious to the devastation and heedless of having been kicked out of Aden a scant three years before, the CEO of DP World offered to restore the port: 'We are exploring areas where we can help our near neighbours in their efforts to restore critical marine and trade infrastructure at Aden and look forward to developing our discussions in the immediate future.'[55] A coercive conquest was once again presented as a project of development.

While Dammam and Ras Tanura had been conjured out of the magic of petroleum, Dubai had traded on its amicable imperial relations with its British protector to surpass its northern rival Sharjah and transform its peripheral coastal position into a central vertex of trade. Aden had a different trajectory. Intimately enmeshed in colonial histories of coercion and commerce, the fate of Aden as a major bunkering port and later as a plaything of regional capital and militaries shows how the modalities of capital accumulation and colonialism sideline some places of trade while valorising others. The decline of Aden is as much about the depredations of regional capital as it is about the end of colonialism.

Making and Remaking the Land and the Sea

> Jeddah woke to hundreds of workers walling off its shoreline. The sea was parcelled off and no one batted an eyelid as city councillors and their retinue of bureaucrats, lawyers, brokers and developers all got their share. Nothing was left for the rest of the population.
>
> The fishermen were the first to suffer from this de facto exclusion from their time-honoured fishing ground ... When they first brought in the tonnes of earth from nearby wadis to reclaim

the sea, Hamed Abu Gulumbo looked around for his favourite place on the shorefront and found it gone.

Abdo Khal, *Throwing Sparks*

The mechanised ports I have written about are undoubtedly seductive, in the way the vastness of engineering and technological modernity, the symmetry of metal and concrete, and the effusion of colour, movement, and sound can be seductive. Container cranes are balletic, large ships awesome. Even the vision of ships at anchor, whether shimmering in the distant haze or on a ship's Automatic Identification System (AIS) screen, gives a sense of worldly transactions, of the hidden movements of money and commodities that make capitalist accumulation and the production and consumption of goods possible.

As far back as 1925, Walter Benjamin was titillated by the sensory profusion of cargo ports. Visiting Genoa on a freighter, he described 'the sounds of unloading freighters all around me as the modernised "music of the world"'.[56] In ports distant from city centres, this music of the world is still played by an orchestra of gantry cranes, containers clanging against one another, and trucks rattling over rails. But the audience for such music is far smaller than it would have been in harbours at the centre of the town. City-centre harbours of the Peninsula are today either sites for hotels and cafés, densely occupied dhow harbours, or ports of transit for cruise-ships, those gleaming white maritime cities carrying thousands of bodies and tonnes of pollution.[57]

So many of the modern ports of the Arabian Peninsula, particularly those on the shores of the Persian Gulf, have had to be built by machines and people in impossible settings. What makes the ports of the Arabian Peninsula so distinct is the preponderance of petroleum and chemical tankers, offshore loading and unloading platforms, and the importance of bunkering to the economies – at least, of the UAE.[58] Of the 97.2 million barrels per day of crude oil and petroleum products, 19 per cent passes through the Hormuz Straits, 16 per cent through the Malacca Straits, and another 5 per cent through the Bab al Mandab.[59] Most of these tankers take on their cargo at the buoys, loading islands, and VLCC and ULCC terminals of the Peninsula. Some fill their load in the Gulf, then top up their cargo in the deeper terminals outside Hormuz.[60] Fujairah in particular serves this function, especially for ships loading the same grade of Abu Dhabi crude, because Abu Dhabi has a pipeline carrying its crude to Fujairah, bypassing Hormuz.

This massive trade in petrochemicals and crude oil has its own environmental problems. A quarter of all oil spills enters a marine environment as a result of tanker transport.[61] Accidental leaks at loading or unloading, ship groundings, and ship collisions can cause oil spills.[62] On many coasts around the Gulf and the Arabian Sea, lumps of tar buried in the sand attest to leakages and spillages of oil. But tankers are not the only source of maritime pollution. Container and bulk ships discharging ballast water – in unregulated or lightly regulated ports – similarly release pollutants, though today ballast and oil/fuel tanks are supposed to be discrete and separated. Invasive species carried from other seas are another unwanted gift of illicitly released ballast water. Oily bilge water, if discharged illegally, is still another source of pollution. When travelling on the sea, in less regulated and monitored spaces, slicks of green, oily discharge floats on the surface of the sea for miles, refracting the sun through a yellowish prism.

Loading lubricating oils sold at bunkering ports, as well as discharging and disposing of sludge (waste product from the purification of ship's fuel), can also release contaminants into the sea. Extraordinarily, trade in tanker sludge is a big business. In 2008, a company in Fujairah could charge US$2 per tonne to take a ship's sludge and process it. But if the quantity of extractable oil in the slop was high, then the company actually *paid* the ship US$2 per tonne for the waste material.[63] If Mary Douglas is right that dirt is matter out of place, then pollution that has not yet entered the marine environment so often enters the circuits of exchange to produce profit.

But long before ships arrive at harbour to load or unload their cargo, ports need to be built. As the story I have told thus far shows, to make the improbable ports on flat shores, channels and harbours have had to be dredged, land reclaimed, and landside structures built. Armies of construction workers and engineers, and later port workers, have to be mustered. These massive projects of engineering and construction presume an epic and infinite ability to provide technological solutions to problems of geology, geography, and morphology.[64] The earth and the sea are assumed to be malleable.

Khor Fakkan port sits on a beautiful bit of land, backed by high mountains and facing the Gulf of Oman. A rocky hill stands tall on a promontory jutting out to sea at the southernmost edge of the town; along with two other rocky atolls nearby, it is a recognisable landmark. The hill also happens to loom tall over the container storage areas of the bustling port, one of the largest and busiest in the Middle East. When I visited the port, in the course of a conversation about expanding port capacity, the container terminal manager – a reserved British man who had spent his entire career in ports in Britain and the Middle East – pointed dismissively to the hill and said that he could 'move that mountain' if he needed more space to store the containers. For him, shaping the land, reclaiming it or flattening it or whittling away at it, was no matter.

This hunger for ever-expanding tracts of land to store containers, imported vehicles, and warehouses or to have longer and more numerous ship berths and gantry cranes has pushed ports the world over out of city centres. The further the ports are from the hubbub of cities, the more they are rendered conveniently invisible and unreachable to most. This inaccessibility shapes not only landscapes but labour regimes and living and working conditions for those who work there (about which more in later chapters). These global ports also necessitate a transformation of the seascape and the seabeds for ever-deeper approach channels to facilitate the movement of ever-more-gargantuan freighters and tankers. This is most astonishingly clear when steaming through the access channel to the container terminals at Jabal Ali. Carved out of a shallow seabed, the approach channel is a narrow conduit to land which ships must strictly follow. Admiralty Charts, continually adjusted and updated by ships' officers with their scissors and glues and bits of printed corrections, show a channel at most eighteen metres deep passing through shallows that sometimes do not exceed five metres. The significance of these depths is that some of the largest ships, especially when laden, can have draughts as deep as seventeen metres. Accounts of ships running aground in these shallow channels, or just outside their marked and buoyed boundaries, are not rare. The superficiality of the waters is not helped by the ever-shifting muddy seabed that is moulded by tides and currents. The *shamal* winds that bring with them illness and bad omens also affect sea currents and shift the seabed in unpredictable ways. The channels approaching Jabal Ali have to be dredged as often as the draught of the ships berthing at the port deepens.[65]

The Gulf is a relatively shallow young sea, formed only in the last 15,000 years as glaciers melted and the Indian Ocean waters rose and poured into the dry lakebed the Gulf had become.[66] Even in the Red Sea, an older, deeper sea, making harbours requires marine engineering and audacious reshaping of the sea and the shore. Here, it is not the sand shoals and muddy seabeds but the treacherous maze of coral reefs running in lines both perpendicular and parallel to the coast that makes navigation and berthing an act of skill, patience, and experience among ships' captains. The turquoise sea at Jeddah is disrupted by churning grey waters skimming the surfaces of coral ridges and islands just under the surface. These are sometimes, though not always, marked with buoys or danger markers. Admiralty Charts of the Red Sea abound with warnings about coral reefs.

Though coral rock and the limestone seabeds of the Red Sea present different technical problems from the muddy shallows and shoals of the Gulf, marine engineering in both seas has transformed the sea, and with it the coastlines. It is difficult to say that much of the coastlines flanking harbours are untouched or 'natural'. So much has been changed in that space where land and sea meet, so many shorelines shifted, seabeds lifted, hills levelled, and lands claimed, that very little remains of the coastline that the fishermen, pearl-divers, sailors, and merchants of the eighteenth or even nineteenth centuries could recognise. With these changes, natural habitats and geographies have also been decimated.

Today there are still places that, because of the sheer obstinacy of their rocky, remote, and inaccessible coastlines, refuse the remaking craft of engineers – Musandam Peninsula foremost among them on the Arabian Peninsula. But land reclamation and dredging have affected perhaps the majority of the shore of the Persian Gulf, much of the southern coast of the Gulf of Oman, and a good deal of the Saudi Arabian shoreline, especially on the Gulf side (by some accounts, a scant four kilometres of mangroves remain on the Saudi Gulf shore).[67] The history of dredging and land reclamation in Belgium and the Netherlands, or the expansion of the Singaporean land mass, all show the extent to which these projects of engineering are central to the conception and maintenance of modern commerce and capitalism.[68]

In the Netherlands, where land was reclaimed from the thirteenth century onwards, the balance of existing governing forces (the bishopric, landowners, the municipal government, etc.) dictated to a great extent how reclaimed land was allocated and used, its ability to generate income or taxes, and ultimately how it influenced the shape of social relations. The reclaimed land was crucial to the subsequent process of capital accumulation in Europe triggered by overseas colonisation and the slave trade. The process of land reclamation in northwest Europe shaped authoritative and exploitative relations at home, but also had secondary and tertiary effects abroad.

That the Dutch had this experience of making land out of the sea has meant that even today, their expertise in dredging is called upon to make and remake coasts overseas.[69] Much of the transformation of the coasts and shorelines of the Arabian Peninsula – especially in port-building – has been effected by firms like Van Oord and Royal Boskalis of the Netherlands and Jan de Nul Group and DEME Group of Belgium. These firms have now been joined by Chinese, Korean, and Malaysian dredging firms as well as older US-based ones – and, tellingly, also by the National Marine Dredging Company, based in Abu Dhabi, which got its start, like so many other firms involved in harbour construction and operation, as a division of the Abu Dhabi National Oil Company. The firm, which is still largely owned by the government of Abu Dhabi, has entered consortiums with international dredging companies in megaprojects such as the Khalifa port and the new Suez Canal.

Dredging can have catastrophic effects. The deep sweeps of seabeds and coastlines disturb the sediments on the seabed and upturn fragile biological habitats under the sea or at the shoreline. Because of the frequency of oil spills, sedimentation of airborne pollution on the seabed, and contaminants from successive wars, disturbing the sea floor reintroduces toxic residues into the water and the pelagic fauna's diets. Coral communities are wrenched apart by dredging cutters and suction pipes. *Sabkhas* and mudflats – which are rich environments for marine and coastal species – are despoiled. The coastlines of the Gulf are quite unstable and shift dramatically with tidal surges and even storms. A former seafarer and trader recounts, in an oral history of Ras al-Khaimah:

> The local system of sweet and salt water, the tides and coastline soils are really complicated. They shift and act upon each other in ways that cannot be foreseen . . . It depended on rainfalls and

> floodwaters, and tides. At Ras al-Khaimah town, the biggest tide is in late summer, in August. Partly this comes from normal seasonal high tides, and then there is often a north wind then, and that makes the tide higher too.[70]

Dredging and land reclamation often have unpredictable effects on these complex and fragile ecological systems. Dredging damages the spawning grounds of prawns and fish through direct physical action but also because of increased turbidity, siltation, and sedimentation.[71] In the shallow Gulf, shorelines are dredged as well as wide approach channels to the berths. As ship sizes balloon and their draughts correspondingly deepen, these dredging projects become Sisyphean, again and again ripping apart a seabed that may have only just recovered from the previous bout of dredging. Land reclamation destroys mangroves, *sabkhas*, mudflats, and shallow-water marine ecosystems and devastates migratory and local bird habitats that depend on these coastal and intertidal systems. Infilling coastal areas with material dredged from the sea introduces sedimented marine pollution into liminal coastal areas and shorelines. In many instances, the change in the morphology of the shoreline also affects wave and current patterns, paradoxically increasing erosion at the shoreline.[72]

The effects of land reclamation are not solely ecological. As shorelines shift and maritime cartographies change, so do sea borders, exclusive maritime economic zones, and other topographic features that are transformed into legal and political categories. Land reclamation can bring with it disputes over the drawing of maritime borders and exploitation of subsea resources.[73] It can redefine what is meant by *international waters*. But land reclamation also creates value *ex nihilo*, giving those major investors access to land-as-commodity conjured out of the sea. Such value creation also gives those who reclaim the land disproportionate profits and the authority to allocate them. In Bahrain, investigative reporters have discovered shell companies established to allow the royal family to profit from land reclamation.[74] The authority to magically create land out of the sea is also a form of accumulation by dispossession, an enclosure of a space held in common – the sea – for the purpose of speculation and sales.[75]

Land reclamation has effects on far shores also, less visible from the vantage point of a port on the Arabian Peninsula. Reclaiming land from the sea requires a great deal of engineering and moving solid materials into place. Dredgers dump vast quantities of soil and sand they have scooped from the seabed in places where new land is being raised out of the water. However, creating new headlands, islands, quays, and breakwaters almost always requires stone or concrete. To make concrete, cement must be mixed with sand and aggregate in varying proportions depending on the particular chemical makeup of the environment for which the concrete is intended.

It may come as a surprise that sand is one of the world's biggest traded commodities by volume (if not value). Of the nearly 59 billion tonnes of material mined every year, 68 to 85 per cent is sand and gravel. The world consumes more than 40 billion tonnes of sand a year – used for construction, land reclamation, shoreline development, and road-building – a rate far faster than the natural replenishment of the stuff by rivers or on beaches.[76] Remarkably, the abundant sand of the Arabian deserts on the Peninsula is thought inappropriate for making concrete. Concrete mixing requires angular sand, which is either marine or riparian, mined from beaches or rivers.[77] Desert sand, eroded by winds, is far too rounded and smooth.[78]

As world cities hunger for construction and trade, sand mining has become a more visible ecological crisis. In 2014, the United Nations Environment Programme sounded the alarm about both legal and illegal sand mining. Quarrying sand from rivers has had such detrimental effects on riparian environments that many states have banned them. In Myanmar, the riverbed sand of most rivers has been shipped to Singapore to feed its hunger for land, leaving the rivers of Myanmar vulnerable to flooding and their banks exposed to erosion. Excavating sand from riverbeds can change the form of the beds and affect flows; it can stir up sediments, creating a watery storm of particles, altering biodiversity and water quality. It can catastrophically transform vegetation and water temperatures and the efficiency and safety of riverine infrastructures (dams and dykes, as well as bridges and crossings and embankments). It can accelerate the washing away of soil from riverside lands and damage the livelihoods of people who depend on the bounty of these lands and rivers.[79] On beaches, it threatens coastal flora and fauna, accelerates shoreline erosion, reduces natural protection from sea storms and tsunamis, and undermines beachside infrastructures.[80] Entire beaches in the Caribbean and Pacific have been stripped of their sand; entire sand atolls – for example, in Indonesia – have disappeared to feed this insatiable hunger for sand. Though fiercely contested, the transnational exploitation continues.[81]

As noted earlier in this chapter, in the 1950s and 1960s, making the harbours in Dubai and Abu Dhabi required quarrying gravel and sand in Ras al-Khaimah, resulting in conflicts over profits. While local residents wanted a share of the bounty, the European mining companies that exploited this resource and the different emirates ignored their demands.[82] Today, significant volumes of the sand and gravel needed for Emirates construction projects come from overseas. India and Australia are two of the largest providers. But as local quarries are mined and new cement factories erected, the demand for imported sand has dropped.[83] In most instances, the profit earned from the quarries remain in the Emirates as more and more local businesses (very often in partnership with the royal families) invest in such extractive industries.

In addition to sand and gravel, the vast quantity of cement needed to make concrete (usually 13 to 15 per cent of the volume of the concrete) is itself a source of great environmental degradation. To make cement, limestone is baked at around 1,450°C in powerful kilns to produce something called clinker. The grey powder that is often bagged and sold to be mixed with aggregates is clinker after it has been ground to dust. Firing a kiln to such a high temperature consumes huge amounts of fuel. Baking the stones produces around one tonne of carbon dioxide per tonne of cement produced.[84] Thus far, no amount of energy-saving additives mixed with the limestone nor efficiency savings in the cement kilns has had an appreciable effect on the energy wastage and carbon dioxide production.

For most of the twentieth century, the countries of the Arabian Peninsula imported their cement from the US or Japan. Jeddah in Saudi Arabia acquired the earliest cement factory on the Peninsula in the mid-1950s.[85] It was followed by Qatar (1965),[86] Kuwait (1968),[87] the People's Democratic Republic of Yemen (1973),[88] Ras al-Khaimah (1975),[89] Oman (1977),[90] and Bahrain (2009).[91] Many of these countries now have multiple cement factories and have begun to export not only their products but their modalities of construction to neighbouring countries. These mountains of sand and cement reshaped already thriving ports in a variety of ways. *When* things began to change matters as much as how. *Where* profit was repatriated matters in seeing who benefitted. Tracing the movement of materials, labour, expertise, and capital across the continents and oceans shows why these ports thrived, and in thriving remade the sea and the land around them, as well as the effect of their expansion and growth in faraway places.

3

Palimpsests of Law and Corporate Sovereigns

They buy countries, people, seas, police, county councils ...
Pablo Neruda, 'Standard Oil Co.', *Canto General*

Aristotle Onassis built his fortune by shrewdly anticipating transformations in the world of shipping. He was one of a coterie of shipping tycoons whose coffers overflowed in war and in peace, including his brother-in-law and longtime rival, Stavros Niarchos. During World War II, Onassis's fleets transported goods and materiel for the Allies at profitable rates. His new business strategy, however, emerged with the end of the war. Where many other Greek shipowners focused on building fleets of bulk carriers, Onassis had commissioned the construction of three megatankers in Scandinavian shipyards just before the war began. These ships, which had been impounded during the hostilities, were released after the war. Onassis (like Niarchos) picked up several T2 tankers at a discount from a US government ship-decommissioning programme and negotiated deals on new ships from recuperating German shipyards.[1] He also fashioned a fleet of whaling factory ships which worked off the Pacific and Atlantic coasts of Latin America. By 1953, his various ships numbered nearly one hundred and had a total carrying capacity of 1.5 million deadweight tonnes.[2] His purchase of tankers in particular was to prove ingenious as world demand for oil rocketed after the Second World War.

In August 1953, an agent of Onassis approached Muhammad Alireza, the Saudi minister of commerce, to broker a deal with the Saudi government that would give Onassis's tankers the exclusive right to transport Saudi petroleum. The negotiations entailed various one-time and ongoing bribes for Alireza himself as well as Minister of Finance Abdullah Suleiman and other courtiers. The agreement was signed in January 1954.[3] A shipping company, Saudi Arabian Tanker Company (SATCO), was to be formed whose tankers would fly the Saudi flag and would have priority in transporting Saudi oil. Onassis was also to establish a maritime college in Jeddah whose graduates would steam on the SATCO tankers.

Once the agreement was publicised, it caused a furore that even Onassis, master tactician that he was, had not anticipated. Aramco, which saw the right to ship the oil it extracted as part of the concession it had been granted in 1933, immediately and fervently objected. In the US, concerns were raised about the possibility that Onassis would ship oil to the Soviet bloc.[4] The Dulles brothers, in their roles as Secretary of State and the head of the CIA and triumphant in their recent overthrow of Mosaddegh's nationalist government in Iran, worried that this deal signalled King Saud's unacceptable autonomy from the US and were troubled by the possibility that he would nationalise Aramco.[5] After all, they reasoned, King Saud had seen a blanket shipping-company boycott of nationalised Iranian oil bring Mosaddegh to his knees.[6] In an address to the Los Angeles World Affairs Council, the patrician Brewster Jennings of Socony-Vacuum Oil worried that the 'adoption of this plan by just those countries which are primarily exporters would bring about a complete change in the pattern of ownership of the world's merchant marines'.[7] Jennings was well placed to know, given his family's involvement with Standard Oil, which ruthlessly monopolised downstream oil processing in the US and beyond. State Department legal advisers even worried that, should the original Aramco concession be challenged, many of its provisions would be discovered to be 'not so ironclad as it might have first appeared in 1933'.[8] Defense Department officials saw Onassis's encroachment on Aramco's shipping business as a threat to the Pentagon's access to inexpensive fuel.[9]

The British had their own bones to pick. Onassis and other independent shipowners threatened the dominance of British Petroleum's tanker business and the slowly recovering British shipping industry. More importantly, the Saud-Onassis agreement gave Onassis the right to carry petroleum from the Saudi–Kuwaiti Neutral Zone. As the Neutral Zone petroleum was being exploited concurrently by Getty Oil and Kuwait Oil Company, a subsidiary of British Petroleum, Onassis's entry into Kuwait could also endanger British interests there beyond Saudi borders. This concern was as much about unfettered British access to oil as it was about maintaining the global prestige of the sterling and the volume of petroleum sales denominated in that currency, as opposed to the dollar.[10]

Shortly thereafter, pressure was brought to bear. A case about Onassis's purchase of decommissioned T2 tankers came to a head around the same time, and a memorandum impugning Onassis's loyalty to the US, written by J. Edgar Hoover some ten years before, was suddenly unearthed and leaked to the press.[11] Onassis's whaling fleet was seized by the Peruvian navy. Most significantly, oil companies worldwide began to tacitly boycott Onassis's ships, refusing to charter them or use them to transport oil. The boycott left half of Onassis's fleet idle.[12] In Saudi Arabia, the CIA conveyed a cheque for $2 million from Aramco to Saudi decisionmakers. It also called upon the services of Karl Twitchell (who had been instrumental in oil exploration in Saudi Arabia and establishing Aramco there) to influence King Saud.[13]

In July 1954, a National Security Council meeting under President Eisenhower issued a memo that specifically mentioned Onassis. The text of memo NSC5428 called for the US to take 'all appropriate measures to bring about the cancellation of the agreement between the Saudi Arabian government and Onassis for the transport of Saudi Arabian-produced oil and, in any case, to make the agreement ineffective'.[14] Preliminary drafts proposed by both the State and Defense Departments explicitly mentioned that any such agreement could potentially interfere with 'the lifting and transport of Saudi Arabian oil for the United States armed forces by ships controlled or owned by the United States Government'.[15] The US's commercial and military interests intersected.

By November of that year, intense pressure from US diplomats and Aramco officials led the Saudi government to suggest arbitration as 'a face-saving solution'.[16] But by December, Aramco felt that it had to concede to the Saudi government by agreeing to place some of its ships under Saudi flags, as long as the Saudi government 'enact[ed] suitable shipping laws' and eliminated preferential treatment for Onassis.[17] Aramco also concluded negotiations with the Saudi government over a new pricing formula which paid the Saudi government retroactive royalty payments going back to 1951.[18] In early 1955, as the discussion of arbitration was proceeding, the Saudi government introduced a new requirement into the arbitration. Brewster Jennings advised the US to take 'a firm line with the Saudi government' and 'be prepared to back Aramco'.[19]

In 1956, the case finally went to the arbitration tribunal in Switzerland. The verdict ultimately depended on the meaning of the word *export* – did the Aramco concession agreement also give Aramco the right to carry the oil away? Aramco argued that 'any attempt to compel Aramco to sell its oil on the condition that the oil must be transported on ships flying the Saudi Arab flag was incompatible with the Concession Agreement and the obligations assumed by the Government in exercise of its sovereignty'.[20] The fundamental principle at stake was Saudi sovereignty.

In its 1958 decision, the tribunal, astonishingly, decided that because Saudi 'law did not contain any definite rules relating to the exploitation of oil deposits, this lacuna was filled by the Concession Agreement, which became the fundamental law of the parties'.[21] In essence, the court of arbitration was declaring that unless the state had clearly set forth the parameters of its future business with Aramco, the concession agreement signed in 1933 had the force of the law of the land and was a document of sovereignty. Further, the tribunal ruled that 'in its capacity as the first concessionaire, Aramco enjoyed exclusive rights which were vested, which could not be taken away from it by the Government by means of a contract with a second concessionaire, even if the latter were legally equal'.[22] Any Saudi claim to jurisdiction over its own borders or maritime business was 'contrary to the needs of international commerce and involved a restriction of the principle of the freedom of the high seas unjustified under international law'.[23] In other words, the high seas had to be 'free' for Aramco to do its business – though not for Saudi Arabia.

Stephen Schwebel, who had been a young lawyer on Aramco's legal team and later became president of the International Court of Justice, celebrated the arbitral decision for the way it had addressed 'questions of lasting importance, such as the exercise of sovereignty, acquired rights that a granting government cannot lawfully retract, competing concession claims and the characteristics and limitations of a government's regulatory powers'.[24] Schwebel, whose writings laud the never-ending victories of multinational corporations in arbitral tribunals, could not have been more right. The Onassis case illuminated the arbitral clash between two capitalist titans, Aramco and Onassis, and the irrevocable losses to public good and sovereign rights that emerged from this battle. Law mattered: to sovereignty, to capital accumulation, and to maritime businesses. In the cases I describe below, colonial legal regimes left their traces in much of maritime law. Legal infrastructures conceived in the North Atlantic continue to be hegemonic, even as centres of capital accumulation move across the seas. The law acts as the powerful adjunct of coercion, according to imperial civilisational hierarchies.

Weaponising Arbitration Tribunal

International commercial arbitrations had long existed as a form of dispute resolution in most jurisdictions, but they expanded during the Industrial Revolution and the concurrent consolidation of imperial control overseas. One history of arbitral tribunals cites as examples disputes over sulphur monopolies in Naples, the slave trade in the US, and ownership of islands and canals.[25] In Britain, parliamentary acts regulated commercial arbitration and established the rules for tribunals. By the beginning of the twentieth century, the Permanent Court of Arbitration had also emerged at the Hague and dealt primarily with treaty disputes between states, global organisations, and private parties. The US began to establish its own legal frameworks and rules for arbitration after World War I.

In the twentieth century, one of the most important functions of such tribunals became protecting alien property (property owned by foreign nationals and corporations) overseas. The expropriations of foreign property that followed the Bolshevik Revolution of 1917 and the Mexican nationalisation of foreign petroleum companies in 1938 provided the impetus in Western Europe and North America to develop complex legal apparatuses, doctrines, and rules to protect the alien property of North American and European investors and firms. The postwar wave of decolonisation only intensified this urge, as newly decolonised states staked claims to their usurped national properties. In many instances, their attempts at changing the terms of existing contracts ran into 'stabilisation clauses' written in after Mexico's nationalisation of oil. Stabilisation clauses froze 'the provisions of a national system of law chosen as the law of the contract as of the date of the contract' to prevent future alterations – in other words, nationalisation.[26] Another condition was the settling of disputes not in the decolonising countries, but in international tribunals. After Iranian prime minister Mohammad Mossadegh nationalised the Anglo-Iranian Oil Company, Iran insisted that any disputes with the Company would have to be settled in Iranian courts, since international arbitration would be 'humiliating and incompatible with the concept of state sovereignty'; Mossadegh had nevertheless found himself facing the Company in the Hague.[27]

International arbitration protected the property of investors, made the contract sacrosanct, and guaranteed confidentiality and secrecy to corporate litigants that did not want their practices exposed to court transparency.[28] The aforementioned Justice Schwebel declared triumphantly that international investment law and its tribunals 'dethroned the State from its status as the sole object of international law'[29] at exactly the moment former colonies were becoming sovereign states. This was no coincidence.

In response to postcolonial expropriations and sovereign oil states' demands for a larger share of their petroleum, the United Nations General Assembly passed resolutions that affirmed the rights of postcolonial states to their natural resources. The response of Euro-American investors was multifold. European jurists, industrialists and policy-makers developed models for bilateral investment treaties which were then adopted by Organisation for Economic Co-operation and Development (OECD) countries. Their terms are at the base of many disputes. These complex treaties often stipulated international arbitration as a means of dispute resolution and almost always designated a choice-of-law clause with the legal system of another (usually European) state as the framework. International arbitration was another mechanism for protecting investors' properties. Aron Broches, general counsel of the World Bank, developed a series of procedures to protect the principle of foreign investment against the demands of postcolonial states in the global South. This principle was enshrined in 1965 in the Convention on the Settlement of Investment Disputes between States and Nationals of Other States. The World Bank arbitration forum, International Centre for Settlement of Investment Disputes, came into force the next year, though it took the proliferation of foreign direct investments in the 1990s to increase its caseload.[30]

The investor-state dispute forum's reliance on administrative procedure veiled the political stakes. While the proponents of the forum boasted about it 'depoliticising' cases, the arbitration procedures in effect stacked the deck in favour of investors and corporate claimants. Investors have sued states against their enactment of environmental or labour protection legislation and to recover lost profits or anticipated future profits. Often their cases are frivolous and speak of endless corporate entitlement; the forum decides for the corporations in the vast majority of instances.[31] As capital accumulation has consolidated in the global South, the corporation is still generally preferred over sovereign states. However, as the story of Dubai Ports World shows, not all corporations nor all states are created equal – global hegemons can get away with limitations on corporations that the governments of the global South could only dream about.

Dubai Ports World

Among the most contentious corporations appearing as complainants or respondents in investor-state dispute-settlement cases has been Dubai Ports World. The company operates seventy-eight terminals worldwide as of early 2019 (see Table 1.2) and often compensates for slowdowns in its domestic business by expanding overseas. DP World is particularly interested in acquiring ports in the Indian Ocean basin. It signed contracts for a thirty-year concession for the port of Doraleh in Djibouti (2006) and a twenty-five-year concession in Aden (2008), as well as contracts to operate container terminals in Karachi, Pakistan, and Mumbai and Kochi in India. The first two of these five concessions were reportedly acquired through bribery.[32]

In Aden, DP World's large cash payment to the beleaguered president of Yemen, Ali Abdullah Salih, bolstered Salih without redistributing any of the port's benefits to impoverished southern Yemen. The deal was so brazenly of no benefit to the city that local political groups objected to it very early on. In the aftermath of the Arab uprisings of 2011, Yemen's anticorruption body called for the cancellation of DP World's contracts in Aden and nearby Ma'alla.[33] That summer, Aden port workers marched in protest at DP World's mismanagement.[34] Pressure brought to bear by the public and the Port of Aden Organisation (which represented the interests of Aden and southern Yemen) resulted in a settlement that saw DP World give up its concession for a payment of US$35 million.[35]

Doraleh, the other DP World trophy, is Djibouti's 'largest employer and biggest source of revenue'.[36] On 8 July 2014, the Djibouti government accused DP World of having secured its concession through bribing the former chair of Djibouti ports, and cancelled the concession. In the arbitral case, DP World was represented by the same law firm that had acted on its behalf in the Yemen case. In 2017, the London-based arbitrators ruled for DP World.[37] Only a year later, Djibouti, citing national security concerns, seized the port. DP World once again called Djibouti to tribunal. Predictably, in August 2018, the London Court of International Arbitration ruled for DP World again; and in April 2019, levied a payment of US$530 million on Djibouti.[38] Djibouti rejected both rulings. The enforcement of the two rulings seems unlikely because just as the dispute erupted, Djibouti signed a contract with Chinese firms to develop a free zone at Doraleh, thus ensuring the protection of an increasingly powerful state.

Whereas DP World has ruthlessly brought Indian Ocean states to court, its activities in the US have been far more constrained by the asymmetry of its relations with that country. In 2006, DP World acquired the ports management arm of the British P&O for £3.92 billion. The acquisition put DP World in charge of six US ports that were then managed by P&O Terminals. While the Bush administration had no concerns with what it considered a commercial transaction with a company from an allied country, a bipartisan group of Congresspersons headed by senators Hillary Clinton and Chuck Schumer did not take kindly to the deal; nor did maritime union leaders and 'serious' US newspapers.[39] DP World tried to weather the storm of anti-Arab protectionism but in the end was commanded by Abu Dhabi to sell its stakes in those six ports. In December 2006, DP World sold those ports to AIG (which only two years later went bankrupt), for a far better price than it had expected.[40] In July 2007, President George W. Bush signed the Foreign Investment and National Security Act, which gave Congress the power to scrutinise corporate takeovers of US assets by foreign owners. Throughout the whole debacle, neither DP World nor UAE officials ever considered using the investor-state dispute-settlement mechanism. The US was far too powerful a patron, far too significant, as the mecca of capital, to be challenged.

DP World has not shown the same degree of equanimity and deference to all the other places where it has sought concessions over container terminals. Unsurprisingly, corporations are not created equal, and state power emanating from the North Atlantic still counts for something. The same asymmetries also appear in the story of how oceanic and subsea features are transformed into legal categories ripe for economic exploitation: legal precedents set by the US define the geographies and topographies of global seas.

Geophysical Features into Legal Categories

Did sea define the land or land the sea?
Each drew new meaning from the waves' collision.
Sea broke on land to full identity.

Seamus Heaney, 'Lovers of Aran'

The most significant of the nineteenth century's exploited oceanic commodities were the products of whaling. Whale ships had been vehicles for passage through far seas, platforms for catching the majestic beasts, and factories for processing them on board. With the industrialisation of fisheries by the late nineteenth and early twentieth centuries, factory ships steamed the seas and exploited distant rich waters. They often became nubs of contention between Euro-American businesses and the peoples of the tricontinents.

These struggles over the 'right' to exploit oceanic resources took on new intensity with the possibility of extracting petroleum from the seabed and subsea soil. Offshore exploration for petroleum and other mineral resources, and later the construction of offshore oil-loading and bunkering terminals, began in the coastal waters of the United States and shortly thereafter in Venezuela. To drill in Venezuela's Lake Maracaibo in the 1920s and later in the Gulf of Mexico, new technologies were invented and tested. These included steel-enforced concrete drilling piles, prefabricated steel drilling platforms, rotary drills, and 'barge drilling', where barges with attached drilling rigs were sunk under the sea (rather than kept afloat on the surface) and used to access the oil below the seabed.[41]

Once the technological feasibility of offshore drilling was ascertained, rights and ownership over these resources had to be justified in order to apportion incomes, fees, and profits. As early as 1942, British and Venezuela reached legal agreements to drill for offshore oil in Trinidad, and their treaty agreement around the Gulf of Paria referred to the 'continental shelf' as a physical-*cum*-legal category to be allotted between the two parties.[42] The technical successes of offshore drilling in Lake Maracaibo and the Gulf of Mexico in the 1940s led to a steep increase in legal claims over offshore resources and the transposition of legal categories onto maritime spaces.

The continental shelf was one of the most important such legal categories, and it arose out of oil exploration in the US. In September 1945, US president Harry Truman issued a proclamation, 'With Respect to the Natural Resources of the Subsoil and Sea Bed of the Continental Shelf', which declared the US federal government's dominion over such resources. Following the proclamation, the first legal case to emerge was not between the US and a foreign state but between the US federal government and California. In late 1945, the US brought a court case against California to determine who had the sovereign right to explore 'vast quantities of oil and gas underneath' the land beyond a three-mile offshore limit.[43] The Supreme Court ruled for the federal government.

The Truman proclamation led to a series of similar announcements overseas – especially in places where the subsea soil was thought to contain petroleum resources.[44] Great Britain followed by issuing such proclamations on behalf of Jamaica and the Bahamas.[45] On 19 May 1949, the Iranian minister of finance introduced a bill to Parliament to facilitate the demarcation of Iran's coastal and territorial waters in the Persian Gulf and the Caspian Sea, to clarify ownership over subsea resources. Only ten days later, Aramco advised the government of Saudi Arabia to proclaim Saudi sovereignty over the subsoil and seabed of the areas in the Gulf contiguous with the state. The proclamation was contingent on equitable agreements with the neighbouring emirates (at that stage, all British protectorates). In response, the British government 'decided to advise the Rulers of those states in the Persian Gulf which are under their protection to take similar action' and drafted the proclamation that these rulers were to issue.[46]

Within days, rulers of the emirates around the Gulf issued their own proclamations of jurisdiction over their seabed and continental shelf: Bahrain on 5 June 1949; Qatar on 8 June; Abu Dhabi on 10 June; Kuwait on 12 June; Dubai on 14 June; Sharjah on 16 June; Ras al-Khaimah on 17 June; Ajman on 20 June; and Umm al-Quwain (no definite date in June).[47] As the arbitrator in a petroleum case concerning Abu Dhabi wrote,

> All of these last proclamations conform broadly in their terms to the Truman proclamation. They mostly contain recitals on the following lines: 'Whereas it is just that the sea-bed and subsoil extending to a reasonable distance from the coast should appertain to and be controlled by the littoral State to which it is adjacent'.[48]

While British colonial officials hurriedly legalised the contours of oil-rich Gulf seabeds, they did not have the same urgency for their colony at Aden, which was not known to be rich in mineral resources. Aden defined its territorial seas and claims over its continental shelf only after its independence in 1970.[49] As a legal expert later commented, 'No new doctrine of international law has received universal recognition so rapidly as has that of the continental shelf. Its being an extension of the border endeared it to nationalistic pride.'[50] But the rapid universalisation of the continental shelf had far more to do with capitalist exploitation of the riches whose very discovery necessitated legal principles to pin them down in that grey zone between 'private' property and 'public' domain.

Because so many of these juridical decisions were made to lubricate the oil companies' entry into these maritime spaces, the outcomes of the arbitration cases in which the ruler of Qatar was involved come as a surprise.

The Offshore

In the space of two years between 1951 and 1953, the ruler of Qatar was involved in two arbitration cases that crucially depended on the definition of maritime limits and boundaries. In the first tribunal, the complainant was Petroleum Development Qatar Ltd; in the second, the ruler was the complainant against International Marine Oil Company Ltd. Rather unexpectedly, the ruler of Qatar won both arbitration cases.

In May 1935, Shaikh Abdullah bin Jassim al-Thani, emir of Qatar, granted a seventy-five-year concession for oil exploration to the Anglo-Iranian Oil Company, which assigned its concession to a subsidiary, Petroleum Development Qatar. Exploration and exploitation of oil resources ceased in Qatar during World War II and picked up again thereafter, with the first oil shipment taking place in 1947. In June 1949, the emir claimed 'jurisdiction and control over an area of the seabed and subsoil lying beneath the high seas of the Persian Gulf contiguous to the territorial waters of Qatar'. Two months later, on 5 August, he signed an agreement with two oilmen representing a British company, Central Mining and Investment Corporation, and a US one, Superior Oil Company of California. The two companies then formed International Marine Oil Company, which in October 1950 assumed 'all the rights and obligations under the Principal Agreement' to explore for oil in Qatar's waters.[51]

Only two days before the ruler was to claim his jurisdiction over the high seas, Petroleum Development Qatar, which had got wind of the competing companies' approach, 'notified the ruler of their intention that the sole prospecting rights conferred on them by the Agreement in May, 1935, covered *inter alia* the land lying under the high seas of the Persian Gulf outside the territorial waters of Qatar'. The company saw the upcoming agreement with International Marine as a violation of their contract with the ruler of Qatar and brought an arbitration case against him. That tribunal decided in 1950 that the Petroleum Development Qatar 'concession did not include the sea bed or subsoil or any part thereof beneath the high seas of the Persian Gulf contiguous with the territorial waters of the State of Qatar'.[52] Therefore, Petroleum Development Qatar was given the right to explore in Qatar's territorial waters, while International Marine 'won the concession to explore further out' on the continental shelf.[53]

The second arbitration case arose when International Marine gave notice of the cancellation of their concession, and then refused to pay the ruler 1 million rupees as stipulated in the original agreement. The company had decided to withdraw because of 'great expenses involved in off-shore operations in the Gulf and what the Company allege to be the increasingly exorbitant demands of the local Rulers' as well as 'uncertain position of the boundaries'[54] and 'the excessive greed of the Rulers'.[55] As always, the local potentates were presented as cartoon villains. In any event, the dispute rested on whether this annual payment of 1 million rupees was an advance payment or an arrears one. The tribunal agreed with the ruler that the payments were intended to pay for the year already past and therefore he was due a payment from International Marine.

What is notable, even astonishing, in these cases is that the tribunals ruled for the Qatari ruler rather than the petroleum companies. The Petroleum Development Qatar case was also important because it established how sovereignty over geophysical features was apportioned, with land and sea posited as clearly distinct spaces and the subsea area as wholly knowable and unchanging, and therefore subject to long-term concession agreements. Perhaps more revealingly, the more important case – the one about apportioning the sea – was in effect about the competing interests of US and UK firms rather than the Qatari public good.

The early years of the 1950s saw a proliferation of such arbitration cases over the right of exploration at sea. The tribunals – held in European capitals and often according to the laws of European states (even when the judges ostensibly rejected these national attachments) – established where and how far rulers of independent and semi-independent states were sovereign over their maritime and land borders. Occasionally a case had to do with competing state sovereignties (for example, the Buraimi Oasis became the subject of an arbitrated dispute over boundaries of Saudi Arabia, Oman, and Abu Dhabi), but more often than not these cases were about European and North American corporations staking claims to territories or aspects of governance usually associated with sovereign states.[56]

The arbitration tribunals ruled (and continue to rule) so often in favour of these corporations that the companies even called the rulers to arbitration when there had been no dispute. In one instance, the British agent wrote to the representative of Petroleum Development (Trucial Coast) Ltd that

> it would be difficult to convince those lesser Rulers of the Trucial Coast, who have not as yet been approached by any other Company, that your object is merely to clarify the present uncertain status of the sea-bed which has accrued to them. They are, unfortunately more liable to fear that you intend to hustle them through arbitration before they are able to enjoy . . . the advice and support of an outside [or non-British] Oil Company.[57]

The language the colonial official used to address the oil company representative is instructive. They were colleagues conversing in familiar tones about the best way to ensure 'our side' got the best deal possible out of the rulers, without getting the rulers' hackles up so much that they appealed to an 'outside Oil Company'. After all, these men (and they were almost always men) had likely been educated together and likely traversed the boundaries between the oil companies and the British diplomatic service with little fanfare.[58]

Again and again, the oil companies acted as indistinguishable agents of their home states or as sovereigns over the oil. The maritime boundaries between states were decided in conversations between competing oil officials in the US or UK rather than between the rulers of those states. For example, to decide the seabed frontiers between Bahrain and Saudi Arabia, British and US diplomats mobilised the officials of BAPCO and Aramco to speak to one another.[59] In many of the contracts allocating Gulf subsea resources in the 1950s, British oil companies called for arbitration of disputes to take place in English forums. A prominent clause of their contracts stipulated that the arbitrators for any dispute be chosen by 'His Majesty's Government and the Company' and for British commercial laws to be sovereign in these cases.[60] British Petroleum, its antecedent Anglo-Iranian Oil Company, and their subsidiaries acted as an arm of the British state because *they were*.[61] The British state owned British Petroleum until Prime Minister Margaret Thatcher privatised it in stages, beginning in 1979. The Arab rulers attempted to play oil companies against one another, often making deals with North American or other European companies to offset the power of the British firm, but the final decision on such matters was often settled in courts of arbitration, where a ruling on behalf of a sovereign state in the global South was as rare then as it is now. Even when arbitrators decided in favour of the rulers, the real beneficiaries were often rival oil companies. Decisions on oceanic and subsea sovereignty were being made in courts ideologically and politically stacked in favour of investors.

Not long after the Qatar arbitration case recounted here, Petroleum Development (Trucial Coast) Ltd called the ruler of Abu Dhabi to arbitration for similar reasons. In the end the ruling similarly gave the ruler the sovereignty over the waters beyond the territorial limits, as in the Qatari cases. But the case is notable for the portentous and pedantic elaborations made by the arbitrator, Lord Asquith of Bishopstone, who found it necessary to preface his ruling with a condescending pronouncement from the haughty summits of colonial superiority: 'It would be fanciful to suggest that in this very primitive region there is any settled body of legal principles applicable to the construction of modern commercial instruments.' Further still, although there really was no reason to apply English law and even Asquith admitted that it was 'inapplicable *as such*', he added that 'some of its rules are in my view so firmly grounded in reason, as to form part of this broad body of jurisprudence – this "modern law of nature"'.[62]

Asquith and many others who wrote about trade in Asia and Africa ignored the enormous significance of legal practice, thinking, and relations in the region – in trade, commerce, and everyday life – before the advent of colonial law. As Fahad Bishara has written in his magisterial account of commercial law and the political economy of debt in the Indian Ocean, law 'left its mark on every actor, artefact, and action'.[63] The avenues in which law worked were broad and variegated. Islamic jurisprudence, commercial regulations, jurist decisions, fatwas – all affected 'deeds, contracts, and receipts, all of which bore the imprint of law'.[64] Onto this complex legal topography European imperial powers attempted to graft their own legal and political systems. To claim the sovereignty of imperium, they had to erase or occlude the extant legal landscape and imagine the legal *terra nullius* of which Asquith witheringly wrote.

When writing about international law, about the tensions between sovereign rights and the right of private property, and – perhaps most importantly – about the laws that govern the high seas, European legal writings inevitably begin with Hugo Grotius. His corpus of work was crucial in establishing a series of dicta that have become central to maritime and commercial jurisprudence. Grotius's notion of 'freedom of the seas' in effect enshrined the right of the powerful to this freedom. Everywhere in Grotius's discussions about this freedom was an occlusion of *which* maritime powers held just the right balance of cannons and guns to exercise this freedom. His writings brought into view a legal argument to distinguish between the sovereign's public rights and private rights of ownership. In this view, ownership of private property was a matter of civilisational hierarchies, whereby a European power might exercise the right to *occupatio* (or appropriation) 'if one finds himself in places without inhabitants, as on the sea, in a wilderness, or on vacant islands' or in places where property was still held 'in community'.[65] An imperial power (read: the Dutch) could treat others' private property as a prize won in conflict, if the empire deemed it necessary.[66]

A significant legal concept emerging out of Grotius's work was the notion of divisible sovereignties of local powers, where 'some of those rights [of sovereignty are] lodged with one possessor and some with another'.[67] In practice this translated into indigenous sovereigns delegating their privileges and prerogatives to their imperial protectors and patrons. Indigenous sovereigns had, before the coming of European powers, 'shared their juridical responsibilities with religious courts, mercantile tribunals, and other imperial jurisdictions, all of which came with their own notions of law, justice, personhood, and property rights'.[68] But they had also retained many privileges and prerogatives, among them access to coastal areas, navigable rivers, and the ability and freedom to navigate by sea, which in many instances the imperia claimed for themselves under the principle of divisible sovereignty.

The Global Struggle over Subsea Resources

> Right ... is only in question between equals in power ... The strong do what they can and the weak suffer what they must.
>
> Thucydides, 'Melian Dialogues',
> *History of the Peloponnesian War*

What becomes clear in reading the case materials about jurisdiction over the seas is that the sovereignty of the states in the global South is defined and fundamentally circumscribed by the encounter with powerful corporate bodies engaged in capital accumulation, according to geopolitical hierarchies defined in and since the colonial era. As the British political agent in Kuwait acknowledged in 1948, the sooner the US and the UK defined these legal parameters, the better they could 'prevent premature claims to the sea-bed off the shore of the Persian Gulf States by other powers' – including local sovereigns.[69] Legal proclamations over subsea geophysical features in the late 1940s instituted new rules of property and claims of ownership over them. In the multilateral conventions that delineated access to the sea, such imperial motives were also clearly on display, whether they had to do with nautical borders or the exploration of offshore or subsea resources.

By 1958, when the first United Nations Conference on the Law of the Sea took place, delegates were faced with multiple and overlapping claims over marine resources. The 1958 treaties, and the 1982 Convention on the Law of the Seas which replaced them, defined the various sovereign claims to the sea or the seabed or subsoil areas, reiterated the 'openness' of the high seas, protected the rights of those who could lay or use submarine cables and pipelines, and safeguarded these and offshore installations with safety zones and regulations about access and damage. The meticulous language of the law veiled the reality that only a handful of powers had the requisite capital, expensive technology, strategic reach, and imperial claims to lay down global communication and energy transport networks, install expensive offshore drilling rigs in deepwater zones, or navigate the farthest reaches of the world's oceans.

In all the conferences in which the representatives from newly sovereign states met the former colonial powers, this inequality in claims and abilities was openly on display. If the old naval powers wanted territorial waters to remain at three nautical miles, independent states from the global South who had been or were still subject to colonial depredations insisted on twelve nautical miles. The definitions of 'adjacent waters' and 'areas beyond national jurisdiction' were sources of contention. In one such conference where the 'needs and interests of developing countries' were specifically discussed, this sense of global fissure was clear. For the world's naval powers, the 'freedom' to navigate close to the shores of newly sovereign nations was a right they could back up with the force of their warships.

Delegate after delegate from the global South pointed to the inequalities enfolded in the neutrality of the law: a 1971 congressional bill (S2801) which allowed the US Department of Interior to issue licences to US businesses to explore the seabeds beyond the continental shelves,[70] the technological ability and capital of 'only the largest multinational corporations [to] exploit the manganese nodules on the seabeds',[71] the fact that decolonisation no longer gave European and North American powers control over raw materials,[72] the concentration of expertise and technology in the global north.[73] The Brazilian delegate argued vehemently that the riches and resource of the sea were 'the property of every human being' and that any profit from their exploitation should be distributed to all states.[74] Of course this proposal was rejected in favour of assigning subsea zones to legal categories that ultimately allowed only the richer nations to exploit them.

For major imperial powers, maritime geophysical features were far more than the 'shoreline, shelf edge, base of continental slope, toe of continental rise, axes of trenches, deepest parts of abyssal plains, and the mid-ocean rift', corresponding to scientific classifications.[75] They were also more than human geographies or the relationships of the coastal people to *their* seas: their habits of usage, the foods they ate, and how they exploited *their* seas. The sea was about translating the commodities underneath it into dollars or sterling.

In the end, after decades of debate, the convention that finally emerged enshrined the principles of 'ownership' and rules of property over common resources. The juridification of the subsea ratified another historic moment of enclosure and pillaging of the commons and transforming commonly held public goods into privately held property. Any disputes were left to international commercial arbitration mechanisms rigged on behalf of large corporations and more powerful states.

Free Zones

> When a poor country establishes an export processing zone, it is showing the world that it is ready to be serious about development.
>
> Richard Bolin, Flagstaff Institute

The excess of law is one aspect of maritime commerce being shaped by legal precepts and institutions. States can also choose to create enclaves where laws and regulations are held in abeyance, ostensibly to spur commerce. A great many such enclaves throng ports. They are now considered a *sine qua non* of free enterprise, promoted by the World Bank and International Monetary Fund (IMF) and copied everywhere.[76] Their primary hallmark is their exemption from customs fees, but they are also enclosed with barbed wire and relatively absolved from environmental and labour regulations, critical scrutiny, and often accountability.

The symbiotic relationship between maritime ports and this kind of legal 'freedom' predates the invention of free zones in the early twentieth century. In the imperial era, Britain designated a string of strategic bases and coaling stations from the Atlantic to the Pacific free ports: Singapore, Hong Kong, Aden, Colombo, certain Caribbean islands, Malta, and Gibraltar had all been free ports under the British Empire's rule.[77] They fulfilled military and naval strategic needs and acted as hubs for transhipped merchandise intended for home ports, overseas ports, or provisioning of ships. They flourished as ports when they sat astride busy trade routes, and they failed in becoming bustling emporia and entrepôt ports when they were at some distance from these routes (as the Malvinas were). Major canal gateways, such as Port Said on the Suez and Colón on the Panama Canal, also acted as free ports.[78] The free ports allowed for the maintenance of long shipping routes and further projection of imperial power and simultaneously captured trade from rival ports, enriching merchants and capitalists allied with the British. Many of these free ports eventually became city-states with cosmopolitan communities of mercantile capitalists, workers, and adventurers.

But British free ports were not the only free ports.[79] In the eighteenth and nineteenth centuries Arabian Peninsula ports acted as informal free ports – unlike the Ottoman ports, which had complex customs arrangements. Since their economies depended on merchant trade, Bahrain, Qatar, and Kuwait only asked merchants for a small subsidiary fee for the local ruler and had no or very small formal tariffs or customs fees (Kuwait required a miniscule 2 per cent tariff on imports).[80] This allowed these ports to grow as important entrepôts on the Arabia–India route. Dubai, which abolished customs and taxes on merchant trade at the end of the nineteenth century, famously benefitted from the mass migration of merchants from the port of Lengeh in Iran in the early twentieth century, when the Qajar king instituted taxes and tariffs on their trade. In the aftermath of World War II, the British protectors of the Gulf emirates encouraged such free-port arrangements, particularly for their favoured and more amenable allies. As I recounted in chapter 2, when the British engineered the decline of the Sharjah Creek in the 1950s, they compensated by arranging for Dubai to act as Sharjah's free port.[81] The British also designated Manama in Bahrain a free port in 1958, just as construction of the modern Mina Salman began there. In the aftermath of the nationalisation of the Anglo-Iranian Oil

Company in Iran and the Suez Canal in Egypt, nationalist and leftist political mobilisation convulsed the island, and the port and free zone in Manama were intended as inducements to the restive Bahraini bourgeoisie.

The first free trade zones of the twentieth century were set up in New York in the 1930s; shortly thereafter, like many legal and corporate apparatuses, the form was exported overseas. Free zones in their various incarnations have become modular technologies for frictionless transfer of capitalist ideology from one place to another. Richard Bolin set up the Flagstaff Institute, a think tank to support the spread of free trade zones, and has argued that establishing them shows that global South countries are ready to be incorporated into the global circuits of capital.[82] At the height of the Cold War, such zones brought with them the promise of capitalist development – at the cost of limiting workers' bargaining power in overseas factory enclaves. They were explicitly intended to shield against the larger appeal of socialist or anticolonial nationalising ideologies.[83] Puerto Rico was the first laboratory for export processing zones, promoted and implemented by an assemblage of US policy-makers, capitalists, their comprador allies, and management consultants. The very name of the project that first introduced the concept there, 'Operation Bootstrap', spoke to the counterrevolutionary intent of the free zones and the mythology of free enterprise embedded in them. In Indonesia and Chile, free zones were first established within a year or two after the overthrow of Sukarno and Salvador Allende, respectively.[84] In the Arab world, the consolidation of conservative forces in the Ba'ath Party (led by Hafez al-Assad) saw the establishment of five free zones in Syria in the early 1970s.[85] The *infitah* (or 'opening up') policies of the Sadat regime in Egypt, which liberalised the economy and encouraged foreign investment, were accompanied by a surge in free zones there.[86] Jordan similarly initiated free zones in Zarqa and the port of Aqaba in the late 1970s.

Country	Number of Zones	Notes
Bahrain	3	One of the free zones is near the port, the other near the airport.
Kuwait	1	The free zone abuts the Shuwaikh port.
Oman	4	Three free zones are located next to major ports (Salalah, Sohar, and Duqm). The last is inland in the Dhofar province and near the border with Yemen.
Qatar	1	The free zone in Qatar has no direct relationship to the port.
Saudi Arabia	None	Saudi does not officially have free zones or special economic zones, but it does have industrial and economic cities, including many 'logistics cities'.
UAE	41	Every emirate has at least one free zone next to its main port, and many have more. The biggest port-side free zones are Jabal Ali (Dubai) and Kizad (Abu Dhabi).
Yemen	1	The free zone neighbours the port of Aden.

Table 3.1 – List of free zones on the Arabian Peninsula[87]

Free zones intentionally create enclaves *within* states, in which some of the sovereign prerogative of states are suspended. In the Arabian Peninsula, many of the free zones that neighbour ports are securitised islands surrounded by moats of highways and barbed-wire fences. These security measures provide spaces in which states intentionally exercise a 'variegated sovereignty'[88] in which there is little or no corporate tax, little or no income tax for noncitizens, no customs or tariffs, and very little regulation. In a sense, they are offshore spaces but onshore, where legal striations allow accumulation of capital without restraints.

Although Arab states were not strangers to free zones by the 1970s, some of the city-states of the Peninsula were not eager to establish them. In many cases, as in Qatar, this spoke to the relative paucity of merchant capital and the outsized role of oil exports instead of cargo trade and transhipment. Even Kuwait, which has long had a vocal capitalist class, did not inaugurate a free zone in the 1970s, despite merchants there clamouring for one. Cargo arriving at such a free zone in Shuwaikh could have been transhipped by land to a ready-made market in Iraq. But the ruler of Kuwait saw strengthening the merchants' hand as a direct threat to his rule and scuppered it.[89] The free zone at Shuwaikh was established only in 1999. Bahrain, by contrast, became a whole-country free zone of sorts, at least for finance and insurance, in the late 1970s and 1980s, benefitting from the regional wars that drove bankers and capitalists out of Lebanon, Iran, and Iraq. In part this would mitigate the effects of diminishing oil production there.

The first free zone in the Peninsula was, surprisingly, at Aden, which in 1970 under a socialist government changed its laws to establish new customs regimes for goods entering South Yemen while simultaneously designating Aden a free zone. The Aden free zone allowed divergent rules of taxation to apply in different locales, giving the state the capacity to differentially allocate social goods.[90] Once North and South Yemen were united, a Yemen Free Zone Public Authority was founded to manage the Aden free zone and develop a container terminal and logistics park nearby.[91] One effect of such free zones has been an emphasis on exports at the expense of local manufacturing.

The utility of these enclaves of variegated sovereignty and liberal accumulation had become such an orthodoxy by the 1980s that the World Bank made them a condition of structural-adjustment programmes for indebted countries of the global South. Whether or not they actually performed as promised, however, is another story.

Jabal Ali

As you approach Jabal Ali from the sea, the coast lies in a haze of dust and humidity. Towers rise high through the shimmering brown air: an aluminium smelter, a refinery, petrochemical production plants. But the presence of heavy industry belies the fact that the Jabal Ali Free Zone is not only a site of goods production but – perhaps as significantly – a hub of trade and services. It is at once an export processing zone, a special economic zone, and a free trade zone. Among the Peninsula states, diminutive Dubai stands out because, spatially, it is a patchwork of twenty free zones (more than half of all free zones within the UAE). Jabal Ali Free Zone is the largest, covering vast tracts of land with its warehouses and manufacturing sites and service offices.

Jabal Ali Free Zone was already planned before engineering on the port began in 1976, though the decree for its operation was not issued until the mid-1980s. In the early 1970s, Dubai's Port Rashid was thriving because it had captured the entrepôt trade diverted from Aden after the British were forced to leave their colony.[92] An extension was needed to accommodate Port Rashid's burgeoning business. In a 1974 interview, Shaikh Rashid's adviser, Mahdi al-Tajir, described the planned billion-dollar free zone at Jabal Ali as an area for warehousing, manufacturing, assembly, and re-export of goods via Port Rashid. He specifically mentioned car assembly plants and the clothing industry, as well as refrigerated storage for meat, vegetables, and fruits. Al-Tajir considered Singapore and Beirut as inferior examples, because both cities lacked the acreage that Jabal Ali could dedicate to free zone facilities.[93] A 1976 article described the port as a complementary project to the free zone (rather than the other way around).[94] The two were, from the very first, a symbiotic whole where the free zone encouraged traffic through the port and the port facilitated investment in the free zone and by extension Dubai.[95] Another factor accounted for the timing of the Jabal Ali Free Zone: the federation of the seven emirates. UAE's federal laws impinged on the city of Dubai's operation as a free port. The founding of a vast free zone so close to the Abu Dhabi border, signalled intent by the ruler of

Dubai and his advisers to maintain a degree of commercial independence from their much more powerful neighbour.[96]

The aluminium smelter in Jabal Ali Free Zone came online in 1979 and a natural gas liquefaction plant opened in 1980. The legal decree that defined the operational rules of the free zone, established the Jabal Ali Free Zone Authority, and issued exemptions from federal tax and tariff regulations was issued in 1980 and implemented in 1985. In 1992, a further decree permitted foreign investors to locate transnational corporations in the zone to take advantage of the tax exemptions and absence of exchange controls, with the ability to repatriate profits.[97] Removing the barriers to foreign ownership was a significant moment in the growth of the free zone. There were also broader geopolitical factors at work: the Iran–Iraq War led Dubai – which had maintained a neutral stance – to become the entrepôt for both countries, but especially Iran.[98] The free zone allowed foreign firms to operate in its territory and export to or import from Iran (or Iraq) with fewer limitations. The UAE's ports and drydocks provided shelter to ships damaged in the Tanker Wars or those that had changed their routes to avoid the upper Gulf.[99] The US wars against Iraq in 1991 and against Iraq and Afghanistan from 2001 onwards only further enriched the Jabal Ali Free Zone. Aside from the war diverting transhipment traffic to the emirate, the free zone benefitted from being a hub for US military logistics and the concomitant exponential growth in contractors.

Just as important in the early trajectory of Jabal Ali were European import quotas on textiles. Successive iterations of the European multi-fibre agreements in the 1970s increasingly restricted importation of textiles from India, Pakistan, Bangladesh, and Sri Lanka.[100] In addition to the quotas, invisible nontariff barriers to textile importation from South Asia included near-monopolies by shipping conferences (read: cartels) on cargo transport to the European Economic Community.[101] Jabal Ali Free Zone provided an escape route from both constraints. Garments manufactured there by Asian textile factories did not count toward the South Asian countries' national quotas, and the port's extensive maritime infrastructure gave manufacturers a broader range of options for transporting their goods to the European market. Jabal Ali Free Zone's textile manufacturing sector had become so large and successful that by 1989 the US was threatening to impose import quotas on UAE textiles. Many manufacturers contemplated moving to Omani territorial enclaves within the UAE, but did not think Oman could match the infrastructural capacity and the relative absence of regulation that Dubai offered.[102]

In 1985, Jabal Ali Free Zone hosted sixteen companies. After it lifted foreign ownership restrictions, out of 720 companies in 1995, only 25 per cent were Emirati.[103] By 2019, it boasted of accommodating more than 7,000 firms. Foreign businesses, polled about why they preferred operating in the zone, cited 'political stability' as their foremost reason. 'Political stability' is of course a euphemism for governance predicated on a docile and policed population and deportable labour. Access to telecommunications, transport and banking services, and the absence of taxes also ranked high on the list.[104]

The free zones provide an offshore ownership structure as well, with foreign corporations able to own 100 per cent of their assets whereas UAE onshore businesses require a local agent, sponsor, or joint venture.[105] Nor is the free zone only a place of commerce. It houses warehouses storing US military materiel as well as humanitarian organisations that increasingly use Dubai as their base of operations for distributing aid in the region.[106] Jabal Ali – port and free zone together – is an organism heaving with commerce and movement and pollution, cloaked in secrecy, protected by scrubland and high-security fencing and underpaid Nepalese security men. Its laissez-faire environment allows capital accumulation for local, regional, and transnational capitalists without even the minimal regulatory scrutiny of onshore Dubai. That less than 1 per cent of the work force in the free zone are Emirati nationals speaks to the regime of control at work there.[107]

Saudi Economic Cities

Pre-oil Hijaz had a well-developed customs regime and no free ports. Saudi Arabia, unlike other Peninsula countries, does not have 'free zones', although 'logistics cities', 'economic cities', and 'industrial cities' proliferate there. The first of these were Jubail (on the Gulf coast) and Yanbu (on the Red Sea), which began as small fishing villages, with Yanbu also acting as the port for the pilgrimage city of Medina. Both were designated 'industrial cities' by a 1975 plan, which also established a separate authority to govern them, the Royal Commission for Jubail and Yanbu. The Royal Commission was modelled after Iran's pre-revolutionary 'Imperial Commission' to administer major projects, circumventing government bureaucracies.[108]

Whereas the intertwined interests of merchant capitalists and rulers (not to mention British colonial officials) had forged a free port and later free zones in Dubai, in Saudi Arabia, the main drivers for the industrial cities' development were large corporations that intended to invest in petroleum refining and petrochemical productions there. The industrial cities on the coast had lighter bureaucracies and better infrastructures, including extensive maritime loading terminals. The first task of the Royal Commission was to deepen the harbours and improve the roads emanating from them.[109] Jubail's proximity to the oil-producing region of the country gave it a head start on the project. Yanbu had originally been chosen as the Red Sea port because in 1975, Saudi Arabia feared that the People's Democratic Republic of Yemen's (PDRY) control of Bab al Mandab might affect its ability to ship oil through the Red Sea. But what actually spurred the construction of Yanbu was the Iran–Iraq War making Gulf ports and terminals more dangerous.[110] A pipeline from the Gulf coast of Saudi to Yanbu then became much more viable.

Predictably, both cities were built by the British marine engineering firm Halcrow, and engineering firms with longstanding relations with Aramco and the US Army Corps of Engineers in Saudi Arabia. Halcrow built the port at Jubail under contract with the Ministry of Communication, while Saudi Arabian Bechtel Company and Saudi Parsons were the primary contractors for other infrastructures in the two cities.[111] As one trade journal boasted, 'The RC [Royal Commission] is staffed with multinational professionals as advisors; all U.S. citizens on the staff belong to SAME [Society of American Military Engineers].'[112] What also distinguished the ports in the industrial cities from, say, Ras Tanura was that the latter was privately owned by Aramco, while Jubail and Yanbu were operated by the Saudi Ports Authority.[113] But Aramco was crucial to the functioning of the two industrial cities, as it provided them with light and power, water desalination, and raw material for petrochemical manufacturing.[114] To encourage the growth of the ports in the industrial cities, the Saudi government banned the transhipment of goods through Jeddah and Dammam and rerouted the needed cargo to the new ports.[115] The legal flexibility surrounding the two cities was the single most important spur for their growth.

While the industrial cities depended on oil terminals and petrochemical industries, the new economic cities sought to take advantage of trade and cargo movement. The planning authority for four economic cities (in Ha'il and Medina in the interior and Rabigh and Jizan on the Red Sea coast) was founded in 2006.[116] Of these, King Abdullah Economic City at Rabigh – with its own dedicated port – is the most visible. Located just north of Jeddah, it is planned to have the second largest cargo port in the Kingdom, after Jeddah. As of 2019, however, marine traffic tracking shows it to host at most around three cargo ships per day. Construction and management of the King

Abdullah Economic City has been outsourced to private businesses: in this case Emaar, Alireza family concerns, the Saudi Binladin Group, and a marine construction firm owned by Saleh bin Laden. The economic cities were intended to be orientated towards services rather than upstream industries, but the first cargo exported from the King Abdullah Port was a consignment of polymers shipped to Singapore in 2014.[117] Two years into the construction, a US diplomat described King Abdullah Economic City as composed of 'a stylish sales centre and several lavish sample villas on the shoreline. These structures were surrounded by miles of open desert dotted by intermittent earth-moving projects such as grading and canal digging.'[118] King Abdullah Economic City was meant to house a population of more than two million; by 2018, two years after its official launch, it had fewer than 6,500 inhabitants.[119]

More than anything else, the economic cities seem to conform to a standard practice of the Saud ruling family: they reproduce diffuse and competing centres of power, with different capitalist constituencies benefitting from the patronage of a given king advocating for a given economic centre. This balance of powers (also observed with the country's security apparatuses) ensures a lack of unity in forces that could politically challenge the royal family. For example, the founding of King Abdullah Economic City ruffled the feathers of Jeddah capitalists, who saw its proximity to Jeddah as a direct encroachment on their businesses.[120]

When Salman bin Abdulaziz became the king of Saudi Arabia, his son Muhammad bin Salman was appointed deputy crown prince and eventually deposed the crown prince, Muhammad bin Nayif, in a palace coup and took his place. Muhammad bin Salman concentrated power in his own hands. He was appointed minister of state, minister of defence, secretary general of the royal court, and chair of the Council for Economic and Development Affairs and was given control over Aramco and the country's sovereign fund.[121] With Muhammad bin Salman effectively ruling Saudi in lieu of his father (rumoured to have dementia), the focus shifted from King Abdullah Economic City and its 'unrealised potential' to another commercial fantasy and legally variegated enclave, Neom.[122]

Neom is to be a new megacity with its own regulatory bodies and judiciary, built in the northernmost part of Saudi's Red Sea coast. It is planned as an opulent sci-fi city of high-tech industry, consumer products and tourism. It spans the borders of Egypt and Jordan, and Egypt has been paid US$10 billion to provide 1,000 square kilometres of its coastal Sinai land to Saudi Arabia.[123] Ignoring major popular discontent about the deal, Egypt has also ceded the islands of Tiran and Sanafir – at the mouth of the Gulf of Aqaba – to Saudi Arabia. Commercial ports are planned for the area, but it is unclear what the economic basis of Neom is or whom the city is supposed to serve, though Muhammad bin Salman claims it will be 'a world hub for everyone in the whole world'.[124] Neom will straddle one of the world's most significant shipping lanes, projecting power into two client states of Saudi Arabia – Egypt and Jordan – and further across the Red Sea coast to East African ports. Neom also sits close to Israel, now a de facto Saudi ally. In this, its myth of origin resembles that of the Jabal Ali Free Zone and port a bit: heralded as the visionary plan of a ruler, it is in reality a means of pinning new territorial boundaries in place, creating a distinct and malleable legal topography while encouraging the unfettered accumulation of capital.

4

Roads and Rails Leading Away

> In striking contrast to the older buildings in Jeddah, there stands . . . the whitewashed Ford and Lincoln showroom, repair shop, and office building belonging to the Alireza family. This powerful merchant clan . . . is concentrating on Fords, Lincolns and Zenith radios. Arabia's first neon sign lights the showroom façade at night, and a gleaming, new, four-door sedan usually stands behind the big glass window, surrounded by colored advertisements of station wagons and convertibles, car styles much admired by Arabs. One order for trucks placed in the United States by the Alirezas was so large that the firm chartered an entire ship to deliver it to Jeddah.
>
> Richard Sanger, *Arabian Peninsula*

In his magisterial *How Europe Underdeveloped Africa*, Walter Rodney succinctly describes how roads and railways in Africa

> had a clear geographical distribution according to the extent to which particular regions needed to be opened up to import-export activities. Where exports were not available, roads and railways had no place. The only slight exception is that certain roads and railways were built to move troops and make conquest and oppression easier . . . All roads and railways led down to the sea. They were built to extract gold or manganese or coffee or cotton. They were built to make business possible for the timber companies, trading companies, and agricultural concession firms, and for white settlers. Any catering to African interests was purely coincidental.[1]

The roads and rail leading away from the sea, and the ports and harbours had – *have* – a symbiotic relationship. What arrives in harbours has to travel inland (if it is not placed on feeder ships and sent off to ports elsewhere). What is being extracted, produced, or traded inland has to be brought to sea to be shipped away. The port and the hinterlands have to be woven together by a network of roads and rails. In the Arabian Peninsula, the exploration and exploitation of petroleum riches was also a significant factor in the development of hinterland infrastructures. But pilgrimage and trade were and continue to be important in road-planning.

In the Hijaz, Jeddah had been the port of entry for pilgrims travelling to Mecca, while Yanbu had acted as the same for Medina. Unpaved roads connected the two holy cities and, before the advent of automobiles, had been used by camel and horse caravans to convey pilgrims from one city to the other. The first railway in the Peninsula connected the Hijaz to the heart of the Ottoman Empire in the Mashriq. During World War I and the British-sponsored revolt against the Ottoman Empire, the railway was repeatedly sabotaged by T.E. Lawrence and his Arab allies. The Ottoman forces regularly repaired the line and used it for military transport. But at the end of the war, the Hijaz Railway was no longer functional.[2]

Railways, even more than roads, were the milieu where imperial conquest and contestation were most nakedly on display. In the early years of the twentieth century, the imperialist US thinker and proponent of maritime power Alfred T. Mahan thus evaluated rail and maritime transport as conjoined strategic infrastructures in the Persian Gulf and Indian Ocean:

> The railroad will be one link, as the Persian Gulf is another, in a chain of communication between East and West, alternative to the all-water route by the Suez Canal and the Red Sea . . . It will therefore serve particularly for the transport of passengers, mails, and lighter freights. On the other hand, for bulk of

> transport, meaning thereby not merely articles singly of great weight or size, but the aggregate amounts of freight that can be carried in a given time, water will always possess an immense and irreversible advantage over land transport for equal distances.[3]

In the Arab world, starting in the latter half of the nineteenth century, imperial contestations were played out in the construction of railways. The Saint-Simonians – the engineering graduates who had helped colonise Algeria – pioneered railway construction in the Mashriq.[4] In Egypt, the opening of the Suez Canal led to a flurry of rail construction to connect the cotton-growing hinterland to the harbours.[5] Access to both harbours and rail allowed port cities like Alexandria to dominate the regional trade.[6] When the Germans were seen to control the Berlin–Baghdad railway, the British and French struggled to maintain competing routes on land and sea. The French managed to buy into the Berlin–Baghdad financing, and through their control of the railways in Greater Syria forged the infrastructural power required for claiming the mandate there after World War I.[7] In the same post-war scramble for power in the Middle East, Lord Curzon unsuccessfully attempted to secure a railroad concession in Iran for British firms.[8] For Curzon, the railway across Iran was a means of 'creating a chain of vassal states stretching from the Mediterranean to the Pamirs and protecting, not the Indian frontiers merely, but our communications with our further Empire'.[9]

Controlling access to ground transport was fundamental to military logistics as well. During World War II, the Middle East Supply Centre imposed major restrictions on civilian travel on rails and roads; these transports were reserved for military and materiel.[10] The entire infrastructure of ground transport created new economies and social relations, new forms of rule and military control. Rosa Luxemburg foresaw this when she wrote that 'railway building and the loans necessary for it mainly served to . . . spread commodity economy' and 'paved the way for military occupation' of strategically significant territories with the excuse of protecting the transport infrastructure.[11]

Roads differed from railways in significant ways. Constructing railways required substantial financing and access to material resources – steel foremost among them – that could be scarce during wars or post-war reconstruction. Roads, by contrast, could be built more easily in times of economic contraction. They needed not be paved, as long as the surface was strong enough to handle hooved animals or wheeled and later motorised vehicles. Before the discovery of oil, the Peninsula's best roads were those serving the pilgrimage in the Hijaz and others connecting coastal towns and villages to major regional hubs (for example, Kuwait and Basra).

In the Arabian Peninsula, automobiles *preceded* graded and asphalted roads. Whether the paths used by cars were made of sand, gravel or oiled surfaces, vehicles had to have sand-tyres fitted. Some early models of cars (Ford) could handle these sand-tyres better than other models (Chevrolet).[12] The entrepreneurial Kanoo family of Bahrain had been among the first to set up Ford dealerships in the Gulf. The first automobiles appeared in Saudi Arabia in 1926, and by 1930 they numbered around 1,200. Most were owned by the government or companies close to the state.[13] The imperial adventurer and adviser to King Abdulaziz ibn Saud, Harry St John Philby, also took advantage of this ready-made market and opened the first Saudi-based Ford Motor Company dealership in Jeddah in the early 1930s. Philby ceded the dealership franchise to the Alireza family in 1941.[14] The Alirezas, in turn, opened the first neon-lit Ford showroom in 1953.[15]

Once oil was discovered in commercial quantities, the oil companies quickly built roads connecting their oil fields, production and distribution centres, oil terminals, and employee housing. These early roads began as oiled-sand surfaces. Newer roads cut through impossibly treacherous mountains at the eastern and southern edges of the Peninsula and through inconstant dune-cloaked deserts in the north and west. The roads brought along the reach of the state, its laws and regulations, its security forces, and its economic plans, agendas, and ideologies.

Roads and rail moved peoples, goods, and militaries. Where oil companies built the roads, they did so to expand their markets and facilitate extraction and maritime shipping. But roads were also built because of Cold War rivalries between different states, which were happy to fund infrastructures that could support maritime commerce or naval bases. And they were built to weave coastal areas and interiors into closely meshed national territories. None of this meant that roads were evenly distributed, or that their distribution accomplished what was intended, but road-building itself was an engine of transformation. As is clear from a compilation of road statistics in the Peninsula, Bahrain's small size and head-start account for the density of roads there. By contrast, the UAE only saw a concerted effort to build landside transportation infrastructures after the departure of Britain. The sparseness and recency of the road statistics speaks to the sparseness and newness of the roads themselves.

Country	Area in km^2	First year reported	km of roads	Most recent year reported	km of roads	Most recent km of road per km^2
Saudi Arabia	2,150,000	1967	8,272	2005	221,372	0.10
Kuwait	17,817	1967	100	2013	7,321	0.41
Yemen	527,967	1981	17,171	2005	71,300	0.14
Bahrain	765	1987	2,614	2013	4,274	5.59
Oman	309,501	1992	25,948	2013	64,051	0.21
UAE	83,600	1993	4,555	2008	4,080	0.05
Qatar	11,571	1999	1,230	2013	9,592	0.83

Table 4.1 – Length of paved roads in countries of the Arabian Peninsula[16]

Oil Roads and Rail

> After four months of unrelenting labor, the dredging of the shoreline and expansion of the port in front of the American compound were complete, and a number of roads were opened. One linked the compound directly to the port and another beside it led west along the beach to Arab Harran. A third road, a short distance from the harbour, connected the second road with the workers' camp.
>
> Abdulrahman Munif, *Cities of Salt*

The story of roads and rail construction in the eastern part of Saudi Arabia where oil had been discovered, and Aramco's role in the development of these connections to the hinterland, are dramatically illustrative. As I recounted before, Aramco needed heavy goods for drilling and extracting oil to be transported to the oilfields. This necessity encouraged Aramco to invest in dredging harbours and constructing wholly new ports in eastern Saudi Arabia. Similarly, roads were required to connect the ports to the oilfields, and eventually refineries and TAPline stations, to the compounds that housed Aramco employees and to the nearby towns and villages that fed and watered the company and provided it with workers. In *Cities of Salt*, trucks arrive shortly before the coming of the paved highways to transport goods and people between the new ports and nearby cities:

> A single truck . . . carried between twenty and twenty-five men with their own and others' cargoes. The trip between the two towns, which were no more than 145 miles apart, usually took about thirty hours, because the truck always got a flat tire or broke down on the road, and in either case it had to be emptied of cargo and men, all of whom had to help unload, push the truck and load it up again. This generally took several hours and often happened two or three times on each trip. In addition to that the truck had to stop and cool down once or twice.[17]

As with the harbours, stoppage of oil production during World War II also attenuated the growth of the transport infrastructure on Saudi's Gulf littoral, but by 1944, both petroleum production and infrastructure construction were again on the upswing.[18] This moment also marked the introduction of the US Army Corps of Engineers' construction programmes in the Middle East. The myriad ventures managed by the Corps, from Morocco to Libya, Turkey, Iran, Saudi Arabia, Pakistan, Afghanistan, and beyond, encompassed building highways, military bases, airfields and other strategic infrastructure projects, including both military and civilian telecommunication networks.[19] In that same moment, King Abdulaziz ibn Saud was urgently extending his hold over the furthest reaches of the Peninsula, and for that roads were necessary.[20] As Pascal Menoret writes, the energetic Saudi road-building projects after World War II were influenced by 'political ambitions, imperial greed, and global networks of expertise, capital and power'.[21] In eastern Saudi Arabia, the US Army Corps of Engineers and Aramco worked with the same contractors (foremost among them Bechtel) to build infrastructures that consolidated the strategic foothold of the US and Aramco's dominance over the extraction of Saudi Arabia's natural resources. For this purpose, construction materials had to be imported into Saudi Arabia, and Aramco's ports were put to work.

From the very first, the new port of Dammam was connected to other oil cities in eastern Saudi Arabia to serve Aramco. This included construction in 1946 of a standard gauge railway from Dammam pier to Dhahran.[22] Extending these connections further inland and beyond Aramco's territories was another matter. In the late 1940s, Ibn Saud demanded the construction of a railroad to connect Dammam to Riyadh, his capital. The British political resident in Bahrain snidely commented to the Foreign Office, 'I suppose Americans feel compelled by His Majesty's obstinacy on the subject to meet his wishes about the railway if possible. He is reported to have told them that if they would not oblige him he would apply elsewhere.'[23] In 1952, the Aramco-designed railroad – on which the Saudi government had insisted – opened, connecting Dammam's cargo port to Riyadh (eventually also connecting other coastal oil cities). The rail traffic and port cargo mutually increased one another, such that Dammam cargo port was already reaching capacity after a year and a half in operation. At the time, there was no certainty that the Dammam–Riyadh rail would continue to be used beyond the early construction boom. One scheme to make the rail more profitable called for drilling wells along the length of its route as a way 'to attract Bedouin from the dry plains and thus start towns [in order to] provide the railroad with traffic'.[24] The plan was never implemented.

In April 1952, James H. Gildea, who had overseen Aramco's railroad construction in 1950, was also tasked to study extending the railway from Riyadh to Jeddah.[25] The *Washington Post* reported that

> Gildea estimates that a total of 1,200 miles of new trackage will be required for the whole operation and that the cost will be in the neighborhood of 200 million dollars. The work will take about five years. Under consideration is the possibility of a loan from the World Bank. Presumably part of Saudi Arabia's oil royalties would be offered as security for financing.[26]

But, because under the Al Saud the public goods allocated to the Hijaz (roughly, Saudi's Red Sea coast) did not equal those given to the Najd (roughly, the interior), and because the economic centre of the country had shifted from pilgrimage on the Red Sea to oil exportation on the Gulf, the Riyadh–Jeddah railway was never built. Nor was the Hijaz Railway ever again revived inside Saudi Arabia, though branches and segments of it outside the country were rebuilt and incorporated into the national rail networks of Jordan and Syria.

As the plans for the development of the railroad began, Aramco also started to produce roads built mostly of crushed rocks (produced by an Aramco-funded plant) or of petroleum waste directly applied to sand.[27] Aramco's infrastructure projects facilitated the export of oil and the importation of necessary materials, but they also provided a market for the company's own refined products. The roadbuilding project created 'an unprecedented demand for Asphalt', while natural gas produced by the company was used in the newly constructed cement plant at Hofuf.[28] The expansion of roads further facilitated the use of automobiles consuming Aramco gasoline, sold in the company's fast-multiplying petrol stations. In Saudi Arabia, Aramco used every opportunity to create new markets for the hydrocarbons it produced.

As Walter Rodney had written, in Africa, road and rail

> were not constructed in the colonial period so that Africans could visit their friends. More important still, they were not laid down to facilitate internal trade in African commodities. There were no roads connecting different colonies and different parts of the same colony in a manner that made sense with regard to Africa's needs and development. All roads and railways led down to the sea.[29]

Aramco's public-relations department boasted incessantly about the company's expenditures on roads used by the Saudi public.[30] But the major ports of Jeddah and Dammam were only connected by road in 1965, and even in 1967, Saudi Arabia had fewer than 8,500 kilometres of roads.[31] Its national road network began to expand only after 1975, when Aramco had been nationalised and oil revenues began pouring into the Saudi treasury.[32] The existing network of roads in Saudi Arabia today is nevertheless unequally distributed: while oil cities are richly endowed with high-grade roads, the predominantly Shi'a habitations of eastern Saudi tend not to see the best of these infrastructures.

Saudi Arabia has not been the only place where oil roads transformed the shape of transportation. The main road in Kuwait before oil had connected Kuwait to Basra. With the advent of petroleum, it was joined by the Kuwait–Fahahil road.[33] The latter was paved by the Kuwait Oil Company, whose headquarters in the town of Ahmadi was located inland, less than ten kilometres west of Fahahil's oil terminals.[34] Kuwait Oil Company was also responsible for building the main road from Kuwait City centre to the oil fields. Kuwait, however, had to wait until the 1960s, after its independence from British protectorate status, to develop its extensive network of radial roads and highways emerging out of Kuwait City's centre and spreading beyond the oil-producing regions.[35]

In Bahrain, before oil, road networks connected the British Political Agency and the Customs House, as well as the ruler's residence at the centre of the island, to Manama in the northernmost part.[36] In the 1930s, the rudimentary roads interconnecting the fishing villages of the island to Manama were subsidised by BAPCO, which had also built a tanker pier near its refinery, as well as an asphalt plant.[37] The roads allowed for workers to be transported from the villages to the BAPCO oil fields and plants. In both Bahrain and Kuwait, petroleum companies had been content to develop those hinterland roads that connected their oil wells to workers' villages or to their refineries and terminals on the coast and no more. In other countries, other logics underwrote the construction of roads.

Roads as Economic Pacification Weapons

> [Dhofar's] isolated position keeps out most visitors and greatly restricts imports and exports. Salalah harbour has little protection against the monsoon winds, so that it is virtually useless for five months of the year. The overland journey from Muscat is impossible for motors and still takes twenty days by camel, while it is even longer and more difficult to get there from Aden.
>
> Richard Sanger, *Arabian Peninsula*

The construction of Oman's earliest roads followed the patterns established in Saudi Arabia. Military logistics and commodity extraction dictated the location of road construction and were very often inseparable. Edward Henderson, who in the 1970s became the British ambassador to Qatar, had in the 1950s been an employee of Petroleum Development Oman, a subsidiary of Iraq Petroleum Company (itself a consortium of several companies, British Petroleum prominent among them). In his memoirs, he recounts how during exploratory trips between Muscat and Salalah, the petroleum company used 'a fleet of six-wheeler Nubian load-carrying trucks, together with Dodges and Land Rovers as personnel carriers for the desert journeys'.[38] These were landed at the deep harbour of Duqm, halfway between the other two cities, all three of which are now major Omani ports. Henderson's oil exploration excursions were indistinguishable from military expeditions, and British officers of the Trucial Oman Scouts were happy to assist his trips. In later years, Petroleum Development Oman built the roads from Muscat to the oil-producing area of Fahud; the roads were constructed by hand, since using local labour was far cheaper than importing expensive equipment.[39] The first roads in Dhofar were constructed by an American oil company during its exploratory work in 1962.[40]

The construction of hinterland transport networks, in Oman and especially in Dhofar, accelerated during the counterinsurgency campaigns against the Popular Front for the Liberation of Oman and the Gulf in the 1960s and 1970s, and the programme of economic pacification that followed the military campaigns.[41] After the British put Sultan Qabus on the Omani throne in 1970, infrastructure construction projects were deployed as means of weaving the furthest reaches of the country together. Transport infrastructures were particularly useful as instruments of pacification because they could be strategically used in wartime while also acting as a milieu for granting state patronage. Thus Dhofar, which had seen the most intense guerrilla revolt of the 1970s, also saw the construction of the new Salalah port at Raysut and the main trunk road from northern Oman to the new port. The company most involved in these lucrative projects was a Palestinian-Lebanese firm, Consolidated Contractors Company (CCC), whose patrons were the powerful Omani courtiers Omar and Qais Zawawi.[42] The Zawawi brothers were Indian Ocean men, with their life trajectories traversing birth in Karachi, education in India, enterprise in Dubai (a Pepsi factory set up in partnership with Shaikh Rashid al-Maktum) for one and medical practice in Saudi for the other, and eventual ministerial and advisory positions in Oman. Their sponsorship of CCC fit well within this trajectory.

Road-building in Oman acted as a means of connecting Muscat to the interior and to the peripheral regions and incorporated the latter into the state while undermining their autonomy.[43] One striking example was the Musandam Peninsula, with its majestic and jagged fjords on the southern littoral of Hormuz Strait, which did not have any roads connecting it to Oman proper until the 1980s and whose maritime smuggling and fishing economy was better connected to Iran's insular holdings across the Hormuz Strait. It is no surprise that one of the first means through which Oman consolidated its sovereignty over this non-contiguous territorial fragment was to establish a naval base there and construct roads to connect it to the country's capital.

The US military and its corporate security extensions were also involved in the programme of constructing strategic transportation infrastructures in Oman. Among the companies most engaged in these development projects was Tetra Tech International Inc. (TTI), headquartered in Virginia, which prolifically produced reports and advice on everything from road construction to oil exploration to digging wells in Oman. TTI president James Critchfield, who had once been a CIA officer, worked alongside the US Army Corps of Engineers to extend the reach of the state into the furthest parts of the Omani territory.[44] By 1975, TTI reports noted the construction of a 230-kilometre road from Muscat to the UAE border, a 90-kilometre road from Nizwa to the coast, and a planned 'paved road network connecting the major towns of Sohar, Buraimi, Salalah, Sur and Muscat'.[45] If the roads defined the contours of Oman's territorial reach, the US programme of construction was sold to the Omanis as an economic boon. As President Carter's National Security Adviser, Zbigniew Brzezinski wrote to the president in 1980:

> In addition to economic and military aid, Oman will receive a substantial further injection of funds into its economy from our military construction expenditures (over $100 million in 1981 but likely to be several times this eventually). This will provide jobs and other economic stimulus; and we will be building facilities (improved air strips, warehouses, water systems, roads, etc.) that will add to Oman's infrastructure. Mr. [Reginald] Bartholomew [then US security adviser and later ambassador to Lebanon] is instructed to emphasize these benefits in his negotiations.[46]

In the end, the US Army Corps of Engineers construction programme cost around US$300 million and provided for four Omani/US naval bases in Khasab (on the Musandam Peninsula astride the Strait of Hormuz), Seeb (30 kilometres north of Muscat along the coast), Thumrait (inland from Salalah), and Masirah Island (on the Indian Ocean).[47] All but Khasab had been at one time a British military or naval facility. Seeb, in addition, had been a thriving commercial port. The Iranian revolution of 1979, the US loss of a stalwart ally in the Shah (who had also provided special operations troops to suppress the Dhofar insurgency), the Soviet invasion of Afghanistan, and anxiety over instability of Saudi Arabia all added urgency to the construction projects and influenced the geographic placement of military and naval facilities in Oman.

The incorporation of Oman's disparate regions into the state's territorial grasp has been facilitated by building ports which required such hinterland constructions. The new port of Duqm, for example, halfway between the existing major ports of Salalah and Sohar, has generated some consternation among the managers and workers of the other two ports: why does Oman need a third port, which will inevitably take some business away from the existing ports? But the putative and actual road and rail and pipelines connecting Duqm not only to the rest of the country but also to Saudi Arabia have proven irresistible to development planners. Not to mention the attraction of such a port in a less inhabited, perhaps even less visible, area of Oman to US naval forces, which have found the Sultanate's naval bases amenable sites for pre-positioning, R&R, and patrolling the Indian Ocean. Notably, a US Central Command (CENTCOM) naval commander considered Duqm useful as a future 'logistics hub and also an opportunity for us to bring ships in there for maintenance and for crew rest'.[48]

Competing Powers and Roads

> Ali got closer to the mountain and watched the Chinese . . . They were not arrogant, nor did they try to avoid Ali and his colleagues; they all slept in the same camp with them and worked together . . . When work hours were over, the laborers returned to their camps. They were a strange mix – peasants, sailors, shepherds. This was the first time they had done such work – cutting through the mountain to pave a road between Hodaida and Sanaa.
>
> Mohammad Abdul-Wali, 'The Chinese Road'

Geopolitical rivalries could also be a factor in foreign investment in port–hinterland road networks, as they were in Yemen.

Yemen's variegated, fractious, and constantly transforming governing structures lent themselves particularly well to projections of geopolitical influence. Aden had been a colony – the *only* British colony on the Arabian Peninsula – until 1967, while the rulers of its hinterland provinces in Southern Yemen had protection agreements with the British. These protectorates and Aden formed the People's Democratic Republic of Yemen in the aftermath of a brutal struggle for decolonisation. The imamate in the north was overthrown by a Nasserist coup in 1962 and became the Republic of Yemen. Intense hostility between the two Yemens belied efforts at unification in 1990 and broke into open warfare in 1994. In the aftermath of the Arab uprisings of 2011, the geographical and political fragmentation of the country has been exacerbated by the intervention of regional and global powers in a civil war whose contours do not necessarily follow the north-south divide.

If war has given the alibi for global and regional intervention in Yemen, the building of transport infrastructures has also been a milieu of geopolitical rivalry. Yemen's mountainous coastal areas and arid hinterland have made road-building there a challenge. While before the twentieth century rudimentary roads connected the coasts to the interior cities facilitating pilgrimage and trade (especially in coffee and animal hides), paved roads emerged after the introduction of automobiles into the country. An account of the 1930s Saudi attempt to invade and annex the northern Yemeni port of Hodeidah describes tribes supporting either Al Saud or the imamate riding on horseback; Saudi armed patrols on camel-back; British and European armed forces (including the Italians and the French) driving armed and armoured lorries transported on warships; and Prince Faisal (later a Saudi monarch), who had been a proponent of annexing Hodeidah, arriving in a convoy of cars.[49]

In Aden, at the same time, British colonial officials planned a major road-building project to connect the Hadhramaut region to Aden Colony. The project alarmed those who had camel-transport businesses in the region, as well as those whose tribal territories were dissected or expropriated by the roads. They worked to sabotage the roads to protect their lands and livelihoods. In response, British colonial officials attempted to incorporate the members of allied tribes into the road-building project by employing them as both construction workers and guards.[50] There was long colonial precedent for such projects of co-optation: where invading European powers had not pressed peasants into corvée labour, some local faction was employed on infrastructure projects in order to guarantee a degree of local buy-in.

The post–World War II era saw a gradual increase in the length of paved roads, both in and around Aden Colony and in the north. Much of the time, roads served as a means of transport for military vehicles or the incorporation of peripheries into the body of the state. In this period, the imamate in the north received support from Egypt, the Soviet Union, and Yugoslavia to build new infrastructures. Starting in 1959, the US also provided economic aid to the Yemeni imam for roads and irrigation.[51] Even after the nationalist coup overthrew the imamate and installed a pan-Arabist regime, the US continued providing road-building aid to North Yemen.[52] The Cold War – both the global contest between the US and the Eastern Bloc and the regional rivalries between pan-Arabists and conservative states – further spurred road-building efforts in North and South Yemen.

In North Yemen, the Soviet Union paid for the upgrade of the port at Hodeidah; Bulgaria and China became actively involved in building roads from the coast to Sana'a and other interior cities. The projects included both Chinese and Yemeni workers, but the technical expertise was wholly provided by the Chinese. The northern Yemeni government also continued to seek US support in road-building. A 1971 memo from a US State Department official expressed the need for 'using [US]AID funds, to make feasibility and engineering studies for Yemeni roads, which might subsequently be built with Saudi funds. American companies could provide the technical know-how and management for such road projects.'[53] The US was directly competing with China and Soviet Bloc countries.

In the south, upon its independence in 1967, the PDRY had 'a well-developed port in Aden, a few good roads around the capital and limited connections by coastal shipping and air to the other centres of population and economic activity, which are scattered along the country's long coastline and in a few fertile – but remote – areas'.[54] Like their rivals in North Yemen, from the very start, South Yemeni rulers appealed to both sides of the Cold War for infrastructural aid. While Soviet influence dominated between 1969 and 1980, South Yemen also joined the World Bank in 1969. As early as 1971 it began receiving loans from the World Bank and aid from the Kuwait Fund for Arab Economic Development for the construction and maintenance of highways.[55] Debt and aid became ways to maintain South Yemen's connection with capitalist world economy, while regional and global funds also used their aid as means of influencing the politics of the country.

While the Soviet Union invested both North and South Yemeni ports that could serve it as naval waystations, the World Bank and Arab development funds saw the roads leading away from the ports as conduits to capitalisation of Yemeni interior. Successive infrastructure projects to build these roads were funded by these bodies, often financed by no-interest loans. Despite the financing that poured into the country, only a fraction of the roads in Yemen are paved and they connect only the largest population centres to one another. Internal conflicts and the dominance of the north since the unification of the country have also led to unequal distribution of roads across the country. Ongoing wars and aerial bombings have only degraded what paved roads there are, diminishing the connection of the ports to the hinterlands.

Federating Transports

> The towns of the Trucial Coast are tied together by a road that is little more than a desert track. In 1931 when a sheikh of Manasir tribe went from Abu Dhabi to Mecca in a Ford car, his trip was considered a great achievement. The number of cars using the road has increased greatly the last few years, and desert-worthy trucks now move about even without benefit of roads.
>
> Richard Sanger, *Arabian Peninsula*, 174

Among all the countries of the Peninsula, the United Arab Emirates was the last to be woven together by a network of roads. This was not only because of the wildly variable terrain but also because the British were not particularly interested in developing the interconnections between the Trucial emirates. As had always been the modus operandi of the British Empire, rivalry between the emirates gave the British more leverage against the rulers.

The idea that the two coasts of what is today the UAE should be conjoined by roads – and to have these road connections serve regional trade via the ports – was not new. The shallow waters and mercurial currents of the Gulf made it inferior to the harbours of the Gulf of Oman, which had been deep and well-sheltered from the sudden storms arriving from the Indian Ocean. In the early twentieth century, when the inter-European rivalry in the Middle East reached a fever pitch, French scholar and adventurer Antonin Goguyer wanted the French to acquire Khor Fakkan port on the Gulf of Oman and build a railway from there to Sharjah on the Persian Gulf side; or, alternatively, to acquire the port of Dibba and build a road to Ras al-Khaimah. Nothing came of this.[56] At the time, it was not unheard of for larger ships to land on the ports of the eastern coast, unload their goods in the better-protected harbours there, and, in the absence of roads, transport them by smaller boats to the west coast.[57]

The dearth of roads meant that, until the late 1960s travelling from Dubai, Abu Dhabi, Sharjah, or Ras al-Khaimah on the Persian Gulf coast to Fujairah on the Gulf of Oman coast often required a boat trip around the Musandam Peninsula, which was notorious for fickle winds and treacherous currents. The overland route was also dangerous as it not only required traversing shifting dunes in some places, but also crossing the Al-Hajar mountain range which was inhospitable to automobiles. This unaccommodating topography meant that at least until the mid-twentieth century, the smaller ports of the eastern coast had more intimate commercial ties and connections across the seas and along the coasts than to the hinterland emirates that claimed them as their own.

Although the coastal areas on both the Persian and Oman Gulfs could be traversed by automobiles fitted with suitable tyres or by four-wheel drive vehicles, these areas did not boast graded and paved roads. Goods that arrived first in the Sharjah Creek and later the Dubai Creek were transported by specially kitted Range Rovers or Bedford trucks throughout the Peninsula.[58] Before the discovery of oil in the Trucial emirates, gasoline was imported from Abadan in tug boats and shipped around the emirates by truck.[59] Only after the injection of petroleum income in the 1960s was a thirteen-kilometre road between Dubai and Sharjah completed, and it took regional intrigue for the road to be extended to Ras al-Khaimah. This modern road was from the very first subject to political manoeuvring between different foreign powers and regional capitalists. The British, the Arab League, and Saudi Arabia all vied for influence on the coast. As a historian of the region, Matt Maclean, writes,

> Egyptian President Gamal Abdul Nasser, British Prime Minister Harold Wilson, and King Faisal of Saudi Arabia were personally involved at various points, testifying to the strategic importance of the Trucial States' development process on a regional scale. In

> the end, the Dubai-Sharjah section was built by the Halcrow construction firm, while the Sharjah-Ras al-Khaimah road was constructed by the Saudi Bin Laden corporation.[60]

Saudi Arabia funded the extension to Ras al-Khaimah in 1969. A road across the Peninsula to the eastern coast of the UAE was built in 1968 and asphalted still later.[61] But the creation of this road itself facilitated the transformation of the small ports on the eastern coast, Fujairah and Khor Fakkan especially, into major nodes of transportation for liquid, bulk, and containerised cargoes in the 1980s and thereafter. This growth was also aided by the Iran–Iraq War, which placed tankers in the line of fire and made crossing through the Hormuz Strait a dangerous venture for most ships, giving more impetus to building infrastructures for loading oil on the eastern coast of the UAE.

Ultimately, the federation of the seven emirates that make up the UAE was pivotal in the road-building project. The roads integrated the factious emirates into a single state and a more tightly knit market served by ports on both coasts. The vast majority of the roads in the UAE were built after the federation and paid for by Abu Dhabi in the 1970s.[62] Even here, geopolitics mattered. As Dubai and Abu Dhabi vied for leadership of the federation and allocation of power within it, transport infrastructures became milieus for this geopolitical contestation. While Dubai chose Jabal Ali, hard against the Abu Dhabi border, as its major future port, Abu Dhabi used roads to the less affluent northern emirates to bind the peripheries closer to its core. These roads also created conduits to new outlets for Abu Dhabi's oil and petroleum products as Fujairah became one of the most important export terminals for Abu Dhabi's crude and refined hydrocarbon products.

Peninsular Connections

Abu Dhabi's political dominance in the UAE after 1971 also translated into an ambition to extend rail connections across the border from the UAE to other countries of the Gulf Cooperation Council (GCC).[63] The UAE's currently planned national rail, Etihad Rail, is intended to connect Ras al-Khaimah, Sharjah, Dubai, and Abu Dhabi on the western coast to Fujairah on the east coast.[64] The national rail is then supposed to link to a Saudi network and onwards to Qatar, Bahrain, and Kuwait in one direction and Oman in the other.[65] In Oman, the GCC railway of the future is to connect to a national link between the ports, interior towns, and mineral-rich areas in the desert.[66] The envisioned cargo transport route ostensibly facilitates the connection of Persian Gulf ports to the Indian Ocean and to the Red Sea, bypassing the contentious Hormuz Strait. The GCC railway was always a geopolitical project as much as a commercial one. It consolidated the paramountcy of the UAE in logistics and transportation while it attempted to weave together the disparate states of the Peninsula, with their oft-contradictory policies and projects and competing economies.

From the start, the GCC rail project faced doubts from the ruling elites of the states over the railway encouraging the mobility of peoples and goods under the state's radar. Some smaller emirates chafed at the possibility of being co-opted by the richer states. The project as a whole was dependent on high oil prices, which made possible specialised rail provisions for building tracks through inhospitable terrains. A crash in oil prices in 2014 and a clash in the foreign-policy imperatives of Qatar on one side and Abu Dhabi, Saudi Arabia, and Bahrain on the other have put paid to the plans of a Peninsula-wide railway. In Saudi Arabia, despite extensive talks about rail projects, the main existing lines are still the Dammam–Riyadh connection and a high-speed railway between Medina, Mecca, Jeddah, and Rabigh, whose inauguration date was pushed back on several occasions[67] but which was finally inaugurated in 2019. The emirates of the northern Gulf – Qatar, Bahrain, and Kuwait – have put out tenders for consulting on rail and have sent representatives to rail-transport trade shows but show no concrete sign of railway-construction projects. In Oman, the planned peninsular connection is on hiatus, though there is talk of a line between Duqm and the interior town of Fahud, the location of one of Petroleum Development Oman's main oil fields.[68] Though there has been some talk of reviving the railway, much will depend on the price of oil and the cold and hot wars waged around the Peninsula.[69] Implementing railways will also depend on the relationships between the states, technocrats, and local and global capitalists.

5

'Mechanic, Merchant, King'[1]

> There are people who do business within the law.
> And others, who love speed, danger,
> Tricks, who know how to
> Twist arms, get fantastic wealth,
> Hurt with heavy shoulders of power,
> And then drink to it!
> they don't get caught.
> they *own* the law.
>
> Gary Snyder, 'Money Goes Upstream'

In 2006, Dubai Ports World acquired Peninsular and Oriental Steam Navigation Company (P&O) for nearly £4 billion. At the time, the *New York Times* described P&O as 'a sinew of empire, a shipping line that ferried soldiers and diplomats, even royalty, on the Victorian mail runs that tied Britain to its outposts far to the east and beyond'.[2] In addition to waxing nostalgic for the old imperial shipping firm, the *New York Times* voiced wonder that the British did not seem to mind so much when former colonials acquired their glorious imperial institutions. Still more striking was the passing of the capitalist baton from a company so identified with the British imperial venture to a firm embodying state-owned transnational enterprise, whose tentacles reached across oceans and seas. The story of P&O's acquisition by Dubai Ports World is the story of the transformation of capital in the Arabian Peninsula. So many capitalists, corporations, merchants, experts, bureaucrats, and political advisers fundamentally shaped shipping in the Arabian Peninsula.

P&O was founded in 1837 as the first major British shipping firm to take advantage of steam technology. The company's deployment of expensive new steamships was subsidised by mail contracts with the British government to deliver post to Iberia and the eastern Mediterranean (the eponymous Peninsula and Orient). By 1853, P&O had also secured the mail contract for India, through its preferred overland route via Suez. When, in the latter half of the nineteenth century, the British Empire consolidated its hold across the Indian Ocean, P&O became the courier to those vast swathes of pink on the map.[3] The company's ships carried passengers, cargo, and mail through the Mediterranean, the Indian Ocean, and beyond.

While P&O may today be the more famous shipping company (perhaps because its logo still festoons ports, ferries, containers, and transport infrastructures), at the height of British imperial shipping in the Indian Ocean, the British India Steam Navigation Company commanded a far larger fleet. A Scottish grocer from Argyll, William Mackinnon, became a shipping tycoon by taking over coastal trade around the Bay of Bengal along with another Scotsman and his old schoolmate, Robert Mackenzie. Mackinnon, who went on to found several shipping companies and whose group of firms was crucial to the consolidation of the British Empire in East Africa and western Indian Ocean, established the parent company of British India in 1856 to take advantage of trade between Calcutta and Burma. By 1862, the firm was flourishing on mail contracts for coastal India and India–Persia routes.[4]

The opening of the Suez Canal proved a boon to these steam navigation firms, who had to find shipping agents in the ever-expanding British dominion. British India's agent in Aden was the firm of Cowasjee Dinshaw & Bros., owned by Parsi merchants who had established in 1854 a shipping business in Aden and expanded its reach through its shipping-agency work as well as lucrative contracts with the (British) Indian Navy.[5] In London, British India Steam Navigation Company's shipping agent was Gray Dawes (part of a family of firms that included Gray Mackenzie and Gray Paul).[6] In 1869, Edwyn Dawes, the founder of Gray Dawes and a director of the Suez Canal Company, foresaw the opening of markets in the Gulf, specifically for transhipment of Persian opium via Aden to China and transportation of pilgrims from Persia to Mecca.[7] Despite the wild optimism of the British-owned firms in those early years, in actuality, the routes from the Gulf to East Africa and South Asia were already well served by dhow trade. Heavy packet subsidies from the British government and expansion or consolidation of the empire in the Gulf, Africa, and the Indian Ocean gave the British firms the boost they needed by the end of the nineteenth century.

In 1914, P&O and British India Steam Navigation Company, which owned 131 and 70 steamers respectively, merged under the former's name. The new chairman was James Mackay, Lord Inchcape (by then Mackinnon and the original founders of P&O had long passed). Inchcape was the sole surviving partner of Mackinnon's merchandising firm in Bombay, Mackinnon Mackenzie.[8] As it is clear from the names of the firms and businessmen, Scottish origins and complex transoceanic networks connected all the firms. By the mid-1920s, P&O owned more than 500 ships. It would put them to the service of the government during the world wars by 'carrying soldiers, guns, food, fuel and ammunition' to wherever the British government needed.[9] After World War II, with the decline in long-distance passenger travel aboard ships, the firm concentrated on its cargo trade and was an early entrant into the tanker, ro/ro (wheeled vehicle shipping), and container markets.[10] It also expanded to providing offshore services and port and logistics management. In the first decade of the twenty-first century, its port-management business, P&O Ports, was one of its most lucrative subsidiaries and owned ports in North America, Europe, and Asia. DP World's acquisition of this tasty business morsel led to a major scandal in the US, discussed in chapter 3.

The story of the creation of P&O and the absorption of some of its subsidiaries by Arab capital is notable in many regards. Shipping is a capital-intensive business and has a fundamentally global character. The litany of firms I have listed were often family firms or were shaped by connections of kinship, had extensive webs of collaboration across vast territories, jealously guarded their domain of operation (using the state's coercive or legal means to fend off competitors), and had a tendency towards monopoly or cartels (in shipping parlance, *conferences*). The transnational firms formed intimate relationships with local capital. Mercantile capital on the Peninsula had from the very first a transnational character, and the coming of oil in the twentieth century gave the merchants of the Peninsula an even longer global reach. Local merchants comfortably negotiated their roles as agents or brokers for foreign capital; eventually many began new businesses in their own right, accumulating capital through setting up factories, organising the circulation of goods, and providing shipping and agency services in the Peninsula.

It was fitting that Dubai Ports World, a firm wholly owned by Dubai's government (and/or ruler), acquired a company so indelibly marked by the history of the British Empire in the Indian Ocean. For both P&O and DP World, the boundaries between firms and states were blurry. Like so many other imperial enterprises operating in the colonies, the interests of British shipping companies were indistinguishable from the interests of the British Empire. In one parliamentary hearing on abolition of slave trade in the Indian Ocean (which was as much about competition with France as anything else), British India's representatives promised that the firm's ships could act as arms of the state:

> In becoming the eyes and ears of the British civil and naval authorities through regular 'patrolling', in encouraging voluntary labour migration through cheap deck passage rates, and in stimulating

> commodity trades to replace the traffic in human beings, mail steamers would be the backbone of 'legitimate commerce'.[11]

The firms – much like the petroleum companies that came after them – fielded officers, advisers, and consultants for their governments. Their shipping agents in Aden and the British protectorate in the Gulf were intimately bound up with the local British political residents and agents and these political officers represented the interests of these firms over local or other European firms.

Although the coming of oil in the 1930s created a new class of Arab capitalists in the Peninsula, especially contractors and construction magnates, many of the old merchant families comfortably slipped into new modalities of accumulation, new sectors, new businesses. But with all the new firms, even when capital itself was 'nativised', certain racialised hierarchies persisted in the management of the businesses. For a certain class of European men of the nineteenth century, going 'East' secured prestige, profit, and profession. Today's shipping businesses in the Arabian Peninsula continue to provide a route to comfortably paid jobs for British, Dutch, and other northwest Europeans with experience in maritime finance, insurance, accounting, engineering, and ports and terminal operation. But the movement of professionals and managers is no longer only eastward. South Asian (and more specifically Indian) experts, managers, professionals, and bureaucrats increasingly populate the middle and even top tiers of corporate structures. Even as local and regional merchants are represented in the ranks of capital, the old and new metropolitan centres are still the locus of a great deal of power.

Tanker and Cargo Shipping Companies

I have chosen three shipping firms founded in the Gulf since the start of the twentieth century to illustrate the changes in ownership of shipping capital. The three firms are BP Shipping, Kuwait

Oil Tanker Company, and United Arab Shipping Company. These three companies represent different origins: a major British imperial venture, Kuwaiti merchant capital, and a consortium of Arab states newly sovereign over their oil resources. The rise of each in different moments of the twentieth century also tracks the historical shifts in maritime transport in the Peninsula over the course of that century, with the dominance of the British eventually giving way to the regional states. The shift in the ownership patterns of these firms also illuminates changes and variations in maritime property regimes.

BP Shipping's parent company was the Anglo-Persian Oil Company (APOC), founded in 1908 in southwestern Iran. The first ship transporting oil for APOC was the 1912 *SS Ferrara*, a freighter that carried the Iranian oil in barrels and which a company engineer described as 'the most terrible thing on God's earth'.[12] The ship's capacity was only 1,650 deadweight tonnes (dwt). By contrast, the world's largest crude carrier, decommissioned and scrapped in 2009, carried 350 times as much. Political transformations – the switch from coal to oil in Admiralty vessels, technological innovations in extraction and carriage of oil, the contentiousness of coal-miners, and the thirty-year wars that remade the world in the twentieth century – led to a major expansion in the production of petroleum.[13] To distribute the cargo, APOC set up a subsidiary, the British Tanker Company, the forerunner of BP Shipping. Between 1919 and 1938, British Tanker Company grew from a fleet of twenty-five ships to ninety-four ships carrying 1 million dwt. The Tanker Company was the only subsidiary of APOC in which the public could invest, and their investment in the early 1920s allowed for the construction of new ships and the expansion of the fleet at the very moment when the shift from coal to oil was gathering pace.

The prodigious consumption of oil in the first two and a half decades after World War II was matched by exponential growth in the discovery of new oil reserves. Even as BP's fleet expanded after the war like other oil companies, it felt an acute shortage of tankers for all the oil crisscrossing the seas. One solution was to charter ships from private owners. The meteoric rise of Greek shipping and the cartoonish glamour of the Greek shipping magnates of that era – Stavros Niarchos, Aristotle Onassis, Stavros Livanos, Minos Kyriakou – transpired because they tapped into oil companies' hunger for tanker capacity. When, after the closure of the Suez Canal in 1956 (and again, for much longer, in 1967), tankers and freighters became far larger and far fewer in number, oil companies feverishly chartered Greek ships, with BP leasing Onassis's entire fleet of VLCCs in 1967.[14] By the mid-twentieth century, changes to tanker shipping ownership regimes were permanent. Most oil shippers changed the balance of their tanker portfolios, leasing and chartering more ships than they owned. This structural change in the tanker business was further spurred by the nationalisation of oil companies in the Arab world, which then asserted control over their own oil transport. BP's tanker ownership reflected these changes. At last count, in 2016, the company commanded only forty-six tankers, carrying 5 million dwt. Many are leased. It also has access to time-chartered and spot-chartered vessels.

Throughout, even with changes in the price of oil, *shipping* petroleum has remained an immensely profitable business for BP. The company's vertical integration (upstream and downstream), vast markets, numerous refineries, and huge number of subsidiaries throughout the world allow BP to profit from oil distribution, despite fluctuations in the price of oil. Given how profitable tanker shipping had been in the postwar period, the British did not want competition from regional shipping companies, but competition they got. In the 1950s, Kuwaiti merchants decided that investment in a new shipping business could 'take the place of the slowly dying long-distance trade by dhow'.[15] The merchants had shipping experience, access to capital, and a state-supported and protected market in oil. As important was the surge in demand for and production of Kuwaiti oil in the aftermath of the Anglo-Iranian Oil Company's nationalisation, and Kuwait's refinery replacing Abadan's as a source of refined hydrocarbons. The British, who controlled Kuwaiti politics via their protection agreement, at first baulked at such a venture and denied permission for the establishment of a rival for BP Shipping. But, eventually – hoping that the new company would order ships from British shipyards – they relented. Kuwait Oil Tanker Company (KOTC) was founded in April 1957 and promptly ordered ships from the Japanese Sasebo shipyard. From then on, the KOTC put its ships at the service of the Kuwait Oil Company (a joint venture between BP and Gulf Oil), under a time-charter system which guaranteed it a stable income over time. KOTC also provided shipping-agency services to other tankers visiting Kuwait, ensuring its domination of oil shipping there. The merchant owners also explicitly excluded the British Gray Mackenzie (seen everywhere as quintessentially representing British imperial interests) from KOTC's agency business. Their opposition was motivated as much by business rivalry as pan-Arabist anger at Britain for its 1956 invasion of Egypt.[16] This tension – cutting profitable business deals with a powerful British firm, BP, while deploying anticolonial language against a rival British firm, Gray Mackenzie – characterised the vexed relationship of the Peninsula's capitalists with the British.

KOTC's business remained fairly stable until the closures of the Suez Canal dramatically transformed the physical structure of the shipping market, with larger ships becoming more prevalent. The nationalisation of Arab petroleum companies and a surge in US demand for oil in the early 1970s also created enormous tensions in the global petroleum shipping business. British Petroleum in this period refused to renew its time charter with KOTC; only an edict by the Kuwaiti ruler requiring Kuwaiti oil to be carried by Kuwaiti tankers saved the company. In the end, the market transformations of the late 1970s resulted in consistent operating losses for KOTC, and the company was fully nationalised in 1979.[17]

Despite its troubles in the 1970s, KOTC had the largest fleet of petroleum crude and products carrier of any of the Arab oil-producing nations. During the Tanker Wars of the 1980s, KOTC tankers were re-flagged by the US, protecting its business as it returned to profit in the 1980s. With the Iraqi invasion of Kuwait in 1990, KOTC chartered its ships to other oil companies (since Kuwait's own oil was burning in the wells) and managed to remain in the black despite the devastation of the Kuwaiti oil industry.[18] KOTC is unique among the many tanker companies in the Gulf in that its founding capital was provided by powerful and affluent merchants rather than the state. The company allowed local capitalists to buy directly into the downstream business of the oil companies in ways not then seen elsewhere in the Gulf. It also flourished because of the work it did for the Kuwait Oil Company, which had been a BP subsidiary. In effect, BP's domination of Kuwaiti oil in the 1950s spun out new forms of capital accumulation, while the shipping experience of the merchants permitted KOTC to develop not only as a ship-owner/operator but also as a shipping agent.

While in 1980 oil and gas transport had been a little over 50 per cent of all seaborne trade by volume, by 2015 this per centage had fallen to just under 30.[19] Today, globally, the largest owners of tankers are predominantly Norwegian companies incorporated in Bermuda and Greek family businesses flagging their ships to Panama and other flags of convenience, both of whom either lease out their ships or operate their own tanker businesses. Most oil companies, whether nationally owned firms like Kuwait Petroleum Corporation (of which KOTC is a subsidiary) or publicly traded like BP, have ceded their ground to these privately owned shippers. This transformation also indicates that the accumulation of capital in tanker shipping is largely occurring outside the region and beyond the reach of independent shipowners there.

A third firm whose fortunes track transformations in shipping in the Arabian Peninsula is the United Arab Shipping

Company (UASC). The firm was founded in 1977 by Saudi Arabia, Kuwait, UAE, Bahrain, Iraq, and Qatar taking over nearly twenty ships owned by Kuwait Shipping Company. To establish its fleet, it also ordered forty new vessels, many of them container ships.[20] Its ambitious start symbolised the surging market for maritime shipping in the Peninsula in the 1970s. The founding of the firm was concurrent with the building of the Arab Shipbuilding and Repair Yard (ASRY) in Bahrain and the massive expansion of port capacity on the Arabian Peninsula in response to port congestion. The conversion of many of the region's freight transport to containers was also a factor in the founding of the firm. UASC is headquartered in Kuwait, but its hub of operations is in Dubai. Of container companies founded in the Middle East, only UASC and the Israeli-owned Zim appear at the top of the 2016 list of liner shipping companies, with Zim at seventeen and UASC at thirteen. Soon after the publication of this ranking, UASC began merger talks with the German Hapag-Lloyd. The deal nearly fell victim to the conflict between Saudi Arabia, Bahrain, and UAE on one side and Qatar on the other, as all states are shareholders in the company.[21] With the completion of the merger in 2017, Hapag-Lloyd became the operator of the new shipping line and the Qatari and Saudi sovereign funds become the fourth- and fifth-largest investors in the new company. The other owners of the company include a Chilean/German maritime firm and the City of Hamburg. The merger catapulted Hapag-Lloyd to fifth place in the list of the largest container-shipping companies.

The conglomeration of secretive family-owned firms, sovereign funds, and state-owned firms creates complex webs of ownership where firms across the globe have a stake in one another's businesses. In a sense, this echoes the Mackenzie/Mackinnon/Gray/Dawes/Paul shipping network of the late nineteenth century, which explicitly served the British Empire. In our time, the blurry boundaries between 'private' ownership and the state – near and far, municipal and national – become most visible in these moments of merger. The ownership regimes and historical transformation of large shipping businesses are also traceable in the histories of merchant families in the Gulf and their vexed and contradictory relationships with European oil and shipping capital.

Merchants and Capitalists

> The Bahreinis are merely merchants and it will be very hard to turn them into industrialists.
>
> W.F. Crawford, UK Foreign Office, Development Division[22]

In a 1967 letter discussing the planning and construction of Dubai's Port Rashid (which was displaced by Jabal Ali port only two decades later), the local British government representative celebrated British power:

> Thus Dubai's first large-scale enterprise is launched with major British participation. BP are large share-holders in the oil consortium which will produce the revenues to pay for it. Costain's are the contractors, and Halcrow's are the consultants, for the harbour. Ninety per cent of the financial credit for the harbour is from British sources and sixty-five per cent of the cover is provided by Export Credit Guarantee Department. For good or ill, we have a predominant stake in the economic future of Dubai. We shall have to be vigilant to protect our interests and to ensure that we do not fall short on our side. If this venture goes well we should have established an excellent lead over our competitors for further business with an expanding economy.[23]

It is not surprising that as late as the 1960s, only just before they relinquished their protectorates in the Gulf, the British still dominated the construction and financing of maritime infrastructures in the lower Gulf. A comprehensive and detailed study of construction projects in the Arab world completed in the 1980s showed that between 1957 and 1981, the largest contracts of British construction and design firms tendered in Bahrain, Saudi, or the UAE were for harbours, docks, and sea defences. In Qatar, Kuwait, and Oman, marine construction constituted British firms' second- or third-largest category of contracts.[24] Among these firms, Sir William Halcrow & Partners and Sir Bruce White, Wolfe Barry & Partners were the most prominent.[25]

While the British dominated the maritime sector in the 1950s, the US proved a major competitor then and thereafter. The average value of US contracts over a five-year period (1977 to 1981) was $8.8 billion, or 31.5 per cent of all foreign contracts awarded to US contractors worldwide.[26] Other beneficiaries of this expansion were Indian, South Korean, and European firms. Between 1973 and 1981, during the oil-boom years, Indian contractors in the Gulf saw a 580 per cent growth in their income.[27] In the same period, nearly 20 per cent of all foreign contracts for Korean firms came from Aramco or the US Army Corps of Engineers' construction projects in Saudi Arabia.[28] Among European firms, Dutch and Belgian dredging companies and the German Hochtief bid on and received maritime construction contracts. Palestinian contracting firms CAT (Construction and Trading Company) and CCC (Consolidated Contractors Company) also had a hand in harbour construction in the region. CAT was the main contractor in enormous port projects in Aden and Oman in the 1960s and 1970s.[29] The résumé of CCC, now headquartered in Athens, Greece, lists harbour projects in Bahrain and the UAE, the construction of Jubail in Saudi Arabia, Ras Laffan terminal and Hamad port in Qatar, and the expansion of Sohar and Salalah ports and the construction of the port of Duqm in Oman.[30]

The fashioning of so much infrastructure was not often without friction. Despite the collective reputation of the larger US and European firms and their diplomats' expansive promotional work, archives and local memoirs are replete with complaints about what poor, badly organised, incompetently executed work some did and the extent of their cost overruns.[31] A local adviser to Shaikh Rashid, Easa al-Gurg, derided the Dubai Dry Dock as built 'at colossal expense', with terrible timing and 'badly planned and executed [engineering], requiring an inordinately high rate of expenditure in maintenance and servicing'.[32] As soon as the Dry Dock was constructed, it became clear that it was not able to 'pay its own way' and had to compete with the larger ASRY.[33] Some contractors readily admitted that the standards of construction to which they adhered in Arabia were inferior to those they obeyed at home.

Even when they did not perform shoddy work, Anglo-American capital often tightly controlled expenditures, limited local merchants' access to the infrastructures they had built, and of course repatriated profits on a grand scale. A member of Bahrain's Kanoo merchant family recounts that in the late 1940s, BAPCO (the Bahraini Petroleum Company) had built a jetty at Sitra but did not allow the merchants to use it for their cargo. Any goods approaching the jetty had to be unloaded at sea unto barges and sailed on dhows around the island.[34] The journey under sail from Sitra to Manama could take up to a day. An Emirati merchant recalled that in Abu Dhabi in the mid-1950s and early 1960s, the 'oil companies discouraged the locals from participating in any way other than as hired hands'.[35]

In Saudi Arabia, the participation of local firms and businessmen in the peripheral bounties of oil created a new class of capitalists – but had to be fought for. Oil largesse spread through intervention by the Saud family or through edicts issued under the names of the rulers but written by Arab nationalists in ministerial posts. Until these forms of pressure from the local elite came about, the contractors in Saudi Arabia were almost entirely US-based firms, Bechtel foremost among them. Even after the aforementioned edicts forced the establishment of joint ventures, the lion's share of the prize went to those larger US-based construction and engineering firms which had long associated with the oil companies.[36] Even US legislation demanded that US agencies (like the Corps of Engineers) and major corporations discriminate in favour of US-based firms.

Among the European companies benefitting from the bonanza of shipping that began after the discoveries of oil, Gray Mackenzie stands out.[37] The firm was part of a group of shipping companies connected to the Mackinnon Group. Established in the 1880s in Bushehr (Iran) and Basra (Iraq), the company gained traction through agency work for British India Steam Navigation in those two countries as well as Bahrain and Kuwait until World War II. Like so many other shippers, the war proved a boon for Gray Mackenzie, which acted as the agent for the British Ministry of War Transport and the United Kingdom Commercial Corporation.

After the war, Gray Mackenzie augmented its staff in Bahrain and transferred its headquarters there in 1951. It also expanded its offices in Kuwait and established a branch in Muscat.[38] With the discovery of oil, it secured contracts with various petroleum companies for the unloading of cargo needed for the development of the fields. This included Trans-Arabian Pipeline (TAPline) cargo in Saudi Arabia (1947); Petroleum Development Qatar work at Zakrit Pier (1951); Abu Dhabi Petroleum's offshore work at Zakum (1962); and work for Petroleum Development Oman (1965). The Company's official historian wrote in 1973 that

> the Company represents many Shipping Companies throughout the Gulf and handles more than 50 per cent of all tankers entering the Gulf, excluding those due to load at Mina-al-Ahmadi, Umm-Said, Halul Island, and Mena-al-Fahal, where the Oil companies provide their own facilities, or delegate their duties to their local counterparts.

Like many other shipping agencies, in the wake of containerisations and transformations in the structure of shipping, Gray

Mackenzie shifted its focus from agency work to management of ports, and its very first port-management contract was for Port Rashid in Dubai.[39] But the process was not all clear sailing. In 1962, localisation regulations in Saudi Arabia forced the company to withdraw. In Kuwait, a similar decree in 1965 forced it to re-incorporate as Kuwait Maritime and Mercantile Company, with Gray Mackenzie owning only 49 per cent of the firm. Gray Mackenzie continues to have a presence in Gulf ports, with its biggest offices in Bahrain, but with the transformations in shipping after the 1960s and the rise of local capital, it is no longer the powerful player of old.

In Aden, the powerful shipping company of Antonin Besse of Aden relied on its agency for Shell Petroleum for the initial expansion of its businesses. The firm made vast profits during World War II as a thirst for petroleum products fuelled a surge in tanker shipping worldwide. Freya Stark remembered her wartime visits with Besse:

> I would escape twice a week or so to the old town of Crater, to see Hilda Besse and Anton sparkling with gaiety and malice. King of the Red Sea coasts and their commerce, ... he was distressed at this time because he could not help making money during the war; it piled itself up *malgré moi*.[40]

Distress or no distress, wars were a bonanza for shipping, but peacetime could also be a time for amassing capital. Besse's import and export business had branches throughout the Red Sea and Indian Ocean (at Addis Ababa, Dessie, Diredawa, Djibouti, Berbera, Jigjiga, Benadir Coast near Mogadishu, Hodeida, Jedda, Port Sudan, Hadhramaut, and Eritrea). He shipped goods from the region to Japan, Germany, Italy, France, England, India, and the US. Aside from shipping agencies, his own shipping business included freighters, dhows, lighters, tugs, and a floating dock. He also engaged in marine and road transport repair, construction, and finance.[41] A large donation from

Besse established St Antony's College at Oxford in 1950. The business that he passed on to his son was nationalised after the decolonisation of Aden.

Already in the 1950s, local capital was trying different strategies to partake of the bounties of infrastructure construction and shipping that had so handsomely profited British, US and European firms. Local merchants became agents or middlemen for Euro-American firms; they received exclusive lucrative contracts from foreign firms, developing secondary industries and commercial ventures around the transportation of oil and bulk cargoes; and they invested their accumulated capitals in new industries particularly germane to the infrastructure boom. Some merchants and family-owned firms did all three.

In each country, the contours of accumulation of maritime and shipping capital differed. In Saudi Arabia, whose two coasts had such vastly different histories, two different trajectories also emerged. Old merchant families of Jeddah, on the Red Sea coast, competed against European firms, while on the eastern coast of Saudi Arabia, new families were enriched through the contracts wrested from Aramco. Sulaiman Olayan (whose family-owned firm is now one of the largest in Saudi Arabia) began working for BAPCO and then CASOC in 1936, having benefitted from English-language education in Bahrain. He started his work as a land transport dispatcher in the early years, when vast tonnage of materials had to be moved from the rudimentary harbours to the oil fields. From there he worked in warehousing for nearly a decade. When Aramco began the construction of the TAPline, as a partner in General Contracting Company, Olayan's first contract was for unloading pipes onto barges off the coast of Ras al-Mish'ab and transporting them to the pipeline construction site for Bechtel. Only a few years later, he became an agent for the Beirut-based Arabian Insurance Company Ltd and was the first to set up a workers' compensation scheme through his insurance company.[42] When he died in 2002, he was one of the richest men in Saudi Arabia; his business remained in the family, with his daughter Lubna taking the reins.

Also on the eastern coast of Saudi Arabia, Ahmad Hamad al-Ghosaibi and his brothers Abdulaziz and Sulaiman benefitted from Dammam–Riyadh railway contracts and used their profits to found a shipping agency and stevedoring business in the burgeoning Dammam port of the 1950s. During the construction of the TAPline, their bonded warehouses served as storage spaces for goods and material for the construction of the pipeline. In effect, servicing Aramco's logistics needs transformed the family into the most affluent merchant family in eastern Saudi.[43] The Ghosaibi business expanded to banking and finance in Bahrain and elsewhere, collapsing spectacularly in 2009 when it became clear that the borrowing and lending practices of the company's Bahraini banks had resulted in vast financial black holes, much of the shenanigans obscured offshore in the Cayman Islands.[44] Maan al-Sanea, a Ghosaibi son-in-law, was one of the businessmen imprisoned in the Ritz-Carlton hotel by Muhammad bin Salman, in his corporate extortion–*cum*–anti-corruption activities.

In Jeddah, the long-established merchant families were pitted against European businesses whose branches in the city served the hundreds of thousands of pilgrims passing through every year. On Saudi Arabia's Red Sea coast, agency work, rather than construction or transport subcontracting, gave the local families a foothold in the burgeoning new maritime businesses. In part this was because Jeddah had for so long been about pilgrimage transport, rather than petro-infrastructure construction. A 1950s account of the city described it as a procession of European firms engaged in trade and transportation (of goods and pilgrims):

> Along the outer boulevard among the legations are the important Western companies doing business in Jidda. These include the American construction firm of International Bechtel, the

> American Eastern Trading Corporation, and the British company Gellatly Hankey, perhaps the best-known trading firm on the Red Sea. The last not only carries on an extensive import and extensive business but does banking on the side ... Beyond the suq, on the main boulevard, stands the modern office building of Jidda's largest commercial firm, the Netherlands Trading Society, locally known as the Dutch Bank which handles the affairs of Indonesians passing through.[45]

The Alireza family, which was and continues to be one of the most important business families in the country, competed with Gellatly Hankey to secure the agencies for various cargo and passenger lines.[46] Gellatly Hankey itself was a fascinating study in the horizontal integration of businesses: it was a shipping agency, a trading company, and something of a bank, and in 1955 it was taken over by the British Bank of the Middle East (about which more below).

Among the families whose businesses soared from an agency start, the Kanoos of Bahrain are noteworthy, not least because contrary to the oft-secretive character of shipping businesses, they have published an extensive and detailed account of their interests and networks throughout the Arabian Peninsula and beyond. The Kanoo family patriarch, Yusuf bin Ahmad Kanoo, had been APOC's agent in Bahrain between 1913 and 1932 (and before oil had been discovered in Bahrain itself). Oil from APOC ships and barges were unloaded in a reclaimed and filled bay, Suwaifiyya, and transported from there to Manama's Central Market. Kanoo had also secured the British mail contract for Bahrain and served as the shipping agent for Netherlands Shipping Committee and Alexandria Navigation Company.[47] In 1962, the Kanoos became the majority owners of Bahrain Ship-Repairing and Engineering Company (the other 49 per cent of company shares were open to public investment). The company's slipway in Muharraq employed fifty to sixty staff and was operated by a Dutch engineer. Until it was overtaken by the much larger ASRY in the 1970s, it served Kanoo vessels based in the emirates of the lower Gulf as well as tankers and barges from Ras Tanura and Khafji terminals.[48]

Kanoo had managed to expand his business through cultivating shrewd connections. The patriarch of the family had extended credit to Abdulaziz ibn Saud, thus establishing his reputation and connections in Saudi Arabia. His sons cultivated US military officers and managed to secure major oil transport contracts with the US during the Korean War.[49] These relations even extended to their rivals. In the 1960s, when Gray Mackenzie was forced to close its offices in Saudi Arabia in response to localisation edicts, 'it recommended its shipping lines to switch to Kanoo'.[50] The Kanoo family parlayed their presence in Saudi Arabia into a licence to manage the Riyadh 'dry port' in the 1970s. The dry port was opened by Prince Salman (later king) to process containerised goods that were shipped to Dammam, transported to the Najd province by train, and cleared for customs in Riyadh. The Kanoos managed the intermodal transportations and the customs-clearing business.[51]

Containerisation and multimodal transport in the 1970s transformed the Kanoo business. Both Port Rashid in Dubai and Port Zayed in Abu Dhabi had container berths from the 1970s onwards, and the first ship to arrive at the latter was a UASC ship (then a Kuwait-based line represented by Kanoo).[52] Just as Gray Mackenzie had done, the Kanoos shifted some of their agency work to port management in order to take advantage of the structural changes in cargo shipping. But the Kanoo family also represented tanker businesses calling at Bahrain and Ras Tanura and held an agency for Japanese tanker owners.

Like the Kanoos, many local merchants had to wrench trade away from European competitors in order to enter the business realm in the region. The obstacles were not only start-up capital or a need for technocratic expertise, but very often British colonial officials' obduracy and rigidity in protecting British business interests from the encroachment of local merchants. Nevertheless, these merchants benefitted from occupying gaps in transport infrastructures which the larger oil or shipping companies could not or would not fill. For example, the fabulously rich Qatari merchant Abdullah Darwish owned a lighterage company in Qatar. Given the paucity of port infrastructures there, lighterage was good business, as cargo was brought to the port of Umm Said (built for oil shipping) and barged over to the port of Doha.[53] Darwish had acquired a great deal of his wealth by acting as a labour recruiter for the construction projects at ports and oil fields in late-1940s Qatar. Petroleum Development Qatar paid Darwish 11.5 rupees per labourer per day; he paid the labourers 3.75 rupees plus food and water, pocketing the rest. During the boom years of the late 1940s, he hired 1,500 workers for two years. 'The labourers were the poorest of Qataris, former slaves and Persians from southern Iran'.[54] Darwish in effect became one of the most powerful merchants in Qatar on the back of such exploited labour. An Iraqi diplomat described him as

> directing the politics of Qatar's ruler, with the whole of the country's economy in his hands. He is the main importer, contractor and agent for every foreign company. He has had a hand in building every structure, and every car and bus driven in Qatar is his. Everything the government or the oil company wants to get done has to go through his hands.[55]

Proximity to the ruler and shameless exploitation of lowly workers paid handsomely, since in this he beat the Anglo-American firms at their own game. This made him something of a thorn in foreign companies' sides, and Aramco kept a long and detailed account of him in its intelligence folders.[56]

Though many of the merchant families and large corporations discussed thus far had their own mechanisms for lending money, as business expanded, they required further access to financial products. Credit and insurance became necessities as the size and reach of businesses grew.

Insurance and Banking

> The current insurance industry in the United States . . . has the same roots as all major insurance systems, in the historical interplay of statistical probability, overseas commerce, and gambling . . .
>
> Arjun Appadurai, *Banking on Words*

On the stage of maritime transport infrastructures, steel, concrete, oil, filth, and the hard materiality of the vessel and the port are often foregrounded. But neither the ports nor the vessels, and certainly not the gargantuan volumes of transnational trade, could exist without some form of financing for the construction of infrastructures and the ships themselves, and insurance, especially for the vessels and their cargo. How a ship is financed, who fronts the money and on what guarantees, what the relationship between the ownership of the vessel and the lienholder may be, and what sorts of insurance decisions and calculations are made all vary according to legal and political contexts.

London has long been a hub of such expertise. It is, of course, the home of Lloyd's, which began as a market for insurance – and specifically maritime insurance – in a seventeenth-century coffeehouse on Tower Street in the City. The business grew to insure not only merchant cargo but also colonial properties and slaves.[57] Lloyd's eventually transformed into a public limited company with a vast amount of operating capital and became a model for other insurance businesses in Europe. As I have already written, other maritime financial services are also based in London, significantly the Baltic Exchange. London also hosts some of the largest and best-known maritime law offices. When one looks closely, it becomes clear that the affluence of the City is a direct legacy of colonialism and slave trade, all underwritten by the British mastery of the oceans.

Though ships today may fly the flags of many registries, many of the rules, regulations and legislations to which global shipping conforms are designed in London, Brussels, and Washington, and they demand global compliance. From these centres emanate not only global insurance brokers, marine financiers, experts on the management of maritime resources and infrastructures, but also legal counsel, auditors, and insurance and financial regulators who aim to regularise the commercial space within which maritime enterprise operates.

Although this metropolitan emanation has been characteristic of modern capitalism for centuries, more recently new nodes of finance, insurance, and other maritime commercial services have risen in the global South. These new nodes, however, often operate under different legal jurisdictions than the cities in which they are located, in a range of offshore arrangements. They are often more closely connected to global networks of capital than they are to their brick-and-mortar hinterlands. These centres, first appearing on the Arabian Peninsula in Kuwait and Bahrain, now include Dubai, whose ambitions are not regional but global. Dubai's International Finance Centre, the home of NASDAQ Dubai (where DP World is listed), now houses over a thousand banks, insurance firm, and capital and wealth-management companies, many of them specialising in maritime trade. China conducts a great deal of its maritime commerce – especially with Pakistan and East Africa – through Dubai's financial centre, and with the aid of accumulated regional expertise located there.

Transformations in maritime finance have reflected even larger socioeconomic changes. Shipping on smaller scales, in dhow trade for example, depended on shares in which the *nakhuda* or seafarers themselves invested.[58] In Europe, the joint stock company was a crucial sixteenth-century capitalist innovation that made possible imperial maritime fleets and the financing of colonialism itself. The construction of larger ships with more expensive steel hulls and new steam technologies in the mid-nineteenth century required the kind of capitalisation that cooperative or small-scale forms of investment and ownership, or even the more highly capitalised joint stock companies, could not support. Borrowing from banks emerged at that stage and took off in the immediate post–World War II period, when the world hunger for petroleum (and the attendant surge in cargo transport) demanded more and more ships to be built and sent to sea.

Of great significance was the emergence of charter-backed financing in the 1920s, first developed by Norwegian tanker builders whose ships were used by oil companies under time charters. This particular form of financing was then refined by the Greek shipping magnates, foremost among them Onassis. Charter-backed financing entailed a long-term charter for a ship, the certainty of whose income over a specified period secured the repayment of the mortgage on the ship. Time charters guarantee incomes for ships because they are based on upfront contracts, rather than the riskier spot-loading or tramp-shipping businesses. Aristotle Onassis developed loan complexes that involved lenders, insurers, shipbuilders, and the oil companies that were his primary charter customers. Once he had secured a charter on an as-yet-unbuilt ship, he obtained insurance for it and used the insurance as a guarantee for a bank loan to pay for the commissioning of a ship.[59]

Since the 1970s, commercial banks have switched from charter-backed financing to asset-backed financing, in effect using the ship itself as security for the loan. This change has reflected the deregulation in banking and attendant innovations in financial products, with all their accompanying risks. The relaxation in rules was also a response to the oil boom of the 1970s, which saw a surge in demand for tankers and consequently for expanded ship financing. Asset-backed financing is less restrictive and riskier than charter-backed lending because it does not require the certainty of future income before credit is extended. With a charter, future shipping income (at least for a specified period) is guaranteed, whereas with the ship as loan security, the lender has no guarantee that the ship can have an income in the future, and if borrowers default they have to forfeit the ship itself. When the shipping cycle reached its nadir in the mid-1980s, many of the borrowers defaulted on their loans and a great many ships were repossessed by banks and had to be scrapped.[60]

Another major transformation in shipping finance came with the 2008 crash. Before the 2008 financial collapse, the top fifteen maritime lenders did not include any Chinese firms. After 2008, credit contracted dramatically and a number of long-standing European commercial marine lenders (including Britain's Lloyd's and RBS) wound down their maritime lending business, while others (Germany's Nordbank and Commerzbank) reduced the volume of their lending. The Korean Export/Import Bank which was already in the top fifteen list, surged to number five in a 2014 shipping-loan portfolio league table. It was joined by three Chinese banks: Bank of China, China Exim Bank, and China Development Bank.[61]

Trade and the construction of maritime infrastructures required different and often more local forms of financing. Throughout the Peninsula, money-changing, letters of credit, mutual lending, and *hawala* fund transfers had long been fundamental components of local and regional economies.[62] Before the 1940s, only Aden and Bahrain had depository banks and Saudi Arabia hosted branches of Dutch and French banks, as well as the British Gellatly Hankey, all of which served the pilgrims from their respective colonies. Many of the merchants in the Peninsula with connections to India used Bombay banks for their businesses. This paucity of banking on the Peninsula itself was in part because the British tightly controlled the establishment of banks in the region. As one political agent wrote to his superiors in 1938 during a negotiation over oil concessions,

> The one thing which I do regard as most important is to insist on His Majesty's Government's approval to any Bank which might be set up in any Shaikh's territory as a result of oil exploitation. A Bank is peculiarly well situated for becoming the focus of hostile propaganda or intrigue, and it seems to me to be of the highest importance that if and when a Bank is established His Majesty's Government should be satisfied that its financial stability is fully matched by the political soundness of its direction.[63]

In Bahrain, which was the seat of British residency in the Gulf, Eastern Bank was permitted to set up a branch in the 1930s. In Saudi Arabia, where the British did not have the whip hand, the National Commercial Bank was the first local bank to emerge in 1938 in Jeddah. The first bank to open a branch in many of the Gulf states was the (British) Imperial Bank of Iran, which soon changed its name to the British Bank of the Middle East (BBME). The bank opened branches in Kuwait (1941), Dubai (1946), and Oman (1948) and secured a monopoly in these countries for eleven, seventeen, and twenty years, respectively. Its officers insisted on the monopoly provision to protect the bank from the 'troubles' they had experienced in Iran – presumably economic nationalism – and from the competition of what they derisively called 'half-baked' Indian banks. In Saudi Arabia, where the Palestinian-owned Arab Bank was the first non-Saudi bank to open a branch in 1949, BBME opened branches in Al-Khobar and Jeddah in 1950 and in Dammam in 1952, and expanded its reach by acquiring Gellatly Hankey in 1955.[64] BBME had a short-lived presence in Abu Dhabi (because of a run-in with Shaikh Shakhbut), re-opening its branch there only after Shaikh Zayid came to power. The firm opened branches in Aden, Bahrain, and other Trucial emirates throughout the

1950s. Unsurprisingly, the bank was wildly successful during its monopoly phase in the Gulf, as it collected ever-increasing deposits (particularly from the ruling families, the merchants, and some income streams of oil companies), paid no interest on most of its accounts during its monopoly period, and invested its deposits in London or Bombay. In the Gulf, it provided short-term loans to finance the massive importation of consumer, commercial, and construction goods after World War II and funded the dhow gold trade from Kuwait and Dubai to India.[65]

In Kuwait, some 25 per cent of BBME's lending supported infrastructure construction. In Dubai, the bank was given a concession to Dubai customs and used the customs income to lend money to the ruler to finance the dredging of the harbour there in the 1950s. It also guaranteed a loan from Kuwait to cover the rest of the harbour engineering programme by using Dubai's customs income as both security and repayment instalments. In order to extend its monopoly, the bank unscrupulously struck a deal with Shaikh Rashid in 1959 wherein 20 per cent of the bank's profit went directly to Rashid's account.[66] But by 1961, new banks were being established by local merchants in Dubai, who partnered with the National Bank of Kuwait and broke BBME's monopoly. As in the shipping-agency businesses, local merchants became more assertive as nascent bankers in the 1960s.

Until the discovery of oil in Oman, BBME's profits there were mainly secured from the business of some twenty merchants of Indian origin who traded with India. The bank's business flourished after the 1947 Indian partition, when a ban on direct trade between India and Pakistan necessitated workarounds for conveying cargo. One was found in the port of Gwadar, then a sovereign enclave of Oman within Pakistani Baluch territory. Omani merchants imported goods from Pakistan or India to Gwadar, whence they were transhipped to India or Pakistan. This lucrative trade was in effect until 1958, when Oman sold Gwadar to Pakistan. After the discovery of oil and the British coup that brought Sultan Qabus to power, Oman's branch of BBME financed the construction of Sultan Qabus port, today in Muscat town centre.[67]

In most of the Arabian Peninsula, local banks (often in joint ventures or under franchise agreements with foreign banks) began to emerge in droves in the late 1950s and 1960s. But the 1970s oil boom and the civil war in Lebanon dramatically transformed the banking and insurance sectors in Kuwait and Bahrain. Beirut itself had been a beneficiary of Nasser's nationalisation of Egyptian banks in 1952, with many banks shifting their businesses there from Cairo and Alexandria. The civil war in Lebanon led many maritime financiers and insurers – European and Arab – to look to new headquarters in the Gulf, where the flow of petrodollars necessitated new banks and banking instruments. Bahrain was especially hospitable to this move. In 1975, the Bahraini government issued a directive to encourage offshore banking units, and it soon had a burgeoning banking business.[68] Only a decade and a half later, it was overtaken by Dubai, whose *laissez-faire* policies, investment in the International Finance Centre, liberal foreign-ownership laws, and streamlined telecommunication and business infrastructures proved irresistible to financiers and insurance firms.

Insurance was another important financial service required for shipping. In most places where merchants engaged in long-distance trade, forms of insurance had long existed: futures contracts, for example, hedge against unexpected changes in prices. Mutual forms of insurance also ensured that some form of compensation was paid out for cargoes that did not arrive at their destinations. However, the reach of the British empire and especially its corporate business vehicles meant that from the nineteenth century onwards, the peculiarities of the English insurance business spread worldwide. Beside London, Macau and Hong Kong became the base of operation for marine insurers on the Pacific, whence Indian Ocean business diasporas (among them Indian Parsis) transmitted these new forms of calculation and finance to new shores.[69]

In the Arabian Peninsula, most insurance companies until the 1960s were local franchises or agencies of European firms. The Kanoos of Bahrain represented Norwich Union. In Saudi Arabia, Gellatly Hankey – which was also a shipping agent for passenger, tanker and cargo companies – represented Lloyd's of London and the Board of Underwriters of New York.[70] Gray Mackenzie in turn secured an agency from Lloyd's for Bahrain. Almost all insurance contracts indemnified cargo and maritime trade. The insurance industry grew in leaps and bounds in the 1970s. As the ports in the oil-producing countries of the Peninsula became congested, more insurance was needed to cover missing cargo resulting from inevitable misplacements, pilfering, and smuggling.[71]

However, despite the dizzying growth of insurable goods, cargoes, and shipping in the Middle East, and even more so in Asia, Europe continues to be the hub of global marine insurance. While the Asia-Pacific region now provides some 28 per cent of all premiums (the Middle East is the source of only 4.1 per cent), Europe remains the source of more than half of all marine insurance premiums. Of insurers, Lloyd's of London earns the largest percentage of all forms of marine insurance (hull, cargo, etc). The UK also continues to be the world centre for protection and indemnity (P&I) clubs, with 61 per cent of all clubs located there. Nordic countries follow with 30 per cent of all clubs, Japan with 6 per cent, and the US with 3 per cent.[72] While marine insurance covers hull and cargo, P&I clubs cover risks from war, environmental, and accidental damage. A report on world shipping centres ranks London as leading the world in shipping finance and laws, while Asian port cities (Singapore, Shanghai, and Hong Kong) lead in other indicators. Dubai is the only Arab port to appear on the list; it does so because of its 'attractiveness and competitiveness' to business.[73]

The concentration of P&I clubs in the UK has notably affected shipping in and around the Arabian Peninsula. During successive wars in the Gulf, Lloyd's Joint War Committee has decided large increases in insurance rates. These increases in turn have affected freight rates and shipping patterns there. The Joint War Committee, other insurance underwriters, and members of the International Underwriting Association determine the world shipping hotspots and issue a list that enumerates wars, strikes, terrorism, piracy, and other possible risks. The list's opaque categories and quantification procedures define which shipping routes and ports are considered 'safe' for loading or unloading and which are thought perilous. The omniscience and omnipotence attributed to the Joint War Committee then influences not only shipping rates and routes, but also the security apparatuses that guard ports, straits, and the oceanic highways.[74]

Advisers, Bureaucrats, and Experts

> New York's imperial
> advance guards (engineers,
> calculators, surveyors,
> experts)
>
> Pablo Neruda, 'Canto General'

> The East is a career.
>
> Benjamin Disraeli

Perhaps as significant as the capitalists, bankers, and merchants involved in shipping are the advisers, bureaucrats, and technocratic experts whose everyday interventions often delineate the parameters of maritime transport. Many hail from the region and know the ruling families through intimacies of friendship or kinship. Many others are ostensibly independent British or American counsellors to the rulers whose degree of independence varies, but generally they seem to have served the interests of Britain or the US, rather than the rulers. Technocratic experts often come from the North Atlantic (though Indians also have had a role in dispensing technical expertise), while bureaucratic and governmental civil service is populated by members either of merchant families or of civil servants of other Arab states (especially Iraqis, Egyptians, and Palestinians).

In the 1950s and 1960s, many of the local advisers to the rulers were either prominent merchants or officers in many of the new businesses: Easa al-Gurg, for example, who advised Shaikh Rashid of Dubai, was the BBME's top officer in Dubai. In 1961 he was appointed a member of the Dubai Port Committee alongside three British officers, three local merchants, and the British political agent in Dubai, Donald Hawley.[75] The appointment was important, as the opening of the Dubai Creek Port in the 1960s marked the beginning of the meteoric expansion of *laissez-faire* trade in that emirate. Mahdi al-Tajir, one of the most influential and gregarious advisers to the ruler of Bahrain, was seconded to Dubai in the 1950s to establish a customs service there, as he had done in Bahrain. Ahmad bin Sulayem of Dubai became al-Tajir's deputy in Dubai.[76] This form of counsel often created dynastic power within families. Ahmad bin Sulayem's son, Sultan, began his first job as a customs officer at Jabal Ali port.[77] He is today the chairman of DP World.

In Kuwait, where the Qatari Abdullah Darwish organised the customs administration in 1949, a great many Palestinian and Egyptian professionals populated the ranks of the civil services.[78] Palestinians in Kuwait were 48 per cent of all employees in the public sector and 41.4 per cent in the private sector.[79] An Egyptian expert amenable to British interests managed the labour department in Kuwait and drew up the labour legislation there in the early 1960s.

This utilisation of Arab talents however did not occur in the lower Gulf, where al-Gurg recalls that on a visit to Egypt, Gamal Abdel Nasser

> asked Shaikh Rashid about the administration of Dubai. Who, he enquired, ran the police, the health department, finance, water, the Post Office, electricity? In each case Shaikh Rashid replied with the name of the British official responsible, employed by the Dubai Government.[80]

Nasser's surprising response, as reported by the nationalist al-Gurg, was that it was excellent for locals to learn the techniques of governance from the British.

But 'learning' from the British, more often than not, happened through British advisers being forced on local rulers. The twenty-six-year-old Charles Belgrave was hired in the 1920s to serve as the adviser to the Bahraini ruler. In the 1940s, he employed underhand, even fraudulent, methods to surreptitiously purchase local land for a British naval base in Jufair. He remained in Bahrain until the late 1950s, when his continued presence, colonial mailed fist, and suppression of nationalist and labour revolts led to widespread popular protest that successfully demanded his ouster. Belgrave had been hired by the Colonial Office to work in that capacity and ultimately served the British.[81] Bill Duff, the financial adviser to Shaikh Rashid of Dubai, was, by all accounts, more independent and was known to have annoyed British political officers in the emirate, when he advised the ruler against accepting certain economic demands of theirs.[82] In Kuwait, the political agent demanded that the ruler, Ahmad Jabir al-Sabah, and his brother, Abdullah, accept British advisers. At first, the Kuwaiti emirs resisted, indicating that they relied on the advice of their representative to the Kuwait Oil Company in London, himself British, H.T. Kemp. The British officials insisted and after Ahmad died, Abdullah was forced to accept two junior British advisers.[83]

British representatives of large firms who resided in the region also 'advised' the ruling families. Neville Allen of Halcrow, who had long lived in Dubai, was known to influence Shaikh Rashid, as did Gray Mackenzie's long-time representative in Dubai, George Chapman. Aramco took this to another level; their officials not only provided formal and informal advice to the Saudi ruling family but attempted to shape the governing institutions and structures there. Those nationalist Arab technocrats who challenged this arrangement – like the Saudi oil minister 'Red Shaikh' Abdullah al-Tariqi – found themselves in a political wilderness.

The work of these foreign advisers and their firms did not only occur in the realm of interpersonal guidance to the rulers. As new government offices, modern commercial infrastructures, and novel economic and social organisations were established, they internationalised management practices and organisational structures. Aramco and the US Army Corps of Engineers brought with them not only accounting standards; engineering specifications; systems of procurement, record-keeping, and management; and legal and contractual provisioning (for example, around rules of arbitration), but also regimes of labour, new (racialised) modalities of hierarchy in housing and workplaces, and novel debt facilities.[84] Many of the merchants/capitalists also chose to conform to new corporate forms, sometimes in order to secure franchises or agencies, at other times to better compete with foreign firms. The house of Kanoo, for example, hired an official accountant (Saba & Company) and a British management consulting firm (Urwick Orr) to restructure the company as early as 1954.[85]

An exemplary instance of the role of foreign and local experts, bureaucrats, and technocrats in the making of maritime infrastructures in the Arabian Peninsula is the story of the Arab Shipbuilding and Repair Yard (ASRY) in Bahrain. The Gulf already had a handful of smaller ship repair yards, one of them belonging to the Kanoo family in the island of Muharraq in Bahrain. However, with the advent of the VLCCs and ULCCs, many of these shipyards were incapable of serving the megaships, either because the yard itself was not large enough or because the approach channels did not have the requisite draught, even for ships in ballast.

In 1969, a former managing director for a Niarchos shipping business, the glamourous Brit Gifford Rossi, proposed a project to the Saudi government for the construction of a drydock that could service the megaships whose numbers were multiplying in the wake of the closure of Suez Canal. His personal friends arranged a meeting between Rossi and the Saudi minister of oil, Zaki Yamani. Yamani suggested that Petromin, the state-owned corporation in charge of exploration for all oil and minerals outside Aramco's concession, should undertake the project on behalf of not Saudi Arabia but OAPEC (the Organisation of Arab Petroleum Exporting Countries). The drydock's business model was based on classified projections of OAPEC oil exports provided by Aramco. In the end, the site chosen for the project was Bahrain.

The project from its very beginning involved a significant number of international participants. Lisnave of Portugal, which at the time owned the world's only dedicated VLCC shipyard; various British shipbuilders and shipyard managers; and German, Spanish, and French architects, shipyards, and construction firms were all consulted. When Kawasaki Heavy Industry pulled out of the project, Hyundai signed up. A manager of Drewry Shipping joined Rossi in setting up the marketing firm that represented ASRY. On the day the cornerstone for the shipyard was laid, 30 November 1974, Rossi presented the ruler of Bahrain with a gold and gemstone model of ASRY, created by Cartier.[86] The drydock started operations in 1977.

Although Rossi's own account of this 'Arabian adventure' does not really discuss the politics that went on behind the scenes, the OAPEC decision to locate the drydock in Bahrain was controversial. Dubai was bypassed; Shaikh Rashid left OAPEC for a time and ordered the construction of a competing drydock in Dubai. But why Bahrain? The timing had everything to do with the British withdrawal from the Gulf in 1971 and the Arab oil producers' fear of Iran's claims on Bahrain. Further, Bahrain had the smallest reserves among the OAPEC states and ASRY provided a source of income for the country. Although much was said about how the drydock provided jobs and technical training for Arabs employed therein, the organisation has always been managed by Europeans (even today, the management team of the drydock is primarily British, along with three Indian technical managers and two Bahrainis). As recruitment advertisements and LinkedIn accounts show, ASRY's workers continue to be mostly drawn from the ranks of skilled workers from Korea, India, and the Philippines.

The Technopolitics of Managing Ports

LinkedIn is useful as a research tool in maritime businesses because it clearly reveals a few trends in the management of ports. First, professional circuits often inaugurate in the ports and terminals of northwest Europe and eventually end in those of the Arabian Peninsula. Port and terminal-operation managerial expertise thus travels from Europe, where regulations are tighter, pay comparatively lower, and unions more fractious. If, in a previous age, the metropolitan governments were invested in placing their technical experts in positions of influence in the Middle East, today the eastward movement of this managerial class is facilitated by the westward movement of maritime transport capital. Today, eight out of ten of the largest container-terminal operators in the world are headquartered in Asia and the Middle East (see Table 1.2). As Dubai Ports World invests in terminals in Rotterdam and London and elsewhere in Europe and North America (not to mention innumerable ports in the global South), it also provides a conduit amenable to the movement of technical and managerial experts from shipping hubs in the global North to the Middle East. British colonial migratory practices also still echo through management structures. South and Southeast Asian technical experts, engineers, and clerical workers fill the managerial middle ranks in these Peninsula's maritime businesses. But South Asians also fill top managerial positions in finance or operations – both of which require technocratic expertise.

The workings of Oman's ports illustrate the geography of expertise and management. The port of Sohar is operated by a joint venture between the Omani government and the Port of Rotterdam (a semi-public, corporatised body in charge of managing Rotterdam, Sohar, Porto in Brazil, and Kuala Tanjung in Malaysia). The container terminal is managed by Hutchison, a Hong Kong–based firm incorporated in the British Virgin Islands. The CEO of the port is British, while most of the rest of the management team are Omanis (as required by Omanisation laws). The port of Duqm in Oman is managed by a consortium between the government and the port of Antwerp. The container-terminal manager for the port of Salalah is a consortium in which the senior partner is the Dutch/Danish APM Terminals (the third-largest terminal operator in the world and the only operator on the top-ten list headquartered in Europe). The CEO of the terminal-operation business in Salalah is British, while his deputy is a US-educated Dhofari. The harbourmaster is a former captain of the Indian Navy. Salalah is touted as one of the most successful examples of labour localisation programmes on the Peninsula; around half of its mid- and top-level managers are Omanis.

While container terminals are managed by transnational firms, most oil and chemical terminals are owned and operated by petroleum and petrochemical companies. Deb Cowen describes the complexity of the maritime logistical system as 'an extraordinary apparatus of management that is neither just public nor private and neither military nor civilian but something else'.[87] The descriptor could as easily apply to the management processes of ports and container, bulk, and oil/petrochemical terminals.

The technopolitics of port management occurs at the point of convergence between automation technologies, algorithmic security, supply-chain streamlining, and a degree of fantasy. The element of fantasy is present in two areas. First, fantastic monsters of terrorism, violence, and insecurity are conjured as threats to port or terminal security, and equally fantastical solutions are offered which subject ports and ships to surveillance, security bureaucracies, and useless red tape. The conjurers of these nightmares of terror are often security 'experts' who, along with their cargo of fear, sell their security expertise. Shortly after the Dubai Ports World bid for the management of six US ports was rejected, a number of professors of management or political science scared up such scenarios of danger using the ever-reliable method of fearmongering dressed up in game-theory models. They argued that terror threats lurked everywhere, and mapped 132 different 'pathways' through which dirty bombs, biological or chemical weapons, or simple explosives could be smuggled into US harbours.[88] The response, according to a sombre Heritage Foundation report, should not be 'simplistic security proposals that focus on inspecting containers and handing out federal port security grants', but rather expanding the inspection power of the Coast Guard not just around the US coasts but around the world, improving the distribution of commercial information, and the nebulous exhortation to 'enhance international cooperation'.[89] The solutions – third-party security companies, complex customs-inspection regimes, and classified threat-modelling algorithms – embed port managers worldwide in global webs of security and surveillance. In effect, a combination of coercive and hegemonic solutions to the threat of security bolsters the power of the US as arbiter and pace-setter of port and maritime security worldwide. These 'security concerns' then shape the commercial landscape by influencing 'transnational regulations, the routing of goods through particular gateway ports or passage points, data surveillance, labour discipline and risk management algorithms'.[90]

A second fantastical element of port and terminal management is meant to address friction resulting from human resistance, the obduracy of the world's environmental and geophysical features, and the very stubborn materiality of the work of transport. Here, the solution is an unrelenting and inviolable faith in new technologies' ability to not only make maritime transportation ever more efficient but to solve all problems of friction. Sometimes the technological innovations are real enough, transforming the face of maritime transportation. The oil tanker was one such innovation. The twenty-foot-equivalent (TEU) standardised container was another. The container technology itself enabled enterprise resource planning, customer-relationship management systems, and supply-chain management systems, including just-in-time technology.[91] But the vast majority of other newfangled technologies are chimerical.

These fantastical management systems are at once hyper-visible and utterly invisible. They are hyper-visible if one is a port manager: trade conferences and trade magazines bristle with advertisements for all sorts of algorithmic software and engineering innovations that will supposedly make the work of ports more efficient, cleaner, more error-free, more frictionless. Among the latter is the hyperloop. The hyperloop is a form of transportation (for cargo or people) which travels through a fully sealed tube, operating free of friction. Whether it can function on a large scale – or at all – remains to be seen. Another fantasy technology is the blockchain. Blockchains are encrypted blocks of data which link to one another to provide a full record of all transactions from the first moment of interaction. What distinguishes blockchain from other recordkeeping technologies is two things: first, each 'chain' contains the entirety of the history of exchanges that have occurred since the beginning. Second, each block in the chain is verified through a complex calculation *every* time a transaction occurs. In reality, verifying blockchains can consume mind-boggling quantities of electricity and time, and their calculative processes are highly repetitive, inefficient, and wasteful.[92] Yet every maritime-transport newsletter boasts of a new blockchain technology that can streamline the process of port management, or customs data gathering, or bills of lading. The blockchain, like so many technologies before it, is seen as the panacea to the problems that plague the supply chain: insufficiency or unavailability of information, incommensurability of knowledge production across platforms, loss of both cargo and related data, and so on. Even the *Journal of Commerce*, in an unguarded moment, compared the rumpus around blockchain to the unfulfilled promises of RFID (radio frequency identification) and lamented the chasm between the promise of technology and the banal reality of its implementation.[93]

But these technologies are also invisible. The extent to which their failures or successes transform practices at ports and terminals can only be measured years after their implementation, when it is almost impossible to isolate their influence as opposed to other factors. The one certain effect of these technologies is a further drive towards automation – however (in)feasible, (un)reasonable, or (in)effective this may be – purging ports of those stubbornly resistant elements: workers. These technologies ultimately centralise power through making its workings unintelligible, capillary, and ever-present.

6

Landside Labour

> They wrap their dry faces with a dirty cloth.
> If they're lucky they have a plastic helmet . . .
> They are canned in a bus,
> then canned in their rooms.
> Their expressions are wiped
> By sun, dust, the law, and by us.
>
> Maryam al-Subaiey, 'The Invisible Army'

Mr C.L. Tucker, the industrial relations officer at the Anglo-Iranian Oil Company (AIOC) in Abadan, arrived in Aden in early November 1948, and immediately had to deal with a major strike that had begun at AIOC and at the port on 16 November and which was to continue until 11 December. Upon leaving Aden he penned a report for his superiors at the company's headquarters in Britannic House in London about the twists and turns of the strike.[1] The report is rich in all sorts of details about inter-firm negotiations and internal company considerations that the Aden Colony intelligence and police reports lack (though Tucker comes across as the quintessential phlegmatic bureaucrat, he also seems like a competent and candid story-teller). The story is an extraordinary account of labour mobilisation, and the responses and reactions to it by the oil and shipping companies, port operators, colonial officials and Adenese people themselves. This significant – but seemingly forgotten – strike is clearly a precursor to the 1950s waves of strikes and mobilisation that themselves laid the groundwork for the anticolonial struggles of the 1960s.

In August 1948, the workers at the Aden Port Trust went on a four-hour 'lightning strike' demanding a 'Corney' wage increase. The Salaries Commissioner, L.G. Corney, had headed a commission of inquiry in early 1948 to examine the wages and salaries of workers employed by the colonial government of Aden. The Port Trust was the most prominent government agency employing workers. Corney's report found that after the end of the war, the cost of living in Aden had so spiralled out of control that most Adenese workers could not subsist on the existing wage structure of the colony. Tucker similarly reported that 'the basic wage rates of unskilled and semi-skilled workers [at AIOC] are low even judged by Eastern standards'. He added that the

> basic labouring rate of 1.6 Rupees a day ... paid to approximately 1/7th of our pay-roll is inadequate to maintain a subsistence level of existence and the next basic rate of Rs.59 a month paid to approximately 1/5th is barely adequate and its deficiency has been disguised only by excessive overtime working.

Tucker also acknowledged that AIOC workers, including those involved in bunkering, were 'further handicapped as unlike cargo labourers they were unable to augment their earnings by pilfering'. Hearing about the Port Trust strikes, AIOC workers presented a petition to the company asking that their wages also be adjusted to reflect the Corney report.

The Port Trust strike was something of a harbinger. Once the potential of the strikes spreading throughout the port became clear, the Aden-based shipping companies, which had formed a shipping conference to coordinate freight rates, now founded a Wages and Labour Section 'as the first line of resistance to the Corney retrospective wage payments'. When the workers for AIOC discovered that, like the shipping conference, the oil company had no intention of making back payments of wages, on 15 November they declared a strike. At first, the Company refused to acknowledge the strike, asking that the letter of intent to strike be signed. A week later, the port workers at Cory Brothers, Halfa Shipping (owned by Antonin Besse), and Cowasjee Dinshaw joined the AIOC strikes.[2] Cory Brothers and Cowasjee almost immediately began issuing notices of termination to striking workers and demanded that AIOC follow suit, but AIOC chiefs in London were adamant that notice not be issued. By the end of November, Luke Thomas porters were also on strike. On 8 December, Dinshaw officials called the police to attack their strikers while, behind the scenes, the officers of both the Port Trust and the AIOC were frantically seeking to find and meet representatives of strikers. The strikers had not named their leaders, and Company officials sought the most visible strikers in the market stalls or Somali quarters and contacted various professionals thought to be in contact with the strikers. Among these was a man described in the AIOC report as 'Sheikh Abdullah, leading Moslem lawyer and member of Legislative Council, who was rumoured to be unofficial adviser to the strikers'.

On 9 December, Antonin Besse, whose shipping company was one of the largest employers at the port and also the shipping agent for Shell Oil Company, sent a telegram to Shell headquarters demanding authorisation for 'strong action' against the strikers. On the same day, streetsweepers in Aden went on a sympathy strike. Arrests at the strike sites and attacks on blackleg labour were ongoing. Then, on the morning of Saturday 11 December, an exasperated AIOC headquarters telegraphed its Aden subsidiary, ordering Corney's recommendations be implemented in line with the Aden government plans. With this announcement – conveyed to the strikers through the trusted Yemeni leader Shaikh Abdullah – two-thirds of the AIOC workers went back to work. But when AIOC announced the decision to the other members of the shipping conference, they were outraged. Representatives from Dinshaw, Cory Brothers, and Luke Thomas all claimed they could not afford the terms to which AIOC had agreed and considered AIOC's capitulation to the workers as 'the surrender of White man's prestige'.

The strike, in the end, secured a number of favourable terms for the AIOC workers, though not the workers for other port companies. By the end of December, Mr Tucker, the AIOC Industrial Relations representative was meeting with the aforementioned Shaikh Abdullah, who 'had now accepted an invitation to act in an honorary capacity as Adviser to the Port workers on formation of Trade Unions'. Tucker added discreetly and wishfully, 'On the question of Trade Unions I discussed at length with Sheikh Abdullah the importance of such organisation being formed on a responsible and representative basis'.

In many ways, the story of the strike illuminates multiple aspects of labour on the ports of the Arabian Peninsula. While the managers attempted to work in concert, they also had competing interests. The AIOC industrial-relations officer was worried about 'allowing ourselves to be manoeuvred into a position where we should have to carry the consent of other employers for any approach we thought necessary'. Tucker believed that 'there is only limited identity of interest between our labour and the port workers of Cory Brothers, Luke Thomas and Halfa Shipping Company as a major part of their working force is cargo discharging labour engaged on piece rates'. But he did not want to alienate the other shipping companies, since so many of them were also AIOC clients.

It was also notable that the locally based shipping companies – one of the most prominent of which, Cowasjee Dinshaw, was owned by a capitalist of Indian Parsi origin – were concerned with the loss of the 'white man's prestige', and that the shipping companies were far more ruthless than AIOC in their dealings with the workers, calling in the police to arrest and beat the striking men and dismissing them from their jobs *en masse*.

But the AIOC, the majority of whose shares were held by the British government, operated under additional constraints. The Corney Commission and the 1948 strike both took place while

Clement Attlee's Labour government was in power in London. Therefore, the company's wish for a 'responsible and representative' trade union, which would act as a liaison between managers and workers rather than as an adversarial institution, converged with the Labour government's wish to encourage trade unions in British colonies. After all, in this feverish Cold War moment, trade unions could also act as a safety valve and prevent the spread of Communist ideologies among the workers. The postwar decades were also the era of decolonisation. A fear of revolutionary contagion was one factor in British encouragement of a more conciliatory union movement in its colonies. Worldwide reconstruction, production, and trade all depended on the movement of petroleum and ships – and cooperation between management and labour was crucial to the circulation of goods and capital.

Colonial racial hierarchies pulsate through accounts of the event. At AIOC and in the port, the managers presumed different degrees of cohesion, defiance, and malleability among differently racialised categories of workers – even if events themselves often proved them wrong. In the reports of the strike, Somalis are described as the 'most difficult section to deal with'. In other places, at other times, 'reliable, hardworking and unimaginative Indians and Pakistanis' are contrasted with 'clever, lazy and politically conscious Palestinians'.[3] The hierarchies were created through different migratory categories. For example, elsewhere in the Peninsula, 'Anglo-American heads, Indo-Pakistani hands, and Arab feet' were said to constitute the labour body.[4] Longstanding ties of migration in the broader region provided pipelines of movement between different coasts and continents. These ties were often attenuated by the states and the paramount imperial powers. The British were masters of social engineering on a global scale, moving prodigious numbers of workers between their various imperial holdings when their plantations, production, or trade required labour. At other times, mechanisms such as passports, visas, labour permits, the machinery of *kafala* – or sponsorship system – and quota systems were used to *prevent* movements of migrant workers.

Support for the protesters seems to have come from unexpected corners of Aden and its hinterlands. The bemused Tucker writes about how hard it was to track down strike organisers and that the best way to find them was to go to the bazaars of Aden. The strikers had been supported by merchants there. The Association of Taxi Drivers had, alongside individual merchants, provided financial aid to distressed workers. Days after the strike, the Adenese streetsweepers had gone on a sympathy strike themselves. The Sultan of Lahej, a hinterland shaikh under the protection of the British, had sent not only financial support but also food and other necessities. Also significant is the appearance of Shaikh Abdullah, who turns out to have been Abdullah al-Asnaj (d. 2015), later the founder of the Aden Trade Union Congress and the People's Socialist Party. Although the strike itself did not seem to have an overt nationalist character, nor – according to Tucker – Communist 'jargon and technique', in some ways it was a bellwether of transformations to come.

If the strike of 1948 was the opening salvo of decades of revolt, it was encouraged by the protests that had preceded it. In 1947, the partition of India had seen unrest among the many South Asians who had long resided in Aden. In the same year, the British government had given a bus concession to an Italian company, which had to be withdrawn within a few days because of the intensity of popular sentiment and protest against it. In May 1948, the Palestinian *Nakba* (the catastrophe of expulsion and expropriation) and the establishment of the state of Israel had seen protests – some violent – in Arab cities, not least Aden. If the Corney report and the promise of an increase in wages acted as a catalyst to the strike of 1948, an underlying sense of frustrated claim-making and a habit of protest had been the necessary ingredients for the strike itself.

Aden, more than any other city on the Peninsula, was the stage on which labour revolt illuminated the contours of labour formation and the disciplining mechanisms used by the state, the empire, and by capital to contain it. Profoundly dependent on landside work and enmeshed in longstanding global networks of shipboard labour, the port of Aden was shaped by this labour. But work stoppages and demand for workplace and political rights everywhere in the Peninsula also proved of great concern to colonial and state officials and to the corporations that depended on their labour for their profits. Control of migration was and is one way the colonial masters and the subsequent independent states have tried to manage worker discontent.

Conditions of Work

> Here is history too. A backbone bending and
> unbending without a word, heat, bellowing these
> lungs spongy, exhaled in humming, the ocean, a
> way out and not anything of beauty, tipping turquoise
> and scandalous. The malicious horizon made us the
> essential thinkers of technology.
>
> Dionne Brand, 'No Language is Neutral'

When Paul Nizan, a future ex-member of the French Communist Party, came to Aden from France in the 1930s to work as a coffee trader, he was outraged, though not surprised, by the disparity of living and working conditions of the different categories of workers. He wrote that 'many native workers have no home and sleep in the open or in ... cafés' while the white managers and Indian clerks are 'hiding in their hygienic lairs, work under the wings of fans, in offices where ... the typewriters endlessly inscribe a small number of little black signs'.[5] Nizan's entire account was alive to the racial differences produced in colonial and company offices; he sensitively described the transformations that Aden's bunkering-port status had wrought.

Like the spaces and shape of harbours, the work taking place in ports of the Peninsula changed with the requirements and qualities of coal-fired steamships, and then oil; the advent of tankers, and then container ships. Coal-fired ships demanded the backbreaking landside labour of coal-heavers loading fuel into the ships' holds. Bunkering ships with oil was more automated, needing far fewer workers whose labour required at least a basic familiarity and facility with machinery, gauges, and mechanised fuelling, and not as much physical prowess as coal-heavers displayed.

Until the arrival of mechanised lading, first of bulk freighters and later of container ships, such physical prowess also defined the work of stevedores who loaded and unloaded bulk goods packed in bags, boxes, or barrels. From very early on, such stevedoring in the Peninsula was contracted and casualised. Tally clerks and casual labourers boarded ships to record every item of cargo and move them off the ship. They worked long hours until the ships were fully unloaded. Sometimes the work-shift could last up to seventeen hours! An eight-hour unloading shift was introduced in Bahrain only in 1962.[6] A labour census in Bahrain from the 1950s pointed out that in marine trades and stevedoring the durations of employment were quite short, as these trades drew on 'foreign unskilled labourers of which there are comparatively high numbers [who] provide a reservoir of casual labour taken on as required'.[7] The same system was still in place by the mid-1970s, despite the massive boom in importation of bulk goods, vehicles, and other cargo. An account of port work in the 1970s mentions that in the Gulf, most of the labourers on the docks were migrants from Iran, Baluchistan, or Pakistan. The same report avers that productivity in the ports of the Gulf was 'considerably lower than the world-wide norm of 750 weight tons [per day per ship] for break-bulk, general cargo and 3000 tons/day for containerized cargo'.[8]

Undoubtedly, the casualised and subcontracting nature of the labour regime was the primary factor in the low productivity.[9]

A 1953 report from the docks of Kuwait clearly recognised that a better-managed port could not depend entirely on subcontracted labour. The report added that 'with the growth of mechanisation it is desirable that the handling of mechanical plant should be confined to directly employed labour'.[10] However, subcontracting gave the shipping companies and ports the alibi they needed to *not* provide their workers with basic wages and benefits. Once citizenship became a norm of governance, with its attached rights – however minimal – nationals began to draw on an expanded repertoire of claim-making for better wages and workplace conditions. Foreign workers (with carefully graded hierarchies of nationality and foreign citizenship) did not have access to this expanded repertoire. As long as foreign workers were cheap, abundant, and deportable, they could be used to build and run the transport infrastructures, instead of expensive heavy equipment and machinery. Walter Rodney had seen the same pattern in the European exploitation of Africa, where, instead of capital-intensive equipment, 'sheer manpower had to take the place of earth-moving machinery, cranes, and so on'.[11]

It was only when these workers were no longer pliant, docile, and easily and cheaply exploited that mechanisation – with its concurrent gains in productivity – was seen as a less troublesome, even less costly option. While such automation had been normalised in the petroleum transportation sector, it took years for Middle Eastern ports to containerise. Containerisation entailed slashing labour rolls, fragmenting dockworker communities, and spatially isolating the ports.[12] Even today, tensions persist between the availability of cheap and deportable labour and the productivity of capital investment. In Khor Fakkan port, often branded as one of the most productive ports in the Middle East, fearless and graceful men climb atop stacks of containers on ships, teetering on the edge and using a flexible pole to unlock one box's corners from the other below it. Above them float the massive gantry cranes that require extensive training and experience to operate. The contrast between the complex gantry and the stevedores' rudimentary poles embodies the tension between automation and cheap labour.

Although the glossy websites of many of the more recent Peninsula cargo ports speak of *plans* for automation (or partial automation), such plans are hostage to the tension I have just delineated. Steady supplies of workers who can be exploited are available in the Gulf. Even if automation arrives, the dystopian representations of windswept spaces devoid of humans tend to be highly exaggerated. Ports will still require drivers, technical operators, cleaners, and maintenance workers. The tension will be refracted through racialised regimes of labour.

The working conditions of the workers who build these infrastructures and who make them function are not the only facet of their lives. These workers also have lives outside their workplace. Today, more skilled workers, whom the British labelled 'artisans', can afford their own rented habitation and are permitted to do so precisely because their skills are in demand. Many more workers are categorised as unskilled or semi-skilled and therefore are more numerous and considered more expendable. Many of these workers cannot afford their own housing and, even if they could, are forced to live in labour camps that are more easily monitored and controlled.

Housing – or the absence or poverty thereof – has loomed large in the lives of port workers and continues to do so. Abdulrahman Munif's magisterial petronovel has searing accounts of 'company towns' in Saudi Arabia in which housing was segregated by 'race' or nationality. A global colour line segregated Southern Europeans, Asians, and indigenous Arabs from their US superiors.[13] US-based oil companies were not alone in importing their home-grown racialised hierarchies to housing. To build the ports and harbours that were often far from city centres, sometimes even offshore, housing misery was exacerbated. On Abu Dhabi's Das Island, where a harbour had to be constructed to prepare for the exploitation of oil there, the same system of segregated and racialised housing obtained. While the British lived in their separate compounds (complete with a golf course), the Asians inhabited smaller-scale housing behind barbed wire and, as a British political agent wrote, 'the local Abu Dhabi labourers . . . are the only people left free and not behind barbed wire'. But, though 'free', they lived in shacks exposed to wind and weather.[14]

The postwar decades saw a boom in construction of major infrastructures in the Arabian Peninsula. At the oil, shipping, and construction companies, their loading terminals, and at cargo ports, it was the woeful day-to-day living conditions and radical inequalities in the provision of basic housing that drove the workers to strike.[15] Even today, labour camps segregate 'bachelor' migrant workers from the population, and the entry of working-class workers to some city spaces are heavily and coercively regulated.[16] The squalid and decrepit labour camps are almost always located outside the city and far from workplaces, far even from the already-distant ports. After unwelcome scrutiny by activists and human rights organisations, many of these camps spruce up their outward façades while simultaneously tightening security and access. Despite these draconian measures, the inhabitants overcome the austerity of camp life through their conviviality, as they are forced by the scarcity of space to cook and eat together. In the end, these camps are spaces of surveillance and control.

Migration

I have a cousin called Hasanain, who was smuggled across the border once. After more than seven hours walking, darkness fell. Then the smuggler pointed to a cluster of far-off lights saying, 'There's Kuwait. You'll reach it when you've walked for half an hour'. Do you know what happened? That wasn't Kuwait, it was a remote Iraqi village. I can tell you thousands of stories like that. Stories of men who became like dogs as they looked for one

> drop of water to moisten their cracked tongues with. What do you think happened when they saw Bedouin encampments? They bought a mouthful of water in exchange for all the money or wedding rings or watches they owned.
>
> Ghassan Kanafani, *Men in the Sun*

In his reflection on the origins of modern forms of labour management, Marcel van der Linden argues that, to understand standardisation, monitoring, surveillance, and other modalities of worker discipline, we need to seek their origins in the management of unfree labour in the colonies.[17] The racialised articulations of class relations so characteristic of colonial regimes of labour are unmistakable in the work of Peninsula ports today. These racialised technologies of rule are created through the management of migration.

The world of manual work – whether skilled or unskilled – on ports often follows hierarchies that conform to the global colour line. Today, skilled workers, for example crane operators, hail from places like the Philippines or India (particularly Kerala) as well as from the country in which they work. Semi-skilled workers, like drivers of trucks on the port side, originate from the more prosperous states of India. The stevedores engaged in more menial work, namely ensuring that containers are locked to one another, and other workers whose labour is necessary to the operation of modern ports, like security guards, come from Bangladesh or Nepal.

If these striations at the ports of the Arabian Peninsula crystallise the prevalent labour regimes there, their historical trajectories also trace the larger transformations in the labour structures of the region. Before mechanisation of many of the ports, Iranians had been the migrant category working at the harbours. Alan Villiers describes their work there:

> Persians seemed to do the porterage, the water deliveries, and most of the coolie work of the port, as well as the harbour in the

> dockyards. There were thousands of them. They were sawing planks out of huge Malabar logs, frightful work in that hot climate; they were unloading the water-booms, driving their asses into the sea to take their dripping loads of water-skins; they carried the firewood, the bags of rice, the packages of dates, and everything else which was being taken to the warehouses of the merchants. Persians and pack-horses were doing the work of the town; the Kuwaiti were doing the work of the sea.[18]

The discovery of oil shifted both work and migration patterns within the Gulf. Oil was exploited first in Iran, and then in Iraq, Bahrain, Saudi Arabia, and Kuwait. Before the Second World War, in many instances, the men of the region abandoned agriculture, pearling, and fishing and moved to the oil fields and the ports that brought in cargoes and exported petroleum and refined products. The seafarers and pearlers of Kuwait and Bahrain were the first to enter the oil industry and the modern ports of their own countries.[19] But from the 1940s onwards, the Trucial Coasts, Oman, and Dhofar also provided a steady stream of workers to the Gulf before the discovery of oil in their own backyards in the 1960s and 1970s.

If they did not work in the oil industry, many of the seafarers from the lower Gulf got jobs as 'coolies' or construction workers in Kuwait, Dammam, or Manama.[20] The British tried to control the movement of people by requiring hard-to-obtain visas, starting in 1927 with Iranians travelling to Bahrain. At the same time, an observer noted that 'it is still very simple for Arabs in neighbouring areas to immigrate to Bahrain and assume Bahraini nationality'.[21] New routes emerged conveying workers from the Trucial states to work in the oil fields of upper Gulf. A man from Ras al-Khaimah recounted how his father, 'like other people, took people going for work up to Kuwait, Qatar, Bahrain and Dammam, and made sure they found people they knew at their destinations'.[22] Established migrant communities lubricated the entry of their countrymen. Many of the migrant workers from the Gulf were quite savvy about the competition for skilled and unskilled labour in the era of infrastructure boom. Some Bahrainis, for example, eschewed a job at home to work in Saudi Arabia, where wages were higher.[23] As the Kanoo shipping magnates of Bahrain wrote, because the oil companies devoured so many of the available workers,

> shipping agents like ourselves had to rely on recruiting labour from the Trucial States (now the UAE) and Oman, particularly as the Sultanate's economy remained depressed until the accession of Sultan Qaboos in 1970. Supervisory staff were just as hard to find. Few Saudis spoke English, so we deployed cargo superintendents from Bahrain. Ship's stevedores were recruited from a labour pool, many also from Bahrain where we maintained a list of labourers, tally clerks and supervisory personnel whom we could call upon when needed. As time went by, entrepreneurs started to compile their own lists of experienced personnel who were available on stand-by. Hence, when a shipping agent required labour, these independent entrepreneurs were asked to provide the necessary 'gangs', usually Iranians or Bahrainis of Iranian descent. These tough labourers dominated the market.[24]

In the migrant-receiving countries, gathering storms of protests pushed the governments to seek out replacement categories of workers that could be more easily disciplined. Historically, the category of 'native' workers on the Peninsula had included communities considered part of the life of the cities: Indians in Bahrain; Iranians in Kuwait; Baluchis in the Trucial Emirates; Somalis in Aden. These communities only became 'migrants' after such categories were invented by modern states to classify and control workers. Restricting or encouraging migration flows was a means of containing worker solidarity and action and forging mechanisms of labour control. If citizenship of a state made 'native' workers more insistent on their demands for workplace and political rights, Arab workers were imported from other states to replace them. But Arab workers' rights were often defended by their home governments. For example, when Kuwait sent a request to Egypt for workers, the Egyptian government 'requested a detailed description of the working conditions under which its subjects will live and may demand certain improvements before it will give permission for Egyptians to accept the employment'.[25] If Arab workers proved problematic, they could be replaced by workers from countries further afield whose governments might not be as vociferous in protecting their migrant worker citizens.

The ongoing protests by nationals of Bahrain, Kuwait, and Saudi Arabia in the 1930s and 1940s in the oil fields, oil-shipping terminals, and cargo ports happened at exactly the moment when the major projects of infrastructure construction and urban expansion were taking off.[26] The subsequent importation of workers from other Arab states was also spurred by the colonisation of Palestine and the expulsion of Palestinians between 1947 and 1949. Palestinians – especially those with skills and English language proficiency – were very much in demand. Great popular political sympathy for Palestinians in the countries of the Peninsula also pushed the states to support Palestinian migration after the *Nakba*.[27] The rulers of the Gulf were motivated to hire Palestinians because of these popular sympathies, but also as a means of encouraging Palestinian resettlement. A specific instance of this occurred in the interaction between Ibn Saud, Aramco, and the Gordon Clapp mission. The aim of the Clapp mission, constituted under the auspices of the United Nations Conciliation Commission for Palestine, was finding a solution that prevented the return of expelled Palestinians to their homes, so as to protect the nascent state of Israel. This entailed finding jobs and new countries for the refugees. The Clapp mission secured the agreements of Ibn Saud and Aramco to hire a thousand displaced Palestinians. Though the accounts often make Aramco's hiring of a thousand Palestinians a story of Ibn Saud's munificence, the employment of these Palestinians proved a boon to the Company (which wanted rid of its strike-prone Italian workers) and to the king himself, who showed his US patrons that he was willing to help them with their regional problems.

Aramco's official company records show that the number of Palestinians it recruited went from being so insignificant as to be not indicated separately in 1948 to 2 per cent in 1949 and 17 per cent in 1950.[28] After Saudi workers, Palestinians were the second-largest category of labourers building the port of Dammam.[29] The workers involved in the construction of the Dammam-Riyadh railway 'totalled 805, including 385 Saudi Arabs, 98 Americans, 203 Palestinians and 89 Italians'. Interestingly, however, 1951 saw recruitment of more Pakistanis (from 2.1 to 5.6 per cent of the total) and a downslope for Palestinians (from 17.5 to 4.5 per cent of the total). By 1953, Pakistanis and Indians were 6.1 and 4.7 per cent of the workforce, in contrast to Palestinians, who now constituted only 4.3 per cent.[30] One cause of decline in the number of Palestinians working for Aramco was the 1956 strike, after which more than a hundred Palestinian workers were arrested 'for alleged political activity'.[31]

While some Palestinians were recruited in their countries of refuge and transported to the Gulf, others made their way there legally or illegally. The route often began in Qamishli, in northern Syria, and proceeded to Tel Kujak, on the Syria-Iraq border. From there, the Palestinian migrants walked for fifteen to twenty hours across the desert to reach villages from which they could make their way to Mosul, Baghdad, and Basra. Once in Basra, guides took them across the desert to Kuwait. Many were abandoned by unscrupulous guides and died of exposure. If they went by sea, they traversed the marshlands of Fao, where many drowned.[32] Many thousands nevertheless migrated to the Gulf, especially Kuwait. In 1955, Palestinian welders alongside Lebanese, Jordanians, and Iraqis were involved in the construction of offshore installations in

Kuwait, and an observer commented on their extraordinary welding skills and strong work ethics.[33] After 1958, however, only Palestinian professionals could get into the Gulf.[34] By 1970, some 189,000 Palestinians lived in the Gulf countries and Iraq. Kuwait hosted the largest number at 140,000.[35] Because so much of the infrastructure construction, urban planning, and state administration in Kuwait was performed by Palestinians, their expulsion after the Iraq War of 1991 was all the more devastating.

Aside from Palestinians (and Jordanians, who were often Palestinian citizens of Jordan), Egyptians and Yemenis outnumbered all other Arab migrant workers. In the 1950s, Yemenis (especially those from the South) had a very strong presence in the political groupings of the Gulf that called for economic and political transformation throughout the Peninsula.[36] By 1958, Kuwaiti statistics show that 87 per cent of workers involved in ocean navigation were foreigners.[37] Many were (and continue to be) Yemenis whose portside and shipboard labour experience prepared them to become boat pilots, stevedores, among other maritime professions in the Gulf cities. After the expulsion of Palestinians from Kuwait in the 1991 war, Egyptians became the largest category of Arab workers there.

The discovery of oil in the Trucial Coast in the 1960s reversed the outmigration of men from the lower Gulf emirates and encouraged the migration of foreigners to work on the infrastructure projects there. It is notable that existing ties of mobility and trade meant that the majority of foreigners working in the emirates were actually Iranians and Indians, rather than Arabs from non-oil-producing countries. In the 1968 Dubai census, 51 per cent of the population and 67 per cent of the workforce were foreigners, with 83 per cent of all workers hailing from Iran and South Asia. Most of these workers were engaged in large infrastructure construction projects. In Abu Dhabi, 44 per cent of the population were Abu Dhabi nationals, 51 per cent were Iranians and South Asians, 3 per cent were from Muscat/Oman, and 920 people (less than 2 per cent) hailed from other Trucial states.[38]

In many of these countries, one response to protests by coalitions of nationals and foreign workers was for the state to fan the flames of division. One way to do so was through restricting employment to nationals (for example, Saudisation of oil-industry employment in 1957 and Kuwaitisation in 1958).[39] Another response was to shift from nationals and other Arab workers to importing migrant labourers from countries whose states did not noisily defend them as republican Arab governments did. Economic liberalisation in India, the bloody war that led to the independence of Bangladesh, and other upheavals in South and Southeast Asia made these countries apt candidates for migration to the Gulf from the 1960s onwards. Controlling the flow of migrants from South Asia – encouraging migration sometimes and restricting it at others – required a variety of disciplinary methods.

The British, who facilitated the movement of Indians until 1947, worked closely with the major oil companies (BAPCO and Aramco in particular) to ensure that the workers were at all times registered and monitored either by the firms or by the government.[40] A draconian visa system decreed into law between the 1950s and 1970s also gave oil-producing states and their employers mastery over the workers. The *kafala* – or sponsorship system – which had originally grown out of pearling work, was adapted by states and booming businesses of the upper Gulf in this early stage. The system made the sponsor, or *kafil*, 'responsible' for the migrant workers they recruited and imported. Originally – in its pearling guise – *kafala* had acted as a system of noblesse oblige, with its inherent tension between paternalism and exploitation. Under the modern regime of labour, where it became a form of discipline without protection, it turned into an encompassing system of exploitation, which disadvantaged the workers by withholding their passports and isolating them from the cities in which they lived.[41]

South Asian workers were often in demand as truck drivers and skilled construction workers on the ports. During the construction of Port Rashid in Dubai, the British mega-construction firm Costains employed 620 men, of whom only twenty were Dubai nationals. As the British labour attaché reported to his superiors:

> As many as 500 are Indians and Pakistanis, some heavy truck drivers being imported especially on contract, but the majority having been taken on locally from illegal immigrants . . . When Costains gave only 6 rials for a 9 hour day on labouring work, local interest evaporated. In September 1968 a strike occurred when Pakistanis demanded better pay and conditions, but work was resumed when the Government deported the leaders.[42]

The deportations of the workers were often brutal, rapid, and irreversible; they often were forced out with months' worth of wages left unpaid. More serious unrest took place on Dubai's offshore platforms, where South Asian workers protested against French supervisors, the hiring of skilled Somali workers, and wages that were kept artificially low.[43] In the 1970s, in Khasab, on the Musandam Peninsula of Oman, a US naval base was built by Pakistani and Lebanese workers, and problems arose when 'the Omani government began to prevent operators of heavy equipment, drivers of heavy trucks, and workers under twenty-five or over fifty-five years old from entering Oman'.[44] In effect, the men were abandoned in an area with very little in the way of telecommunications, living amenities, or connections with locals. Their contact with locals was seen as a threat by the government of Oman, which worried about contagion of intransigent ideas. It also wanted to insulate itself against charges that foreign workers were getting jobs that should have been reserved for nationals. The forms of abandonment and forced isolation suffered by Asian workers on Khasab were not new. Such involuntary segregation was often exacerbated on construction sites at ports and naval bases which are deliberately located far from city centres. Loneliness was a condition of work for many of the migrant workers.

Worker barracks and camps were not the only horrors visited on these migrant workers. Again and again, accounts by Indian and Pakistani migrant workers paint pictures of brutal employers who often refused to pay on time (or ever), uncaring home states, and a host state which, if it ever attended to the migrant workers, did so only to crush their protests. Part of the blame also fell on unscrupulous recruiters, who kept migrant workers indebted to them by charging them large upfront fees. When cyclical programmes of Saudisation (or other forms of localisation) of labour were introduced, thousands of migrant workers were often sacked without any recourse and went without several months of wages. They would be abandoned to their own fate, without the ability or resources to return home. In 2017 after one such Saudisation plan, sparked off by the precipitous drop in oil prices and the subsequent economic slowdown, the government of India itself repatriated thousands of stranded workers.

In 2015, foreigners accounted for the majority of the population in Bahrain (52 per cent), Kuwait (69 per cent), Qatar (90 per cent), and the UAE (88 per cent). (Oman and Saudi Arabia were exceptions, where foreigners were 45 and 33 per cent of the population, respectively.) In all these countries, South Asians outnumbered all other foreigners, with 7.4 million Indians, 3.3 million Bangladeshis, and 3.2 million Pakistanis residing in those countries (with half of Bangladeshis and Pakistanis working in Saudi Arabia).[45] It is difficult to track down how many of these workers are employed in the maritime or port businesses, as the sending countries and the employers either do not have aggregate statistics or jealously guard such information. But, in my own experience of different ports of the Peninsula, it was clear that certain migrant communities dominated particular categories of jobs. Punjabi men seemed to outnumber others in landside stevedoring work in the ports of the UAE, while Indians did the same work in the port of Salalah in Oman. In Saudi Arabia, the pilots guiding the container ships to their berths were Yemeni, while other Arabs seemed to operate the cranes. Southeast Asian men operated cranes in Jabal Ali and Salalah. In every port I visited, the people on the berths and involved in unloading or loading ships were men, although Abu Dhabi apparently now boasts a woman crane operator of Emirati origin.[46] Jabal Ali port claims that in its Terminal 3, to operate the remote-controlled quay cranes and rail-mounted cranes, it has recruited respectively 30 per cent and 70 per cent Emiratis, of whom, rather symmetrically, 30 and 70 per cent are women.[47] Intriguingly, in spring 2018, Hutchison, which manages the port of Dammam, began advertising for Saudi women to train for gantry-crane operation.[48] The advertisement required no prior experience and only a secondary-school diploma. Perhaps this insistence on the recruitment of women into the labour force is a new form of categorial discrimination, where now South Asian workers are replaced by women from the Peninsula.

Protests in the Peninsula

Over the course of the years, as I researched this project, whenever I mentioned the extraordinary ferment of protest in the ports and construction sites of the Gulf from the 1940s onwards, I was met by surprise. Thanks to Munif's *Cities of Salt* and Vitalis's *America's Kingdom*, the protests of Aramco workers are more familiar to Anglophone readers,[49] and we know a little about the use of protests as political (rather than workplace) contention in Bahrain and colonial Aden. But strikes in Qatar and Abu Dhabi and other Gulf states are less familiar. Anthropologist Ahmed Kanna writes of a 'politics of non-recognition' towards migrant worker protests in the Gulf in recent years; this non-recognition extends back in time to the waves of protests led by nationals of the states on the Peninsula.

Politics or workplace protests?

> Our struggle – even today – is not a labour struggle only; and time has come to transform our fight into a political one.
>
> Sayyid Ali al-Awwami, Saudi National Movement

What distinguishes many strikes at docks on the Arabian Peninsula is not only the depth of worker grievances about workplace conditions (as in the story that opens this chapter), but also the weaving of these workplace protests into political demands. Whether mobilising against colonial masters or authoritarian monarchies, strikers often justified their demands for better working conditions, rights, and dignity as being not only about bread-and-butter issues but also about politics. This perhaps explains the extent to which the Gulf monarchies were so terrified of workplace agitation.

Politics for the strikers extended to what happened in the broader Arab world.[50] This was even more urgent for dockworkers, who work at the very boundaries of their state, experiencing the materiality of international trade in their hands, on their backs, in what they unloaded. Palestine, in particular, was and continues to be a catalyst of political claim-making among the populace (even as the rulers have gradually shed their pretence of support for the Palestinian cause). Detailed narratives of such workplace strikes told by the strikers themselves tend to be rare – at least for the earlier decades after the discovery of oil. Madawi al-Rasheed interviewed one Aramco strike participant who wrote about his life at the company:

> We worked together. I met people from ʿAsir and other parts of Najd. It was amazing. We had a communal kitchen, it was our 'restaurant'. We called it *matʿam abu rubʿ*, because they charged a quarter of a riyal for the meal. The food was awful. But the Najdis would not say anything. They were shy; they would not complain. They would not ask for more money or food. They

> just left the Indians to eat there. Later in the 1950s they began to demand things from Aramco. When *al-lajna al-'ummalyya* [the Workers' Committee] told us to ask for more cash and better food, we did not respond. People were not beggars. But when they told us to ask for political rights, we all responded and joined the strikes in 1953. I sent money to my family. All I wanted to buy for myself was a radio. I wanted to hear about what was going on in Palestine and Egypt. Palestinian workers told us about their problems. We listened to the news together. (Interview, March 1999)[51]

Oblique accounts offered in the archives show that workers were deeply aware of the strategies of racialisation and hierarchies of labour meant to keep them in place. In Aden, during an Aden Port Trust dockers' strike, the workers demanded paid transport to Britain once every five years. While the colonial officers dismissed this as a case of impudence by the natives, it was clear that the workers themselves saw their labour on an equal plane with their British counterparts, for whom paid transport was a perk.[52] This demand for equality arose wherever the British or US companies had imported racialised regimes of labour, and led to worker protests and strikes. Housing, the quality of food, and the dramatically unequal rates of pay were often the source of grievances of the indigenous workers.[53]

Everywhere on the Peninsula, clamouring for 'more cash and better food' or housing shaded into demands for meaningful political participation. In 1950s Bahrain, general strikes called by a Higher Executive Committee (of four Sunni and four Shi'a activists) took place as part of a campaign to get rid of the arrogantly autocratic Sir Charles Belgrave.[54] Belgrave who had been the adviser to the ruler for nearly thirty years, not only represented British colonial rule, but was also a symbol of British military aggression against Bahrainis' Arab brethren. After all, 1956 was the year of the Suez War, the assault on Egypt by Britain, France, and Israel. The Bahraini Labour Federation claimed some 6,000 members[55] and could bring to a halt, if not oil production, then its shipping. The offices of Gray Mackenzie – and other British establishments – in Bahrain were burnt down.[56] The leaders of the strike were detained, put on a show trial and exiled to St Helena, as the ruler was terrified by them either remaining behind or going into exile in Egypt where they could conspire against him.

In Kuwait, after the 1956 Suez War, workers at Ahmadi port brought oil transport and loading of British and French tankers to a halt, and protests and sabotage were so extensive that a nightly curfew was instituted.[57] In Aden the same year, when Antonin Besse made a large donation to Oxford University, his workers went on strike to 'protest at the donation to England of so large a sum of the firm's money'.[58] Adenese workers appear in the archives as some of the most persistently mobilised workers in the Peninsula. March and April of 1956 saw over 100,000 work-days of strikes in Aden, most of them in ports or shipping. A US consul described the leadership of the unions as young Arab men 'imbued by the spirit of nationalism'.[59] By October 1956, when the Suez War began, the protests and strikes reached a fever pitch.

In April 1963, when the short-lived union between Egypt, Syria, and Iraq was announced, Qatari dockworkers went on strike in jubilation. Their strikes were supported by nationalist merchants, while 'police patrols and the bodyguards of the ruling family in Doha were reinforced by armed tribesmen drafted in from the interior'.[60] The 1963 Qatari strikes were sandwiched between general strikes in 1961 and 1968, which were more centrally about workplace issues. Das Island (Abu Dhabi) offshore and oil-terminal workers also had workplace demands in 1965, and 'the strike was notable for the solidarity of Abu Dhabian workers across nationalities and for their rejection of the authority of the Ruler's representative on the island'.[61] The archives are also replete with workers' calls to transform the Shaikhdoms into republics!

The continued Israeli dispossession and subjugation of Palestinians looms large in accounts of strikes on the docks and terminals. After the 1967 war, during massive demonstrations in Al-Khobar, Dammam, Ras Tanura, Qatif, and Dhahran, the US consulate and air field there were attacked and US flags were torn down.[62] In April 1970, 'during the unloading of a barge containing a consignment from the United Kingdom, employees of INTAP (a Kuwaiti contracting firm) discovered a sack to which was affixed a small metal tag bearing the imprint of a six-point star.' The sack was reported to the police as violating the Arab boycott against Israel, and twenty-three Iraqis, twenty-one Jordanians, eleven Lebanese, and one Syrian stopped work 'and induced thirty-four Indian/Pakistani labourers to cease work at the same time'. After five days, the men returned to work, on 14 April, when they were persuaded by the Arab Boycott Office representative, the police, and the ruler's representative on the island that the tag was actually the customs tag of Nigeria rather than the symbol of the Israeli state.[63]

Pan-Arabism was not the only political current circulating among labour strikers. It is rare to find references in the colonial archives to indigenous workers who may have had Communist sympathies, but this has more to do with a will to portray Communists as *foreign* agents rather than acknowledge the sympathies of local workers with the ideology.[64] In the late 1940s, a 'Syed Hasshin Siddik' was deported by Aramco to Aden via Bahrain because 'he was reported to have made inflammatory and communistic speeches to Adenese workers in Dhahran'. Even the British officers in Bahrain seemed exasperated by the deportation and wrote,

> It should be pointed out that all oil companies, and especially Aramco, grow hysterical when faced with a rebel or agitator. The latter always delivers 'inflammatory' speeches and are, as a matter of course, 'communistic'.[65]

In Bahrain, Marxist ideas were introduced by representatives of Iran's Tudeh Party in the early 1940s and spread by members of the Iraqi Communist Party. The Bahraini left helped organise successive strikes throughout the postwar decades which wove together workplace demands and political mobilisation (including major strikes in 1968 and 1972 that paralysed the port).[66]

Because the Communists were often thought to be foreigners, expulsion and deportation was used to discipline them, as with 300 workers, primarily Iraqis and Jordanian/Palestinians, who were expelled from Kuwait in 1959 because of their political sympathies.[67] When in June 1965, Pakistani and Indian workers went on strike in Muscat 'and the Omani labourers came out also', thirty-three Pakistanis thought to be the leaders were 'repatriated' by the company. The British labour attaché wrote ominously,

> With the present attempt to line up pan-Arab and communist efforts in the labour field, it would be unwise to discount the possibility of communist attempts to infiltrate the Indian-Pakistani labour force in the Gulf.[68]

No labour force was safe.

Starting in the 1970s, however, pan-Arabist and Communist fervour were increasingly suppressed by ever more repressive and authoritarian non-oil-producing Arab regimes which were simultaneously liberalising their economies. In the Peninsula itself, even the ostensibly socialist People's Democratic Republic of Yemen (PDRY) was turning to the World Bank and Arab monarchies' development funds to finance infrastructure projects there. The Iranian Revolution, with its promise of an Islamist alternative, did not find the same kind of organic sympathy with labour movements in the Gulf. Even economic grievances by Shi'a populations of Bahrain and Eastern Saudi Arabia were cast within the contours of a poor people's politics, rather than labour activism. The exceptions were the protests of the 2011

Arab uprisings in Bahrain, when the interests of the Shi'a minority, represented strongly in Bahraini labour unions, and the calls for the transformation of the Bahraini regime converged.[69] In the end, the result was the expulsion of many Shi'a members from the unions and sectarianisation of the organisations.

Forms of protest

> The masses of people moved as one man, and their voices rose to reach the farthest places, even drowning out the sound of the gunshots and the screams that came from the other direction . . . The concrete posts shook like empty branches and were uprooted like dead trees. In moments the barbed wire was buried under the sand, and the human waves plunged forth.
>
> Abdulrahman Munif, *Cities of Salt*

Port workers in the Peninsula faced the most gargantuan obstacles to protest. Some of these obstacles are familiar to port workers elsewhere: casualisation of labour and increased distances between ports and city centres fragment worker communities and undermine cohesiveness. Strategies of divide and rule deployed by states and colonial powers pit nationals against foreigners, Arabs against other Asians, Communists and nationalists against one another or against 'loyal' citizens. Despite these barriers to mobilisation, the archives teem with accounts of protest. Strikes and labour withdrawals were most prominent in the 1950s and 1960s – the era of decolonisation. The short, sharp anger of direct action, including machine-breaking, violence, and rioting, was far more frequent thereafter, when the full force of repressive measures against labour strikes had circumscribed protest in almost all Peninsula countries. Nevertheless, the two could be combined.

One particular story told by the British labour attaché is worth quoting in full, given that it illuminates the state and employers' divisive policies in response to labour protests, the repertoire of resistance chosen by the workers, and the force of ideas and practices that could (but did not always) spread within and across national boundaries in the region:

> In May 1963 a series of strikes took place which came as a complete surprise both to the companies and to the Government [of Abu Dhabi]. The strikes were well-organised and were marked by an unusual feature – outbreaks of violence in which Europeans and Indians were injured. The leaders were mainly Abu Dhabi nationals who had worked on oil installations elsewhere in the Gulf. At the Jebel Dhanna [oil] terminal all non-European workers employed by the contractors went on strike and the strikers took control of the camp, holding the managerial personnel. At Tarif, where the movement was clearly connected with the outbreak at Jebel Dhanna, about 100 strikers with sticks besieged the ex-patriate personnel in the offices and mess hall. There were also disturbances at the Santa Fe base camp. On May 31st there was an outbreak on Das Island. The strikers' demands, which were identical in all sectors, were for a 50 per cent increase in wages, equal pay with Jordanians and Lebanese, and the use of local men for certain jobs done by ex-patriates, e.g., heavy truck driving. The strike petered out in June after local state authorities were prodded into action ... My view is that no subversive organisation existed prior to the disturbance, but that the troubles were sparked off by the general strike in Qatar which, despite efforts at intimidation, petered out in early May. The Qatar strike was originally caused by demonstrations approving the tripartite declaration on unity signed in Cairo by Egypt, Syria and Iraq. It is known that the Qatari oil workers tried unsuccessfully to solicit support from the oil workers in Bahrain and it would seem highly probable that support would have also been sought in Abu Dhabi – for which Qatar was serving as a base. Furthermore, at the end of April, Qatari workers at Umm Said were openly saying that the time had come to end Sheikhly rule in Qatar and set up a republic,

> whilst at the end of May the oil workers on Das Island were similarly talking of setting up a 'New Republic' in Abu Dhabi.[70]

The elements of the story are astonishing: solidaristic organising and the use of violence, political and workplace demands, the transnational transmission of protest, and the ultimate broader failure of the protest. In the absence of labour unions or oppositional political parties, such staggeringly courageous action could not be sustained and very often resulted in ever more repressive measures against the organisers.

In all protests, the rulers' security forces deployed indiscriminate violence against the workers at every turn, providing an alibi for their British and American patrons. While deportation was the most frequent form of punishment for non-nationals, imprisonment, exile, and execution were meted out to citizens. Security forces for the smaller emirates were often recruited from categories of peoples who would not have a natural sympathy to strikers and were led, even after the nominal independence of many of the states, by British officers. Many of the latter had been fearsome figures having served in wars of pacification elsewhere, most famous among them Ian Henderson, the Butcher of Bahrain, whose brutal methods were used to suppress dissent and mobilisation in the 1990s. Torture was rife in the prisons of the Peninsula and beatings were doled out at the workplace, during strikes, in worker barracks, and on city streets. Once electronic surveillance technologies became more frequent methods of policing populations, they were used to not only track dissidents but to also ensure the orderliness of workplaces and places of gathering. Perhaps most striking is the extent to which forms of protest, especially direct action, have survived such repressive measures.

A more recent form of protest against workplace injustices has been to bring pressure to bear on employers through the courts or via human rights organisations. In 2004, Nepalese logistics workers were imported by Jordanian recruiters under contract with KBR (a subsidiary of Halliburton company and a provider of logistical support to the US military) to haul cargo for the US military in Iraq. The Nepalese had been told that they were going to Kuwait to work, but found themselves in the bloody frontline of the war on Iraq. Their convoy, carrying goods from Kuwait to US forward operating bases deep within Iraq, was ambushed and several of the logistics workers were killed. Their families sought justice from the US court system, but their case was eventually thrown out on procedural grounds.[71]

In the absence of trade unions, human rights organisations, both transnational (like Human Rights Watch and Amnesty) and more regional or local ones (like the Filipino Migrante International), have also taken up the cause of the workers, but naming and shaming only goes so far. Long-lasting organisations in which the workers themselves take the reins and engage in sustained disruptions of production and circulation are far more effective in the long run.

Unions as channels for protest

It is unsurprising that the rulers in the region resisted calls for labour unions issuing from the workers or any embryonic organisation that could serve as a channel for worker grievances. After a very successful strike at Aramco in 1956, the Saudi Arabian government banned not only strikes but also labour unions, a ban that still stands and, if anything, has become more draconian as the decades have passed. It is, however, more surprising that at least in the 1950s the British pushed for the institution of trade unions in Bahrain, Aden, and Kuwait.

This push becomes more explicable once the character of the British labour movements comes into play. In all instances in the Peninsula where the British permitted the establishment of a labour movement, they asked the Trade Union Congress of

Britain to act as a model for these unions. British unions had been 'anti-Communist by conviction [and] hostile to any idea of using strikes as political weapons'.[72] Writing about Qatari demands for unions, a British labour attaché claimed that 'although there are obvious dangers of subversion by extremist elements, trade unionism could prove to be a major factor in the gradual political evolution of the Arab world, in internal social reform, and in blocking the course of international communism'.[73]

The British used several tactics to circumscribe militant, activist unions. In both Bahrain and Aden, the unions were originally established as vertical, or company, unions rather than sector-wide unions, as demanded by the representatives of the workers themselves. In Aden, the port workers finally succeeded in 1958, after several years of segmented shipping-company unions, to transform the smaller organisations into the General Union of Port Workers. They nevertheless did not succeed in getting the Port Trust Union to join the mergers.[74]

Like Aden, in both Bahrain and Kuwait, unions were not sectoral but limited to a given company and exclusive to nationals. When in 1968, an amendment to the Labour Law was passed that allowed foreign workers to join the unions as full voting and officiating members, the oil and shipping companies feared that the legislation could 'rally non-Kuwaiti workers behind it' and drive up the cost of contract work for the companies. This in turn drove the British and US government representatives to come up with successful strategies to defeat the amendment by having it withdrawn.[75] It is crucial to note – given that the xenophobia of national workers is so often highlighted in accounts about labour mobilisation – that in Kuwait, the nationals actually wanted unity between Kuwaiti and foreign workers. They even compared the legal distinctions between nationals and foreigners to South African apartheid.[76] Although in the end the efforts of the workers came to naught and the new law limited foreign worker participation in trade unions to non-voting and non-officiating membership, today there are again efforts at forging bonds between nationals and migrant workers. Despite the legal limits on migrant worker unionisation, national unions are increasingly engaging in alliances with unions representing foreign workers that are based in their home countries.[77] Such alliances can allow the home-country unions to act as a conduit of representation for the non-represented migrant workers. To what extent such creative solutions can succeed still remains to be seen.

By the late 1960s, the British had realised how central the labour movements in Bahrain, Kuwait, and Aden had been to anticolonial struggles and domestic protests against repressive regimes. Thus the British changed their position towards labour unions in the Gulf protectorates. In 1968, as the British prepared to withdraw their militaries and cede nominal control to the states of the Peninsula, the US labour attaché in Beirut suggested that the British may want to put into place unions before they left. His British counterpart, Mr Morris, wrote that

> he saw no prospect in existing circumstances of any industrial trade union movement in the Western European sense. Any growth of trade unions would be essentially political in character, and was accordingly a matter of internal judgement by the rulers. The attempt by the British to stimulate trade unions in 1955 in Bahrain had had unfortunate political consequences.[78]

Unions are still absent on the ports and docks of Saudi Arabia, Qatar, and the UAE. In Oman, a labour union was formed at the port of Salalah in 2009 which, due to political constraints in Oman and repressive political measures (especially after the Arab uprisings of 2011), focused on 'strong dialogue and sound negotiations'.[79] The corporatist character of unions in Oman is a form of state co-optation.[80] In Salalah, regional politics also played into the emergence of the union. While some of the port managers I met openly espoused Dhofari nationalist frustrations against being ruled from Muscat, the unions appealed to the munificence of the Sultan in the capital as a means of gaining a foothold in their workplace. By invoking the state as a patron and protector, the unions were making a Faustian bargain. Even when allowed to come out into the open, being beholden to the state means that the union's ability to disrupt the order of things is severely disadvantaged. After all, if the state's economy depends on such core businesses as the port or the oil terminals, work stoppages are seen not only as a challenge to the employer but also to state security.

More often than not, however, it is not the workers who appeal to the states to act as benevolent protectors, but the companies. Repeatedly, the oil and shipping companies, terminal operators, and logistics firms looked to the state to unleash violence against protesters. Under the British, the diplomatic language of colonial rule used the rulers' supposed preference as an alibi for colonial violence. The companies depended on the state for legally banning labour stoppages, worker assemblies, or workplace dissent and openly called for brutal police action against workers. In the late 1960s, an Aramco officer voiced his gratitude to the Saudi ruling family for the anti-strike law which he said 'has been the principal reason for stabilized industrial peace during the past twelve years'.[81]

Having replacement workers black-leg strikers was one of the milder forms of punishment deployed by the states. In August 1968, during an oil-company strike, the deputy ruler of the Qatari proffered workers to replace the strikers. But the oil company politely refused the offer, 'partly because marine operations could be dangerous with inexperienced workers, and partly because the Company did not wish to provoke sabotage on its equipment'.[82] Intrusive surveillance of workers was another modality of control. The ruler of Sharjah's British-managed security department ran security checks on local workers hired by contractors to construct naval bases and ports.[83] Finally, police beatings, detentions, and violence were so frequent that they were often uncommented upon, except by those subjected to them or when the violence was so spectacular as to not be ignored.[84]

Deportation of foreign workers and exile of labour activists were other forms of punishment. But there was a danger associated with exiling labour leaders, as they could take their activist practice and experience with them. The giant of Saudi Arabian labour activism, Ishaq Shaykh Yaqub, was one such character. While working for Gray Mackenzie in al-Khobar, he became embroiled in the pivotal strike of 1953 and was exiled to Bahrain, where he joined political protests there.[85]

This circulation of labour dissent, of ideas and strategies and politics, was crucial to the age of revolt in the Peninsula, now so frequently forgotten or suppressed or overshadowed by other revolutions, other wars, elsewhere in the Arab world.

Chokepoints and Counterlogistics

Landside workers may be subject to fragmentations and repression and increasingly automated out of work, but they still hold the possibility of mobilisation in their refusal to work. In the years of ferment of the 1950s and 1960s, the protests that most rattled oil companies, governments, and colonial officers were those that could bring the production and circulation of oil to a halt. Both the oil plants and the terminals had 'strike plans' that, in the event of work stoppages by nationals, enlisted European workers to continue production and provide oil-loading and bunkering services.[86] Not all jobs at the ports were so easily replaceable. During a two-day period in 1961 in Doha, pilot-boat crews stopped work, preventing tankers from berthing. This had the effect that oil was still produced, but only as long as the storage tanks at Umm Said had excess capacity to take it. After two days of production, those tanks would be full. Within this two-day window, the Qatari police, populated by extended members of the ruler's clan and other loyal families, violently suppressed the strike.[87] A strike that hampered ship loading was a chokepoint preventing the smooth flow of oil.

Chokepoints are places on land or at sea where huge volumes of cargo slow down to pass through narrower conduits on their way to their final destinations. Chokepoints can be straits or ports where the speed of unloading of ships is not matched by the speed of landside transportation conveying the cargo away from the port. Chokepoints can slow down circulation, affecting the speed of 'value-in-motion'.[88] Occupy activists' 2011 port blockades in the San Francisco Bay Area used counter-logistical tactics at the port chokepoints to create a new modality of activism. Pro-Palestinian activists' 2014 blockades against Israeli Zim ships unloading at the port of Oakland borrowed the tactic from those 2011 protests and emulated earlier transnational solidarities of dockers refusing to unload apartheid South Africa's ships.[89] In response, the Zim ship changed course and unloaded its cargo at another port up the coast. It also soon funded a Zim artists' residency aboard its container ships to 'artwash' its political origins.[90]

Port blockades or refusal to load and unload ships have in the past been successful in drawing attention to international campaigns. When Dubai Ports World took over the management of the new London Gateway terminal and logistics park in the Thames Estuary, it refused to recognise a union representing the workers there. Dockers in the Netherlands and other ports threatened to blockade ships coming from London Gateway, and the union Unite launched a campaign around the port, describing it as a 'port of convenience' that undermined worker well-being, health, and safety.[91] Ultimately, strong transnational activism and a court case brought by Unite forced DP World to recognise the union, though no contract with the union has been signed at the time of this writing.[92]

But blockades, as performatively rich as they are, even as they 'give our blockaders a sense of where they stand within the flows of capital', ultimately are only a set of tactics. Even disregarding whether or not they are effective now or in the long term, like any other tactic they can be appropriated for less than salutary politics. Here, I want to tell the story of the *SS Cleopatra*, a packet ship owned by the Khedival Mail Line in Egypt which arrived in New York in April 1960. The Seafarers International Union (SIU) declared a picket at Pier 16 on the East River and refused to unload the ship. The International Longshoremen's Association honoured their picket and joined the boycott of the ship. In Egypt, activists and eventually Nasser himself declared this an action in sympathy with Israel, and Arab trade unions sent messages of protest to the two US-based unions. The head of SIU argued that 'the trade union action [was] based on Cairo's denial of freedom of the seas to many United States ships' carrying Israeli cargoes or touching at Israeli ports. He further reported that SIU had received staunch support from Omer Becu, the legendary labour activist and secretary general of the International Transport Workers' Federation in Brussels, Belgium.[93] When the Khedival Mail Line brought a court case against the SIU, a federal judge refused to ban the picketing of the ship. [94] The press reported that

> nearly 3,000 American tourists in Israel for the holiday season today gathered at a reception in Hamlin House in Tel Aviv and adopted a resolution congratulating the New York maritime workers and longshoremen for their boycott of United Arab Republic shipping in New York Harbor.[95]

The news of the picket angered Kuwaiti dockers, who sent a message of support to the International Confederation of Arab Trade Unions and declared that, in retaliation, they would boycott loading any US-flagged tankers at Ahmadi or Abdullah oil terminals. A retaliatory boycott of US ships also went into effect at Port Said and threatened to spread to the ports of Syria, Saudi Arabia, Iraq, and Lebanon. In the end, intense negotiations brought the Arab boycott of US ships and the SIU's boycott of the *SS Cleopatra* to an end by 7 May 1960.[96] That was not the last time that the ostensibly radical, cohesive, and militant dockers' unions in the US would stand on the side of US security interests. Only a decade later, the SIU boycotted a Swedish ship because Sweden had sent supplies to North Vietnam during the war.[97]

Ultimately, the boycott was on both sides a political action. In the era of decolonisation, Arab dockers stood in solidarity not only with one another but also with the perceived leader of the Arab anti-imperialist revolution, Gamal Abdel Nasser. For their part, the US unions defended the national security of their own state and that of Israel, choosing to turn a blind eye to the massive upheavals of the era of decolonisation and how it was rearranging political and social relations across the world.

7
Shipboard Work

> For a ship . . . is no limited monarchy, where the sturdy Commons have a right to petition, and snarl if they please; but almost a despotism.
>
> Herman Melville, *White Jacket*

> The crew are the only true comrades a ship has at sea. They polish the ship, they wash it, they stroke it, they caress it, they kiss it – and they mean it, because they are not hypocrites where their ship is concerned.
>
> B. Traven, *Death Ship*

Even astute analysts like C.L.R. James and Michel Foucault have seen in the ship a kind of affirmative *topoi*: the former a utopia, the latter a heterotopia. While imprisoned in Ellis Island, James, writing about Melville's *Moby Dick*, described the workers aboard a ship as 'a world-federation of modern industrial workers [who] owe allegiance to no nationality . . . They owe no allegiance to anybody or anything except the work they have to do and the relations with one another on which that work depends'.[1] I do not disagree with James about Melville's *Moby Dick* being perhaps the greatest American novel ever written, but an autonomous, self-constituted, sovereign working class is as far from the hierarchies of ships as one can imagine.

Foucault, in turn, analyses heterotopias as places of imagination, discipline, and violence, recognising brothels and colonies as examples. And the ship is certainly that. Yet his brief essay suddenly veers into a romantic finale:

> . . . if we think that the boat is a floating piece of space, a place without a place, that exists by itself, that is closed in on itself and at the same time is given over to the infinity of the sea and that, from port to port, from tack to tack, from brothel to brothel, it goes as far as the colonies in search of the most precious treasures they conceal in their gardens, you will understand why the boat has not only been for our civilization, from the sixteenth century until the present, the great instrument of economic development (I have not been speaking of that today), but has been simultaneously the greatest reserve of the imagination. The ship is the heterotopia par excellence. In civilizations without boats, dreams dry up, espionage takes the place of adventure, and the police take the place of pirates.[2]

Something in that account ignores that the imaginative life on the ship is founded on a substratum of mind-numbing, boring, repetitive labour for everyone, including the officers, and back-breaking toil for the seafarers. Marcus Rediker's excavation of the historical etymology of 'spinning the yarn' points to the continuity of monotony and hardship on the ship from the age of sail to the age of steam. Rediker describes the work needed to re-weave rope yarns to make them re-usable for hoisting sails. As they sat to engage in this weaving that tore into their hands and made their bent backs ache, sailors told one another stories to lubricate the passing of time. Rediker adds that labour on the ship is 'collective, lonely, and noncontinuous. Ships were isolated for long periods, and the crew lived in close, forced proximity. Many times there was nothing to do . . . Captains therefore created "make-work" of various kinds to fill the porous workday.'[3]

It is something of a cliché aboard ships that, when you have finished sanding off the rust and repainting the hull of the ship, you have to start from the beginning. The decks of ships are far more pleasant places to work than the engine rooms, but they are still exposed, and if steaming through the Mediterranean is pleasant during most times, even walking on the deck of a ship lashed by monsoon rains or the storms of Bay of Biscay is still immensely dangerous. The work is more repetitive and tedious and menial the lower a seafarer is in the hierarchy of the ship. If there is pleasure to be had from working at sea, it cannot come from mopping the deck for months on end. And there is no exposure to sun and sea air if you are clad in a hardhat and a mask and wearing heavy overalls. When the oil pipes inevitably leak into the bilge or ballast water, bucketing out oily water may be part of the daily duties. If there are no yarns to be spun, there is also scant possibility of telling stories over the deafening sound of the electric grinders or power hoses. An ordinary workday can include standing under a storm of rust and paint flakes, necks craned backwards as overhead beams are scraped and scrubbed. The essayist John McPhee described the work thus:

> Chipping rust is a job for people made of neurological nylon. They use hand-held jackhammers – needle guns, chisel guns, Bumble Bees, triple-scalers. They dislodge rust and they create sound. Wherever they are, wherever you are, you can hear them . . . Depending on where you are, the chippers can seem to be hovering aircraft, they can seem to be splashing water, they can suggest a dentist drilling in a cavity hour after hour.[4]

Working in the engine rooms requires abundant skill. Writing about the work onboard ships, Trotsky romanticised the machinists of the ship as 'industrial workers in sailor's uniforms who form a minority among the crew, [but] nevertheless dominate the crew because they control the engine'.[5] The vast underbelly of the ship is always hot and loud and throbbing with the motion of the cylinders and the rotation of the massive one-metre-wide drive shaft. The oil-purifying room is the hot, humid inferno at the heart of the engine room, where the engine and lubrication oils have to be heated to 135 degrees centigrade before they can grease the machinery. The handful of people who work in the engine room are all engaged in reparative or regular maintenance. Copious artisanal skill is required for maintenance in the engine rooms, as any damaged pieces have to be hand-machined. Thus, on the one hand, the spectacle of computerised monitoring screens and so much automation and, on the other hand, the exquisite blacksmithing skills required to fix objects that run an awesomely powerful engine.

Even in the wheelhouse, many of the tasks are deadly tedious. Admiralty Charts need to be regularly updated by gluing on new strips of paper marking out changed routes and conditions of travel. Endless reams of paperwork have to be filled out – for the company, for inspectors, for the countries of transit, for the countries of arrival, and for anyone else requiring signed and stamped bits of paper. One captain told John McPhee, only half-jokingly, 'If a ship doesn't have a good copying machine, it isn't seaworthy'.[6] There are always crew members staring out to sea to look out for boats or ships that may not be picked up by radar or the Automatic Identification System. On both my journeys, when we arrived in the Gulf of Aden, procedures aboard the ship subtly changed. Safety measures were put into place and on every shift, the crew member who stood watch in the wheelhouse became more focused, tenser.

The crew members stared out to sea, and they saw through the haze and heat and shimmer of the Indian Ocean boats, porpoises, buoys that it took me at least another five or ten minutes to identify. They joked with me about seeing fast-moving skiffs, playing on the fear of pirates that was rife. But they could *see* afar. Their eyes had become so accustomed to gazing at the sea through the coruscation of air and water that they picked up small boats that were, for some reason, too small for radar, and could tell the difference between a school of dolphins and a fishing boat. In the lonely waters of the Gulf of Aden, the ability to distinguish the tiniest trace of movement was a crucial skill.

Joking about piracy had its own poignancy. Where pirates had captured tankers or bulk carriers in the Gulf of Aden, the seafarers had been the inevitable losers. Too often, hijacked seafarers remained in captivity for long periods, sometimes years, as the ships' owners refused to pay a ransom even as they collected insurance on the ship. Many captive seafarers starved and became sick; some died in captivity. Their captors, themselves poor, starved, and exploited, could be brutal or kind to them; in many cases, they showed solidarity and sympathy. But life aboard these captive ships, often deliberately grounded on the coasts of Somalia by the pirates, was an exercise in endurance. Piracy is, ultimately, a business and the people who ran the racket were likely dressed in suits and drove shiny big SUVs in Nairobi or Singapore or another cyber-connected and well-to-do regional capital. The pirates were exploited by those distant 'businessmen'.

I was told by the crew members who had steamed on different kinds of ships that tankers and bulk carriers felt less safe when going through pirate seas than the fortified ro/ros (roll-on/roll-of transporters of wheeled vehicles) or tall container ships. The decks of tankers and bulkers are closer to the surface of the sea and are vulnerable to skiffs coming alongside and pirates climbing the side with grappling hooks and rope ladders. Container ships have higher freeboards, making them less accessible. The seafarers told me that the flag under which the ship steamed made some ships more vulnerable to piracy and some more protected by naval escorts. Some ships – Russian and Israeli crafts foremost among them – carry armed security guards aboard, but the ships I took were flagged to Britain and, despite the availability of NATO and EU escorts, relied on high-pressure hoses and ordinary security measures for safe passage through pirate waters.

These moments of preparation for piracy are far from the humdrum everyday, but they are also infrequent. What broke the boredom of being at sea on a far more regular basis were port visits. Port visits are not tedious, but they are exhausting and stressful. A constant refrain of the seafarers with whom I spoke was 'twelve ports in China, every eighteen hours'. The requirements of productivity are perennially diminishing the turnaround time at the port. Even where the port stay is longer, the stressful navigation of ships through congested channels to port is no way to break the boredom: it is drudgery. In my second journey, my ship was the first ultra-large container vessel to arrive at the port of Mersin in Turkey after an expansion of the port and the deepening of the approach channel. The opening in the breakwaters that extended out to sea from the berths was still a little too narrow for the ship, and the captain, as skilled and experienced as he was, visibly tensed during the navigation to shore. At congested ports, berthing the ship requires not only the skills of the ship's officers and crew, but also an implicit trust in the pilots and tugboat captains who guide the ship into spot in what is the equivalent of parallel-parking along a vast dock.

Arrival at port was no moment of rest for the seafarers. Many had to work with the dockers and stevedores and crane operators to ensure the smooth lading and unlading of the ship with containers, bulk goods, or liquid cargo. This is because of the understaffing of ships and the automation of ports. At most ports, the turnaround time was less than twenty-four hours and, if a port is far from the city centre or has onerous immigration procedures for leaving the confines of the port itself, then a visit to the city is not particularly effortless or expeditious. The reputation of some cities, like Hong Kong, makes a mad dash nevertheless appealing. Some ports are entirely off limits to visiting seafarers. In the ports of Saudi Arabia, the state does not grant seafarers permission for entry (at one time, this only applied to non-Muslims; during my visit, I was told no one could go into the city). The port of Khor Fakkan does not have a border crossing, and therefore cannot accommodate entry for non-nationals or anyone who may need a visa or a seafarers' card to exit the port grounds. In other ports, shipping companies may not permit their seafarers to go ashore because of often nebulous or outdated security fears. For some shipping companies, Beirut has been off limits since the 2006 Israeli war on Lebanon and the ensuing internal conflicts – to the great regret of all seafarers who have heard legendary stories about the city's nightlife. In August 2016, CMA CGM withdrew permission for sailors to exit the grounds of the port of Mersin because of the attempted coup in Turkey a few weeks before.

Work hours differ from ship to ship and shipping company to shipping company, but on the ships on which I travelled, officers and crew worked in alternating four-hour shifts, twenty-four hours a day. That means the seafarers can only sleep in (less than) four-hour chunks. The ship is often physically arranged in a way that reflects the pyramidical character of order and discipline onboard. The captain has his own floor (or shares a floor with the first mate), with large rooms and expansive seating areas. As the ship floors descend, the rooms become smaller and the crew members have to share their spaces with at least one other person (often with two or three others). Officers and crew dine in separate quarters and are fed different foods. The European officers receive meals of 'meat and two veg' while the ship's cook prepares curries for the crew members (I have to confess that, although it seemed that the curries were prepared with leftover meats of the officers' meals from the previous day, they were far superior in taste to the meals served to the officers). The officers and crew have different sitting rooms with varying leisure equipment. The gym is shared by the officers and crew members, though differing perceptions of embodiment and masculinity mean that European officers use the weight-lifting equipment more than the Asian crew members.

Hierarchy and routine rigidly structure even the leisure time onboard, especially for the crew. Rules on ships differ, but many shipping companies now ban drinking socially, so, if the captain turns a blind eye, the crew are forced into their rooms to have a beer at night. Filipino seafarers used to famously ask for karaoke equipment aboard ships, and sing-song socialising was a beloved pastime. I attended one karaoke party on my first trip, and it was an enjoyably giddy event, with the seafarers lustily belting out to Asian-pop versions of famous hits. But this is also changing: as more shipping companies secure satellite internet connections for their crew members, more seafarers retreat to their cabins to browse the internet, watch porn, or contact their families. The new access to internet was something for which the officers and crew members of my second ship journey were grateful. After all, now they did not have to wait for arrival at port to browse the web, or for a nightly bulk transmission for their emails to friends and family to be sent. But the satellite internet connection has clearly transformed practices of sociability on the ship, especially for crew members whose contracts often require them to spend nine months at sea (the officers' contracts had far shorter durations at sea). Anthropologist Johanna Markkula, whose father was a Swedish captain and who herself spent some time onboard Swedish ships, writes about how during times of tension aboard the ship, crew members retreated from communal activities like 'sports tournaments, barbecues, parties, and karaoke nights' into their cabins and reconnected with their families.[7]

This bifurcated contracting system, which has been particularly exacerbated since the 1970s, also means more divergent wage systems between officers and crews of the world's biggest shipping companies. Most shipping companies headquartered in Europe depend on Filipino crew members. The Philippines has now developed an extensive maritime training network for crew and officers, and the country depends on the remittances of its labour diasporas, and especially its vast numbers of seafarers.[8] The ships on which I travelled also had a single Filipino officer each. These men ate with the crew members rather than with the European officers, and their socialisation also took place in the crew's leisure room rather than with the officers.

The officers and the crew lived separately not only because of their place in the organisational hierarchies, but also because of geographical divides in their countries of origin.

Lascars, Asiatics, and Others

> Sailors are free laborers, they are free, starved, jobless, tired, all their limbs broken, their ribs smashed, their feet and arms and backs burned. Since they are not slaves, they are forced to take any job on any ship, even if they know beforehand that the bucket has been ordered down to the bottom to get the insurance money for the owners.
>
> B. Traven, *The Death Ship*

The dual-wage system, in which officers of European extraction get paid one rate and worked on more amenable contracts and the ship's crews on another wage scale and worked on a more draconian contract, has a precedent in the work of lascars. The term *lascar* refers to a seafarer from the European colonies who served on merchant vessels owned by the European. The early official definition reeled off 'Indians, Asiatics or other Natives from the Territories of the East India Company'.[9] The first lascars were hired by Dutch ships in the seventeenth century to staff naval artillery; the name *lascar* derives from Persian *lashkari*, 'soldier'. By the eighteenth century, the British were hiring lascars to 'replace European crews decimated by disease, death or desertion'.[10]

Although the vast majority of historical accounts of lascars are about South Asian seafarers, Adenese (and Yemeni) sailors were a substantial subcategory of such seafarers, and African and Chinese sailors were also sometimes labelled thus. The employment of lascars on British and other European ships was precisely about the racial hierarchies of labour that structured colonial regimes of exploitation. As the sailor Alan Villiers – who had plied many sea routes, including dhow trade routes between the Persian Gulf and East Africa – wrote in the 1930s, once 'slavery had become uneconomic [it] was better to own a man's work than to own and support the man himself. To own his work, you had not to support him'.[11] The choices free/wage labour offered were no choices at all if the end result was desperate exploitation, intensification of racialisation, apparatuses of debt that kept sailors obligated to work in particular ships and for particular *serangs* (a combination of labour recruiter and ship's bosun), and abject poverty as the alternative to back-breaking work.

The recruitment of lascars was from the very start a disciplined form of exploitation of racialised labour. In the eighteenth century, lascars were paid one-seventh of English seafarers' wages, and their mobility was circumscribed by law. From 1790 onwards, British ships could only hire English sailors on westbound ships west of Suez, preventing Asian seafarers from entering Europe (though the measure was spectacularly unsuccessful). In 1823, laws were specifically promulgated against lascars that

> while confirming that Lascars were British subjects, denied their Britishness for employment purposes except in certain parts of the world, or during wars; it deemed them to be less than a European, which endorsed their employment at discriminatory wages and conditions; and it authorised their forcible expulsion if they were unable to obtain work. The Act was in force until 1963.[12]

Race was always explicitly and implicitly invoked in the wage rates of lascars, in their contracts, and in the discourses about them.[13] However, it was not only the state that discriminated against lascars. Thick veins of racism run through the disposition of the National Union of Seamen (NUS) of Britain towards lascars. They invoked the language of 'British heritage' in shipping and demanded that the lascars – who, as colonial subjects, were legally British – not be recognised as such. The deals negotiated by the unions in 1891 saw English firemen aboard ships paid £4 per month to a lascar's £1.20 (paid in rupees, not sterling). The Merchant Shipping Act of 1906 responded to union demands and legislated for expanded accommodation space and improved diet for English seafarers, but explicitly excluded the lascars.[14]

In 1919, laws were passed to deport unemployed lascars from Britain, even though they were British subjects. Many were rounded up and forcibly shipped to India (or Aden, which was a waystation on the route to Bombay). In 1925, the Special Restriction (Coloured Alien Seamen) Order required that *all* 'coloured' seamen register with the police. Destitute 'alien' seafarers were to be deported. In a haunting precursor to the Windrush scandal of 2018, the police forcibly registered so many British subjects that protests arose from organisations and institutions representing black British citizens and Indian subjects of the Empire. During the Depression, when the British government proposed to subsidise tramp shipping, the NUS and its allied unions demanded that no subsidy be given to shipping companies that hired 'non-domiciled Asiatics and other coloured seamen'. In 1943, the All India Seamen's Centre protested to their British union brethren about their silence on the lascars' discriminatory work hours and nonreceipt of overtime, pensions, sick pay, or workers' compensation in the event of injury. They received no response.[15] As late as 1965, British legislation and regulation allowed for discriminatory wage and contractual measures for non-white seafarers, lascars foremost among them, with the 'forced labour' provisions applicable to lascars and 'Asiatics' in effect until in 1970. Adenese seafarers were included in these categories; Aden remained a British colony until the end of 1967.

Adenese lascars were first recruited not aboard British ships, however, but by the French Messageries Maritimes in 1869. Messageries Maritimes was at the time the world's largest shipping company and the biggest rival of the British P&O.[16] In 1856, the French had established their own coaling station next to P&O's coaling station (first inaugurated in 1842); once the Suez Canal opened, they had a fortnightly mail service bunkering at Aden.[17] While they refuelled at the port, they also recruited seafarers. Many of the Adenese lascars were from villages of the interior or the highlands who used seafaring as a way to support families and maintained their connection to their villages no matter how far they travelled. Messageries Maritimes only required that the seafarers carry their British discharge books or police identity cards and, unlike many other European shipping companies, did not seek to verify the Adenese's passports.[18] Adenese lascars were taken onboard as firemen or stokers.[19] It was a job often given to lascars on the racist assumption that hailing from hot climates inured them to the infernal working conditions of the stokehold. In the interwar years, some 50,000 lascars plied the seas on British merchant vessels; many thousands more worked for European and US ships. Up until the 1960s, lascars made up to a quarter of all crew on British ships.[20]

Before limitations on lascars' ability to jump ship increased in the twentieth century, they often abandoned ships that had abusive masters, floggings onboard, and dire working and living conditions. This was the only recourse available to workers who were ostensibly free but, because of work/life conditions and legal strictures, were confined to a form of servitude. Jumping ship was an escape.[21] But in response to white union demands and as a means of disciplining the sailors by the state, starting in the early twentieth century, increasingly draconian entry requirements were introduced in many ports around the world, whereby simply having a sailor's card does not suffice for seafarers to leave the grounds of the port.

Circulation of Revolt

Though the circumstances of work were dire and racially structured, lascars served as conduits for the circulation of ideas about revolt around the oceans they traversed. I began the previous chapter with the story of the 1948 Adenese strike, which immobilised the port. As I mentioned before, the British Petroleum industrial relations officer who wrote about the strike attributed it to the cumulative force of preceding protests. He also wrote that 'Arab and Somali seafaring workers who during the [Second World] War had seen conditions in other ports and also obtained higher wages were not slow to communicate this knowledge to their fellow workers in Aden'.[22] Adenese travelled not only as seafarers but as migrants. We now know a great deal about Hadhramis in Southeast Asia and Yemenis in Djibouti and other far ports.[23] But Yemenis travelled even further afield. On his dhow journey, Villiers met a 'curious old Seyyid' who spoke a foreign language neither Villiers nor the other sailors understood. Villiers soon found that the language was Polish, which the man had learnt in Hamtramck, Michigan, a Polish suburb of Detroit where he had lived while working in an automobile factory. The Yemeni had made his way to Detroit aboard ocean steamers, on which he had been a stoker for eight years.[24]

Perhaps the largest diaspora of Adenese seafarers was scattered in British ports, where, as I have already recounted, they were subject to many discriminatory practices. The passing of the 1919 Aliens Restriction (Amendment) Act resulted in lascars being rounded up and deported to India or Aden. On one ship, some 150 Adenese and 63 Punjabi lascars

> insisted on land leave in Aden, on halal meat, and on the immediate payment by the India Office of the debts they had incurred with their creditors who were also on board. They were infuriated as they felt they had been cajoled into returning to India

> with false promises. The shipmaster pointed out that the port captain had told him he was 'very sorry to oblige me to sail with such a crowd of Bolshevicks [sic] aboard'.[25]

There was no surprise that lascars were considered seditious Communists. Many Indian seafarers had become active in the emerging Communist movements there, and, with the establishment of Indian seafarers' unions in the 1920s, in the trade union movement as well. Because they could transmit ideas of revolt and bring news of mobilisation, their very 'mobility became an asset to political movements and a source of anxiety for states'.[26] But they did not only transmit ideas. They were thought to have also been involved in gun-running and dissemination of clandestine or prohibited publications.

The Yemeni communities of Britain were not only mobilised by Communists but also by Free Yemen Movement and other nascent nationalist organisations. For example, in 1928, a police informant wrote to the British authorities in Aden about how a ship's agent travelled throughout Britain on behalf of Imam Yahya's struggle against the British. The informant wrote,

> From Marseilles he came to London, Cardiff, South Shields and Hull all in England. He instructed to all Arab seamen that there is a war between the Imam Yehia Zaide and the British. He made a grand speech in no 1 Sophia Street, Docks, Cardiff to Arabs and showed the letter of Imam Yehia Zaide he had with him and which requested all Arabs to help Imam Yehia Zaide with money. They all helped him and collected a reasonable amount.[27]

Whether or not the letter was simply conspiracy-mongering or dirty tricks, it indicated the political force of the Yemeni seafarers in their diaspora and their mobility in different European ports.

The community of seafarers in Britain also revolted in response to discriminatory legislation and racist union activism against them. For example, in 1930, the British passed a law that required Arab and Somali seafarers to have passports or other papers in order to work on ships. The ensuing riot by the seafarers resulted in a large number of arrests.[28] By the late 1930s, the Colonial Seamen's Association and other Communist-led organisations specifically aimed to recruit among non-white seafarers. The extent of Communist Party recruitment and mobilisation was such that Harold Moody, the president of the League of Coloured People, told a newspaper that 'the coloured people of Cardiff are mainly Communists, simply because no one else has seen fit to give them a helping hand'.[29] Thus it was not surprising that, when the Royal Indian Navy mutinied in Bombay in 1946, they found solidarity across the seas. When the anticolonial mutiny was reported in the papers, and as the mutineers telegraphed ports far and wide, 'other ships stationed across the Indian Ocean as far as the Andaman Islands and Aden also refused to conduct their work'.[30] Though the mutiny fell victim to the conflict between the Congress and Communist Parties in India, it heralded an age of anticolonial revolt that eventually faded into the ravages of capitalist retrenchment in the 1970s.

Global Hierarchies Aboard Ships Today

> The constant hardships of the sea life, with its wholly inadequate food, its broken rest often in wet and always insufficient clothes, its exposures to fevers and all sorts of tropical ills – these things must take their tolls. Every sailor in that ship, except one sixteen-year-old boy, was grey; most of them iron-grey. Many looked old, but there were no old men.
>
> Alan Villiers, *Sons of Sinbad*

In the wake of the heady era of decolonisation in the 1960s arrived the much gloomier 1970s. The decade saw the cataclysm in the petroleum markets which came with the nationalisation of oil and cartelisation of the Organisation of Petroleum

Exporting Countries (OPEC), the start of the reversal of social-democratic gains in most of the global North, and in the global South the consolidation of authoritarianism combined with liberalisation of hitherto statist economies. By the end of the decade, container shipping had become not a novelty but a welcomed technological modality, completely changing the look of ships and harbours. Oil extraction and circulation had also changed. Overcapacity in shipping encouraged economies of scale, leading to very large ships. Tankers, bulk carriers, and other freighters all grew in size by orders of magnitude. Euro-American oil companies also accelerated their divestment from their shipping businesses and instead chartered tankers from independent shipping companies.[31]

The means by which the economic and political upheavals were transmitted to the bodies and daily lives of seafarers were twofold. The first significant transformation was the diffusion of techniques of discipline from the tanker business into the new and expanding container terminals. These new techniques included automation, the whittling down of the number of work forces on the docks and aboard ships, and the acceleration of turnaround times at ports. Second, national deregulation in a great many countries of the world allowed national shipping companies to move their ships to 'open registries'. Ships steaming under flags of convenience in turn led to transformations in working conditions, including the creation of a dual wage and contracting system aboard ships.

Working on tankers

In the logbook we wrote: 'cyclones and storms';
we've sent the S.O.S. to other ships,
and gazing, pale, at the Indian Ocean
I doubt if we'll ever reach Batavia.

Nikos Kavvadias, 'A Midshipman on the Bridge in an Hour of Danger'

From very early on, the technologies of tanker transport were a mechanism for disciplining workers on ship and on shore. Tanker terminals were often miles from the city centres, sometimes miles from the shore. Automation was a built-in feature of tanker loading from very early on. This reduced the cost of stevedoring at ports and made tankers a more attractive venture for shipowners. Aristotle Onassis's liking for tankers was precisely because one could

> hook up a hose, turn a valve, and a tanker was loaded in half the time it would take to pack a freighter's hold, using clumsy slings and cargo winches. It took dozens of stevedores to load a freighter and these men cost money, thanks to strong unions controlling such ports as New York and London. Oil could be siphoned aboard with as few as six men. If the unions weren't looking.[32]

Three operators, not six, were required for this kind of loading: one oil worker at the tank farm turned on the tap, another at the switchgate manifold regulated the flow to the tankers, and 'a man in a little office on the jetty beside the tanker supervise[d] the loading'.[33] The automation and the reduction of required staff seemed to be a perfect model for the ghost ports yet to come. Already in 1967, McKinsey Consulting was advising London ports to model their container-shipping businesses on the VLCC and ULCC business, whose economies of scale and automatic pumps reduced the cost per unit of transport.[34]

The regime of work aboard tankers was, also from very early on, uncannily similar to labour on automated container ships. A 1956 *New York Times* report described the life of tanker men:

> At sea, the tanker man lives pretty much as does the freighter man, except that there is more of it. For the big tanker spends little time in port. She is in this afternoon, to start spilling out her cargo, and after eighteen hours is off again tomorrow, for a

> month or two . . . The oil-loading ports in faraway lands are isolated, not near the white lights. A man can use up most of his day in port getting to and from the nearest hot spot.[35]

The tanker, then, is a model of the kind of logistical work with which we are so familiar and which has fundamentally eroded the working conditions of seafarers. The consolidation of bulk cargo in containers has created the conditions of automation at sea and at ports which tankers had pioneered.

Flagging

> The so-called flag of convenience, the convenience being that taxes could be avoided, insurance could be to a considerable extent ignored, and wages attractive to ship-owners could be paid to merchant sailors drawn from any part of the world.
>
> John McPhee, *Looking for a Ship*

To sail under a flag of a country transforms the ship into a quantum of sovereignty of that country. Not all ships fly the flag of their home ports. In the Indian Ocean in the eighteenth and nineteenth centuries, in order to avoid confrontation with French privateers, vessels of the East India Company flew the red Arab flag. In turn, the Company allowed local merchants to sail under its flag to lend them something of its maritime power and prestige.[36] By the late nineteenth and early twentieth centuries, slaving ships from the Arabian Peninsula sometimes flew French flags in order to avoid having to submit to British maritime inspections. The Sultan of Oman in 1895 granted the French a coaling station in his domain in return for dhows of Muscat flying the French flag. As the British tried to fend off the French establishing a strategic foothold on the Peninsula, they used the pursuit of slave ships as an alibi to harass and stop ships flying the French flag, including those which may have had nothing to do with slave trade but had otherwise evaded obeisance to the British claim to rule the seas.[37] The Muscat Dhows Dispute arose out of this imperial contestation over Arabia. The British who took the arbitration case to the Hague questioned the French right to grant dhow captains the use of the French flag. The case ultimately decided for the British; *however*, it affirmed as a general principle the right 'of every sovereign to decide to whom he will accord the right to fly his flag and to prescribe the rules governing such grants'.[38]

Once the law formalised the legality of 'flags of convenience', it was only a short time before it was used as a method for evading laws, strategic advantage, and cutting costs to benefit trade and profits. In World War I, the US flagged out more than a thousand merchant vessels to Britain. Standard Oil of New Jersey flew the flag of Danzig over the ships of its German subsidiary to avoid having them seized for reparations after the war.[39] Open registries, however, came into being with the Panamanian, Liberian, and Honduran flags. The Panamanian open registry was established via legislation in 1916, allowing any ship to be registered to Panama through a Panamanian consul at a foreign port. A US freight company which transferred its ships to the Panamanian registry was explicit about the benefits:

> The chief advantage of Panamanian registry is that the owner is relieved of the continual but irregular boiler and hull inspections and the regulations as to crew's quarters and subsistence. We are under absolutely no restrictions, so long as we pay the $1 a net ton registry fee and 10 cents yearly a net ton tax.[40]

Among those who benefitted from Panamanian registry were Aristotle Onassis and a great many shipping companies who wanted to avoid taxation, inspection or regulations. The vast majority of Onassis's ships were flagged to Panama, and Onassis took advantage of this arrangement to hire whom he wanted aboard his ships at wages not comparable to those of other tanker companies. Alongside Panama, other Central American registries, like those of Honduras and Costa Rica, modified their registration processes to attract the banana boats of the United Fruit Company and other fruit importers. Throughout the 1940s, tankers and banana boats proliferated under these flags, Panama foremost among them.

The conditions for the establishment of the Liberian registry speak to the intimate ways in which the open-registry system conveniently sat within a new post-war liberal capitalist order. The establishment of Liberia's registry occurred under the auspices of the former US Secretary of State and ambassador to the United Nations, the patrician Edward Stettinius, who took his extensive transnational connections to making a tidy profit from colonial exploitation of Liberian resources. Stettinius and several financier friends from the US founded a private development firm in Liberia. The firm entered a profit-sharing agreement with the Liberian government, whereby of any profits earned on the company's nebulous businesses, 65 per cent was reinvested in the corporation, 25 per cent was given over to the Liberian government, and 10 per cent was donated to the charitable Liberia Foundation.[41] With input from a shipowners' group and Esso's shipping managers, Stettinius's company drafted the law and designed the registration processes for a Liberian registry in 1948. This registry was a private firm, operated by Stettinius and his business partners, and a share of the profit from the registry went to them. Today the Liberian registry has been renamed Liberian International Ship & Corporate Registry and is headquartered in the US state of Virginia. The first ship to be registered under the Liberian flag was a tanker owned by that other famous shipping tycoon, Stavros Niarchos, and chartered to Getty Oil of California. From the very first, the registry was a venture for channelling profits to the US; Liberia has benefitted very little from it. As early as 1948, the International Transport-Workers' Federation (ITF) protested the 'evasion of taxes, currency regulations, and safety, social and labour standards' which the open registries, or flags of convenience as they came to be called, made possible.[42]

The processes of cost-cutting, the trough in shipping business, and the national deregulations of the 1970s saw an exponential expansion of ships sailing under flags of convenience. The latter came about when European states established a secondary or 'international' registry to relax crewing rules and slacken health and safety standards aboard ships. The requirement to hire nationals to staff the ships was also set aside under deregulation and with the open or international registries. From the 1970s onwards, the number of foreign crews on ships proliferated, and some countries began to specialise in supplying shipboard labour. While the top five ship-owning countries – Greece, Japan, China, Germany, and Singapore – together marshalled 49.5 per cent of all shipboard tonnage, in 2015, the five largest suppliers of officers and crew, were China, the Philippines, the Russian Federation, Ukraine, and India. The number of seafarers in that year was estimated at 1.6 million, and Chinese officers surpassed the number of Filipino officers, though the latter still dominated among crews.[43] Filipino seafarers are an astonishing 14 per cent of all seafarers.[44] Arbitrage on the international wages of crews earns shipowners handsome profits.

Working conditions aboard ships are wildly variable, with ships flagged to European ports offering far better accommodations, food, and wages than ships flagged to open registries. A great many seafarers have fallen prey to unscrupulous shipowners who abandon sailors aboard faulty vessels in foreign ports, with no pay and no way to return home. B. Traven's novel *Death Ship*, about a rust-bucket destined for the deeps in an insurance scam, may be only a more colourful and literary rendering of the plight of a great many seafarers. When hijacked by pirates, seafarers are often left at their mercy, abandoned by ship-owners unwilling to pay ransom.[45] Ships have always been international spaces, with sailors of many nations working together. Today's internationalisation is different. A vessel can be owned by Greeks, chartered by a French shipping company, flagged to Liberia, officered by Chinese or Eastern Europeans, and staffed by Filipinos. This internationalisation of the ship, its forms of discipline, and dual wage structures also result in less worker cohesion aboard ships compared to landside workers. Seafarers' weakening ability to strike is reflected in the statistics of the Strike Club, a marine delay insurance club established in 1957 to insure against maritime strikes; it has since expanded to cover other kinds of delays, such as those created by port closures and accidents onboard or on shore. Strike Club statistics for 2015 to 2016 show no shipboard strikes while recording strikes by stevedores, other port workers, land-transport operators, and others.[46]

I want to tell a final story about one such strike in the era of internationalisation. The *MV Saudi Independence* was an East German ship built sometime in the 1950s.[47] In the late 1970s, it and two sister ships were acquired from East Germany by a Saudi shipping firm based in Jeddah, Orri Navigation Lines International, which operated a number of tankers, bulk freighters, and bunkering barges and offered stevedoring and other portside services. The ship had departed from Jeddah and had arrived in Piraeus, Greece, via the Suez Canal. From there it had steamed to Antwerp and Bremen. The owners demanded such deep cost-cutting from their captain that the vessel had become a hunger ship. A report by the Commission for Filipino Migrant Workers recounted that as the ship travelled from port to port, the

> shipowner always promised that the food supply would be replenished in the next port. But already after some weeks, the captain at that time was dismissed because of his efforts to improve the food situation on board the ship. His place was taken by a Filipino captain. Soon after he was sent back to the Philippines for the same reason. Later, during the second trip to Europe, the Filipino first mate was also dismissed after making a

> complaint over radio on the lack of food. Finally, the radio officer was also dismissed. The need became so great that the crew had to improvise making a fish net to try to catch fish and supplement their meagre rations of food with fish. At the same time, the shipowner very shamelessly sent a telegram ordering more savings and limitations on food supply. There was in fact no food supply.[48]

The Filipino crew members at last revolted and on 18 May 1981, as the ship arrived in the port of Rotterdam, went on strike. The crew complained to the inspector from the International Transport Workers' Federation and demanded that Orri Navigation Lines sign the ITF Collective Agreement. Orri, in turn, brought a suit in the District Court of Rotterdam to force the sailors to terminate their strike and for ITF to cease representing them. The Rotterdam District Court and subsequently the Court of Appeals both ruled in favour of the owner. When ITF and the strikers ultimately took the case to the Court of Cassation, it dismissed the appeal. The grounds for the dismissal was that because the ship had hired these Filipino crew members, then the rule applicable to them was Philippines law, and as the latter prohibits strikes 'in vital industries such as public utilities, including transportation', the crew members had to return to work.[49]

None of the worthy-sounding legal accounts of the case tell us what happened to the workers aboard the hunger ship. This silence is symptomatic: the bodies whose hunger earned profit for the shipowners and upon whose backs the law was made are erased out of the history entirely. The ships were scrapped in 1984.[50] Orri Lines still thrives and has offices in a great many international ports.

8

The Bounties of War

> The great empires of Europe, through their colonies and spheres of influence, spread authority, order, and respect for the obligation of contract almost everywhere; and where their writs did not run, their frigates and gunboats navigated. Methods were rough, division of benefits was unfair, and freedom was not rated high among the priorities; but people, goods, and ideas moved around the world with less restraint than ever before and, perhaps, ever again.
>
> Dean Acheson, *Present at the Creation*

Routes of War; Wars of Routes

Months before the tripartite invasion of the Suez Canal in 1956, the British Foreign Office commissioned a report from British Petroleum and Shell, presumably drafted in preparation for war, on the shipping of oil from the Middle East.[1] Among other things, the government wanted to know whether the canal's capacity could keep up with the meteoric increases in oil production by the British oil companies in the Arabian Peninsula. The report indicated that it could not. How this knowledge may have influenced British policy is not clear. A few months later, British, French, and Israeli forces invaded Sinai and took control of the Suez Canal. It is safe to say that the British government had not anticipated the secondary effects of its invasion of Egypt on global shipping. The invasion led to the closure of the canal between November 1956 and

May 1957 and dramatically influenced relations of trade, forthwith and forever.

In the immediate aftermath of the invasion, Syria and Lebanon banned any British or French ships loading at their ports; loading at Haifa was considered far too dangerous; the closure of the Suez Canal left ships stranded in the Great Bitter Lake. Ships carrying oil from the Middle East now had to round the Cape of Good Hope, and South African ports saw a huge rise in ships arriving there. Imports of beef from Rhodesia into Cape Town surged with the need to feed the multitudes of sailors arriving there.[2] Maritime freight rates worldwide spiked, with Gulf of Mexico–Rotterdam rates increasing from US$14 per tonne to US$18 and doubling on the Gulf of Mexico–India route, from US$19 to US$38.[3] Everyday patterns of life in Europe changed, with one *New York Times* headline lamenting the shift in British tea habits as ships steaming from India now had to go further distances, resulting in higher tea-leaf prices.[4] The fuel shortage in Britain brought factory closures and layoffs, sharply increasing emigration to New Zealand, Australia, and Canada.[5] The US slapped Britain and France on the wrist for the invasion, denying Britain a much-needed IMF loan. But it also brought ships out of mothballs to transport coal and petroleum to Europe and specifically to the UK (the closure of the canal had led to a shortage of dry cargo carriers for coal transport).[6] Kuwait Oil Transport Company was founded in April 1957 to provide an alternative to BP Shipping, which had become the object of hostile public scrutiny in the Arab world.[7] The canal closure saw an intensified interest in pipeline construction. European states began exploring the possibility of oil extraction from West and North Africa. The urgent need for more efficient cargo transport accelerated the containerisation process that had begun in the early 1950s.

Early 1957 saw a striking increase in the construction of VLCCs capable of rounding the Cape of Good Hope at greater economies of scale. The long route around Africa also avoided the nationalist government of Egypt, perhaps even deliberately punishing it for its gumption in nationalising.[8] Only weeks after the re-opening of the Canal and the ignominious withdrawal of the tripartite powers, British and other European ports were preparing for these larger ships.[9] The re-opening also gave a new alibi to the British naval presence in the Arab world, and the Royal Navy shifted its main Middle Eastern naval base from Cyprus to Aden.[10]

A decade later, on 5 June 1967, Israeli warplanes assaulted Egyptian airfields. Nasser closed the Suez Canal to all traffic on 6 June. The *New York Times* immediately published an assessment of the effects of the closure on shipping:

> For a ship traveling from the Persian Gulf, where many of the Arabian oil ports are, to Britain and Western Europe, the voyage around the southern tip of Africa will take 16 days longer, add 4,800 miles of travel and increase the overall cost of the voyage by as much as $20,000 [approximately equivalent to $143,000 in 2017].[11]

The *Times* estimated that, of the fifty ships passing through the canal in 1966, half had been oil tankers. Italy and France were most directly affected (as 60 and 39 per cent of their oil, respectively, came through Suez), while 'Britain, which depended on Canal shipping for 60 per cent of her oil 10 years ago, now has cut that total to 25 per cent, primarily because of new African sources of petroleum'.[12] By the end of July, the cost of purchasing tankers had already increased, and the shipping rates had doubled for some tankers carrying oil, with the 'Persian Gulf-to-Britain run . . . most severely affected'; further increases in rates were being forecast for the autumn.[13] In that same period, Iranian oil began to find East Asian customers, particularly in Japan, whose economy was rapidly taking off.[14] Those North African fields – especially in Libya – whose opening had been accelerated after 1956 provided necessary petroleum for Europe. The Soviet Union also took up some of the slack on shipments to Europe. The growth in ship sizes which had begun in 1956 accelerated, but in 1967, the freight market had an overcapacity that it had not had in 1956. Therefore, after an initial spike in freight rates after the war began, the prices on routes returned to pre-war levels.[15] In one case, the freight rates for the Ras Tanura–Rotterdam routes was 10 per cent below pre-war levels.[16]

The 1967 closure of the Suez Canal resulted in a loss of markets for the Indian and Pakistani economies, which depended on export shipments to Europe through Suez, but was a boon for South Africa.[17] Innovative oil-swapping models were invented to accommodate the route closures over the long term. For example, USSR provided oil to Kuwait's and Abu Dhabi's customers in Western Europe, while the two Arab emirates supplied equivalent amounts of oil to the USSR's customers in East Asia, in lieu of Soviet oil transport via the canal.[18] In response to the supposed oil boycott against Western countries, including the Netherlands, the port of Rotterdam encouraged and subsidised the construction of refineries, bulk liquid and petrochemical terminals, and other downstream port infrastructures. Today, the largest global shipments through and from the port of Rotterdam are petroleum products. All this after the fearmongering about the precipitous drop in petroleum exports to Europe, especially after the oil-boycott rhetoric after 1973.[19] It is noteworthy that the nationally owned Kuwait Petroleum Corporation upgraded its refinery and petroleum-transport infrastructure in Rotterdam despite the supposed boycott.[20]

Where the war proved most catastrophic, however, was its bookending of the era of decolonisation, especially in the Arab world. Writing in July 1969, the imperial apostle Bernard Lewis recast the anticolonial movements of that time as trifling pawns in the great Cold War chessboard:

> In May 1967, the prospects for a southward expansion of Soviet influence seemed excellent ... With the Suez Canal and Aden at its disposal, the Soviet Navy would soon have established supremacy in the Red Sea, and the regimes on both shores would have been due for realignment or replacement. The way was open to further penetration in southern and eastern Arabia, and especially in the Gulf, where Iraq was already in the revolutionary camp and Iran could be isolated and threatened at its weakest point. *All this was stopped by the June war.*[21]

For Lewis, 1967 marked the pivotal moment during which the counterrevolutionary and reactionary forces that so often served (and were protected by) the imperial powers got the upper hand. The ascendance of those conservative forces meant that despite the bombastic speeches about an oil boycott, the *New York Times* observed in December 1973 that 'the tanker loading at Arab terminals and arrivals at some European ports have never been higher'. The *Times* drily noted that 'the feeling of crisis may also reflect some exaggeration by companies looking for higher price levels' and that Lloyds had reported *increases* in tonnage exported from Ras Tanura in Saudi Arabia, Jabal Dhanna in Abu Dhabi, Mina Ahmadi in Kuwait, Khor al-Amaya in Iraq, and Bandar Mahshahr in Iran.[22] It took eight years, the War of Attrition, and the 1973 War, plus an intensive dredging operation, before Suez was reopened on 5 June 1975. By then, the Arab world had irrevocably changed, and regional geopolitical power had shifted from Cairo to the Arabian Peninsula.

The Utility of Regional Wars for the Peninsula

The regional wars that followed the 1967 war did not have the same dramatic effects on shipping routes as the closures of the Suez Canal, but nevertheless they profited maritime commerce in the Arabian Peninsula.

When, during the 1973 war, Israeli aircrafts and warships struck the Mediterranean ports of Latakia and Tartus in Syria, they effected a transformation in the geography of shipping in the region. Israeli bombing targeted all infrastructure in the ports, including fuel and petroleum installations and transportation facilities. The damages were reported to be as high as $386 million; one analyst claimed that 'it will doubtless take years for Syria to regain its level of economic growth'.[23] Ships were diverted from the two destroyed Syrian ports – as well as the port of Aqaba in Jordan – to unload their goods at the port of Shuwaikh in Kuwait for transhipment by trucks to Jordan, Syria, and Iraq. Kuwaiti newspapers reported that all berths at Shuwaikh were in constant use and Kuwaiti merchants were complaining about a warehousing shortage at the port.[24]

The 1973 war's effects on regional ports was a harbinger of what was to come with the Lebanese civil war of 1975 to 1991. This war's constantly shifting alliances (both internal and external); the syncopated rhythm of its violence which moved across the country at different rates and times; its unpredictable fits and starts; and the accumulating uncertainty around how it might end gave the war a different quality than past bursts of violence in the country. Once the Beirut docks were burnt down by the Phalange militia in 1975, each warlord set up his own port along the coast. A *New York Times* reporter described the fifteen or so private ports as 'a row of stone piers built out into the sea with cranes mounted on the ends ... Freighters steam in all day, unloading containers of smuggled goods in full view of the coastal highway'.[25] But businesses were more skittish about staying in Beirut. Bechtel, then the 'largest foreign employer in Lebanon', dispersed its Beirut staff to Saudi Arabia, Kuwait, and Jordan.[26] By 1977, most major international firms had moved their headquarters to Dubai and Sharjah. Shipping shifted to Syrian, Greek, and Cypriot ports as well as Peninsula ports.[27]

Kuwait, Dubai, Sharjah, and Bahrain were major beneficiaries of the banking and insurance sectors deserting Beirut. In

1975, Bahrain passed regulations that transformed the island into an offshore banking centre, serving interests outside the island and in particular filling gaps that the Saudi banking sector could not. Kuwait banks began to serve Saudi Arabian and Iraqi investors who were turning away from Beirut, and in 1979, Kuwait and Iraq signed a haulage agreement for transhipment of goods to Iraq through the port of Shuwaikh, financed by these new investors.[28] Dubai, whose history of entrepôt trade was well-suited to merchant banking, took on that mantle in the Gulf, and by 1978 hosted 55 banks with 350 branches.[29] Sharjah was also trying to compete with Kuwait and Dubai and attract capital and banks from Kuwait and Saudi Arabia who no longer could route their businesses through Beirut (by 1978, seventy-nine US and European banks had applied to set up branches in Sharjah).[30] The massive rerouting of petrodollars from Beirut to the Gulf resulted in a frenzy of construction and consumption, with the attendant exponential increase in imports, which further heated the economies of the port cities. Port congestion all around the Peninsula led to plans for construction of new berths or wholly new ports.

In addition to workable and well-appointed harbours, the availability of finance and insurance and good telecommunications and road infrastructures were also necessary for the dizzying growth of the port cities of the Gulf. The period between 1975 and the start of the Iran–Iraq war saw a surge in new port construction, with Mina Salman and ASRY drydock inaugurated in Bahrain, the ports of Shuwaikh and Shuʿaiba expanding in Kuwait, and Port Rashid's new berths becoming operational. The congestion at many of the larger ports in the region – including at Basra, Jeddah, and southern Iranian ports – were relieved by the Gulf ports picking up the slack.[31] Maritime transport in the Gulf flourished.

Tankers, Wars, and Tanker Wars

> The sea has been entirely packed with stray shells. It is changing its marine nature and turning into metal.
>
> Mahmoud Darwish, *Memory for Forgetfulness*

The process of nationalisation of oil companies and the eventual cartelisation of OPEC led to the entry of the oil-producing states into not only production but transport. A sales manager for a Belfast shipping company complained that after touring Saudi Arabia, Kuwait, Abu Dhabi, and Iraq, the country's oil technocrats had indicated that 'instead of large tankers, the Arabs would want smaller vessels to carry refined petroleum products, such as kerosene and gasoline'.[32] By entering the downstream business, the producers were trying to capture some of the added value from which European and North American oil companies profited. The oil producers also founded their own shipping companies, which placed large orders with East Asian shipyards for new VLCC and ULCCs.[33] The seas surrounding the Peninsula, especially in the Gulf, were thick with tankers in the 1970s. The Iran–Iraq War changed this.

The heady 1970s were followed by a gloomy early 1980s. While most ports on the Peninsula suffered from a recession in the early 1980s, Port Rashid and Jabal Ali in Dubai, Sharjah's Khor Fakkan, and Fujairah grew.[34] Dubai, which had always had strong bonds of trade with Iran, quickly became the country's entrepôt; its trade with Iran immediately grew by 40 per cent.[35] Fujairah's position on the Gulf of Oman and beyond the strait of Hormuz meant that at the height of the Tanker Wars (about which more below) it acted as a major bunkering and petroleum-loading terminal, far less affected by the tit-for-tat tanker bombings of Iran and Iraq in the Gulf. With Dubai as Iran's port of trade, Kuwait served as Iraq's cargo transhipment port, especially for arms and ammunition.[36] Aqaba in Jordan,

Shuwaikh in Kuwait, and Dammam in Saudi all received cargoes for Iraq. Dammam even reserved quays specifically for Iraqi cargo.

In the first four years of the war, shippers from other nations became hesitant about travelling to Iraqi or Iranian Gulf ports because of the staggering increase in insurance rates for ships in the war zone.[37] Iraq rerouted much of its oil exports through pipelines terminating on the Red Sea terminals of Yanbu or on the Mediterranean coast of Turkey, but Iran still exported the vast majority of its petroleum by sea, loaded at terminals in the Gulf.[38] In 1984, the war between Iran and Iraq had reached a stalemate on the battlefield. France delivered five Super Étendard planes and an armoury of Exocet missiles to Iraq, which it could then use to bolster its weakened position on the sea. In the first six months of that year, the Iraqi air force attacked ships loading at Iran's Kharg Terminal twenty-four times, with many of the incapacitated tankers belonging to foreign shippers. The Iranian regime, which had regularly blamed Kuwait for its logistical, financial, and military support for Iraq, began attacking Kuwaiti tankers. The first such attack occurred on 13 May 1984 against *Umm Casbah*, which was carrying Kuwaiti oil to the United Kingdom. By the end of 1984, Iraq and Iran had attacked fifty-eight and nineteen tankers, respectively.[39] The response to these attacks was an increase in insurance and freight rates for tanker transport throughout the whole of the Gulf (though oil prices actually fell from US$36 per barrel in 1981 to US$17 in mid-1987).[40] Iran was disproportionately the target of international opprobrium.

The reciprocal attacks accelerated in early 1985 and were at their most intense in 1986, with Iranian focus shifting heavily and noticeably to Kuwaiti tankers by the end of the year. In late 1986, Kuwait approached China, France, the US, and the Soviet Union asking to reflag Kuwait tankers. As soon as the Soviet Union indicated that it would lease three of its tankers to Kuwait, the US announced in March 1987 that it was reflagging

Kuwaiti tankers. In the end, ten Kuwait crude vessels and four LPG carriers were reflagged and renamed by the US.[41] In addition, to avoid attacks by the combatant navies, convoys of commercial and naval vessels began to form to steam through the Gulf. The convoys themselves, however, fell victim to mines, and the commander of the US Navy Middle East Task Force had to admit that the US Central Command had not 'seriously considered mines in planning Gulf operations'.[42] By 1988, the Gulf bristled with eighty-two Western and twenty-three Soviet naval vessels, including combat ships and minesweepers.[43] Given how little they disrupted assaults on tankers by mines or missiles, the warships seemed to be protecting the abstraction of shipping routes rather than the ships themselves. When the war ended in 1988, Iran and Iraq had attacked ships 411 times in total, with Iraq responsible for 60 per cent of the attacks. Sixty per cent of the ships had been tankers.[44]

The primary effect of the Tanker Wars was the securitisation of the flow of oil and the militarisation of shipping routes.[45] Fascinatingly, another effect had been the justification of the US naval sovereignty overseas, even in defiance of the country's own legal corpus. As a US military lawyer, Michael Snipes, pointed out, reflagging the Kuwaiti tankers went against two different legal determinations. The first precedent Snipes invoked was the *Benito Estenger* case.[46] In that case, in 1898, a Spanish shipowner who lived in Cuba had transferred the registration of his ship to a British owner and flown the British flag, 'but with Spanish officers and crew, and her former owner on board as supercargo', in order to protect his ship from US seizure during the Spanish–American War.[47] The US had nevertheless seized the ship. When the shipowner petitioned the court for the release of the ship, the US Supreme Court ruled that reflagging in times of war was not *bona fide* and that the US could seize the ship as a war prize. On the basis of the Prize cases, Snipes wrote that 'belligerent parties have the right to capture the ships and goods of each other on the high seas'.[48]

Thus the US had no legal basis to interfere with Iranian attacks on Kuwaiti tankers, because Kuwait had by its action become party to war. Further, Snipes argued that because the crew members of reflagged tankers were Filipinos and the officers were Europeans or Kuwaitis, the US was breaking US laws forbidding flags of convenience.[49] On this Snipes was on shakier ground: US law only forbade flags of convenience on coastal trade; a 1963 court case had in fact effectively moved flagging to open registries from a grey area to firmer legal ground. But perhaps more importantly, these precedents did not matter one way or the other: the law is malleable in the service of power, and in reflagging Kuwaiti ships, no matter how many US laws and legal precedents were violated, US sovereign power was extended overseas.

Desert Storm and After

The political and maritime landscape emerging from the Iran–Iraq war was the setting for the Desert Shield/Desert Storm operations. The Iraqi regime invaded Kuwait in 1990 as a way to cancel its debts to Kuwait and open an access route to the Gulf's open seas from its main port in Basra. In the immediate aftermath of the Iraqi invasion, Jabal Ali was once again the greatest beneficiary of the war. Kuwaiti businesses fleeing the invasion set up shop in the Jabal Ali Free Zone, while Dubai Ports World rented 750,000 square metres of office space and warehouses to Kuwait Petroleum Corporation and acted as a warehouse for goods meant for KPC's port at Shuʿaiba.[50] For the US, Desert Shield/Desert Storm were an occasion to flaunt the 'New World Order' under its hegemony as well as, more mundanely, to exercise its military's logistical reach and prowess across the world. The 'powerlift' – the massive haulage of goods, personnel and materiel required for the rapid ramp-up of forces in the Gulf – became a dress rehearsal for future deployments of US forces to far regions. The global hegemon had to make an expeditious show of force across the seas. The powerlift allowed it to do so.

In the ramp-up of forces in 1990, US military and chartered civilian aircrafts transported personnel or smaller and more compact items to the battlefields' staging areas. Tanks, wheeled vehicles, heavy armaments, and other bulky goods were transported aboard ships from ports around the world. Hundreds of ships left sixteen US ports and fifteen foreign ports (especially Rotterdam) and hauled millions of tonnes of cargo to the countries of the Gulf.[51] The US Merchant Marine fleet was requisitioned first, but the US Transportation Command also chartered a large number of foreign-flagged ships (from the Danish shipping giant Maersk, among others), for the delivery of the materiel.[52] The ports of Dammam and Jubail became the staging ground for US forces. Doha, Dubai, Fujairah, and ports in Oman turned into maritime nodes for logistics, fuelling, and victualling. Local shipping agencies, like Kanoo in Bahrain, served the US Navy in handling military materiel and securing marine insurance.[53]

The newly constructed port at Jubail proved handy when Dammam and Dhahran's port and airfield were quickly overwhelmed. Prince (later King) Abdullah of Saudi Arabia boasted to a researcher about migrant workers' labour camps in Jubail housing 60,000 to 70,000 US and Saudi forces at the peak of preparation for war, noting that the US 'had lawyers, real estate specialists, accountants . . . ready to work with us on all aspects of their temporary tenancy'.[54] The Saudi director of international security for Jubail marvelled that the US military logistics expert arriving in Jubail

> knew exactly where everything was and where he was to go. In fact, he had maps of the area which were much more detailed than anything we had, down to the last pipeline, storage tank, road, and building – even in areas that we are not privy to, such as the Naval Base.[55]

Although the US was eager to continue its presence on Saudi soil after Desert Storm, the Al-Khobar bombings of 1996 reduced overt US presence there; as I shall recount below, however, the US expanded its bases and especially its naval presence in the region. With the advent of the War on Terror, the logistical pieces at the ports in Kuwait, Bahrain, Qatar, the UAE, and Oman – as well as further afield in the Indian Ocean and Horn of Africa – were in place and ready to be used for supplying the wars in Afghanistan and Iraq. More than any other war, fighting the forever war on its multiple and multiplying battlefields depended on the US ability to marshal access to maritime transport infrastructures in the Middle East, the Indian Ocean, and beyond.

The Importance of Bases

Naval bases often have intimate relations with nearby ports. Rivalries over access to certain bodies of waters may be over either commercial or strategic advantage. As I write, regional powers, Qatar and Turkey on one side and the UAE and Saudi Arabia on the other are competing for access to commercial ports in the Red Sea. In their strategic calculations, Berbera, Somaliland and Bosaso, Puntland (Somalia); Assab, Eritrea; and Suakin, Sudan, are not only commercial ports but strategic outposts and possible sites of current or future naval bases. The UAE alone has military bases in Assab, Mogadishu, and Berbera, Somalia. Djibouti hosts military bases of China, France, and Japan and the largest US military base in Africa.[56] The EU, NATO, and Ethiopia also have presences there. Saudi Arabia plans to build a base there. Its Doraleh port is also hotly contested between Dubai and China. Yemen's war-worn ports are claimed by regional powers patronising local forces, even as the war goes on.

The base competition in the Red Sea and Horn of Africa echoes the European competition over footholds in the Gulf a century ago. Long before this flurry of transport and naval infrastructure construction, the theoretician of American maritime imperialism Alfred T. Mahan had argued that naval fleets in the Persian Gulf, 'based upon a strong military port' could 'flank all the routes to the farther East, to India, and to Australia, the last two actually internal to the Empire'.[57] Such a force need not have a permanent presence, since navies have 'the quality of mobility which carries with it the privilege of temporary absences; but it needs to find on every scene of operation established bases of refit, of supply, and, in case of disaster, of security'.[58] The British established many such bases on the Peninsula: in Aden, Sharjah, Bahrain, Oman, and elsewhere. These bases, as with subsequent US bases, were often welcomed by the local potentates. In 1966, on the eve of the decolonisation of Aden, the British government issued a white paper on withdrawing its military forces from East of Suez. Reflecting on this impending withdrawal, Michael Howard wrote in the official organ of Chatham House,

> The oil-rich feudal enclaves which remain around the Persian Gulf may still consider British protection to be a lesser evil than the social revolution threatened by their 'progressive' neighbours, but one need be neither a liberal nor a Marxist to regard these as embarrassing, if inescapable, liabilities rather than Imperial assets.[59]

But protecting needy local rulers and acting as a sentinel on the trade routes around the Arabian Peninsula were not the only reasons for setting up bases east of Suez. Cold War rivalries – much of which were the product of the fevered imaginations of monomaniacal security experts on both sides – also spurred US strategic planners' base-building. After the eviction of Britain from Aden, the new Aden government granted Soviet naval vessels access to port facilities there, though it rejected a more formal basing arrangement.[60] In the 1970s, the Soviet Union began shipping oil to the Aden refinery for production of fuel for its naval vessels in the Indian Ocean.[61] Starting in 1968, 'a Soviet fleet made an unprecedented tour of the Indian Ocean and Persian Gulf, visiting Aden, Basra, and other ports'.[62] The alarm at the simultaneous withdrawal of Britain from and the presence of the Soviet Union in the Indian Ocean gave the US the pretext for setting up bases there. In the 1970s, Britain leased the island of Diego Garcia, in the Chagos Archipelago, to the US who wanted the islands 'swept' and 'sanitised' of all humans. The deportation of all residents was intended to free the naval base of any local pressures.[63] All the inhabitants of the island were evicted, and the most significant US pre-positioning base in the Indian Ocean region was established there. The Cold War competition over bases led to paranoia and pedantry on the part of the US military planners. In a document titled 'Soviet Global Military Reach', for example, the CIA director quantified Soviet naval visits to friendly ports: Syria hosted 122 such port visits, South Yemen 74, Tunisia 18, and Libya 14 port visits each.[64] Aden was a particular worry to the US military and intelligence planners because it hosted Soviet naval intelligence and communication facilities (though no bases).

The clients of the superpowers around the Indian Ocean also contested access to Red Sea ports. When in 1977 Somalia invaded Ethiopia, regional powers ranged on opposite sides, with US allies, Saudi, Egypt, and Sudan standing behind Somalia. Soviet Union and Cuba sent forces to support Ethiopia. As a result of the re-arrangement of forces in the Horn of Africa, and with the Shah of Iran's financial and military aid to Somalia (via Oman, where the Shah's regime was also aiding Sultan Qabus's counterinsurgency), the Soviet navy was evicted from Berbera in 1978.[65]

The 1979 overthrow of the closest US ally and client in the Gulf, the Shah of Iran, was pivotal for the future of US military and naval posture in the region. Until this moment, the US had primarily depended on client regimes to act as regional gendarmes on its behalf (Israel in the Mediterranean and Iran in the Gulf) and had used arms sales as a means of accessing bases in Saudi Arabia, Oman, Turkey, Morocco, and Somalia.[66] In response to the revolutionary transformation of Iran, and just before the Soviet invasion of Afghanistan, President Jimmy Carter devised a new Persian Gulf security framework, the Carter Doctrine, on 23 January 1980:

> An attempt by any outside force to gain control of the Persian Gulf region will be regarded as an assault on the vital interests of the United States of America, and such an assault will be repelled by any means necessary, including military force.[67]

The framework emphasised a need to improve ties with the Gulf states and Saudi as well as with Pakistan and Turkey, and to strengthen relations with Somalia and Djibouti. It also called for Saudi Arabia and other Gulf states to finance 'regional security needs' – presumably of the US. In other words, the aim was to form a united front against revolutionary Iran and get the local clients to pay for it. Militarily, the framework required an increase in US overflight rights in the region, an expansion in US military presence and regular exercises, expansion of strategic air- and sealift and access to bases, 'overbuilding of regional facilities', and prepositioning bases throughout the region and in the Indian Ocean.[68] A task force established in 1980 formed the kernel of the US Central Command (CENTCOM), whose official founding was announced in March 1983.

Among these Arab states in the Gulf, Bahrain and Oman had long offered the US access to regional waters and ports. In Bahrain, the US had taken over the Jufair naval base from the British in 1971. Oman was the only state in the region to sign a formal basing agreement with the US during this period; the US quickly went to work building bases on the island of Masirah in the Indian Ocean, and at Khasab on the Musandam Peninsula, which juts into the Strait of Hormuz. The US also secured pre-positioning and staging areas and hospital-ship arrangements in most of the Gulf states, as well as at Berbera; Mombasa, Kenya; and several locations in Morocco.[69] Diego Garcia's importance in this period only increased, with eighteen prepositioning ships anchored there.[70] In CENTCOM's early years, the US encouraged Saudi Arabia to upgrade its naval facilities at Ras al-Mish'ab, Jubail, and Jeddah and its civilian ports in the latter two cities.[71] The military construction programme directed by the US Army Corps of Engineers offered 'a visible indicator' of US resolve to protect its regional clients.[72] Conveniently, it was also a conduit for the diffusion of US business expertise and a source of lavish income, as President Reagan began privatising many Pentagon functions.[73]

The operations to protect hydrocarbon shipping during the Tanker Wars were one of the earliest arenas for CENTCOM flexing its muscles in the region, however ineptly. The Iraqi invasion of Kuwait and the subsequent Desert Shield and Desert Storm operations were heaven-sent occasions for the Command to consolidate its hold in the Peninsula. After 1991, the US signed a number of bilateral military agreements with states in the region and opened major bases in Kuwait, Oman, and Qatar. CENTCOM's regional headquarters was located in Qatar and the US Fifth Fleet and CENTCOM naval headquarters were in Manama.[74] Assessments of the US logistical effort in Desert Storm and Desert Shield showed that the most inefficient element of warfighting there had been 'unloading capacities at the ports and movement beyond the ports'.[75] The 1990s saw a flurry of civilian-port construction and expansion and bolstering of hinterland transport facilities, which allowed commercial and military interests to converge.

Today, after the War on Terror exponentially expanded the US presence in the Middle East, Indian Ocean, and Africa, the US Navy owns and leases land at Jabal Ali for warehousing and logistics and leases land at Fujairah for refuelling and prepositioning.[76] It also owns land in Kuwait and Oman and extensively in Bahrain (in Manama, at Jufair, at the Mina Salman pier area, and at Shaikh Isa).[77] Camp Lemonnier in Djibouti and Diego Garcia in the Indian Ocean are important not only to CENTCOM but also to the newly established US Africa Command.[78] Jabal Ali is the US Navy's busiest port of call, receiving up to 200 warship visits per year.[79] The very characteristics that make Jabal Ali a logistical dream – its securitised perimeters, its proximity to the Maktoum Airport, its massive warehouse complex – also make it the perfect staging ground for transporting goods from and to Afghanistan.[80]

Public unrest and mobilisation against US bases in places such as Bahrain and Saudi Arabia have led to both states and the CENTCOM itself looking for ways to make the bases less visible.[81] One way to do so is to move military facilities into the bellies of gigantic ports like Jabal Ali or tucked away covertly in far harbours. Another is to move offshore. CENTCOM officials have described this new posture as becoming 'more maritime', with 'a tailored, lighter footprint supported by access to infrastructure that enables rapid reinforcement'.[82] Stripped of its managerial-military jargon, this means that US forces are hidden offshore aboard warships with their Automatic Identification System [AIS] turned off. But they can swiftly arrive onshore at the Peninsula's many ports at the invitation of their loyal regional clients. US protection of regional powers has shielded the Peninsula monarchies not only from external invasion but, more importantly, from local demands for democracy.[83]

The Riches of Military Construction and Logistics

In places like Saudi Arabia, the major infrastructure projects that put in place oceangoing harbours, oil terminals, railways, pipelines, and the like were interdependent with military ventures that built bases, roads, telecommunications facilities, and military or naval transport installations. Aramco and the US Army Corps of Engineers, and the contractors who served them – Bechtel, Fleur, Parsons, and others – shared knowledge, intelligence about the locale, and vital equipment. Bechtel regularly briefed the CIA on what went on in Saudi Arabia; in return, the CIA passed the company information it needed for securing contracts.[84] Petroleum Development Oman's operations were sometimes indistinguishable from the operations of the Trucial Oman Scouts, since so many of the officers of both organisations had served both the British colonial venture in the Arab world and the oil industry there.[85] Among the private firms that have benefitted most from the regular wars the US fights in the Middle East have been logistics companies based both in the US and the region.

US Army's Logistics Civil Augmentation Program contracts are legendary in the bounties they distribute among already rich US-based companies with Pentagon connections.[86] These multi-year, multi-sited, multi-billion-dollar contracts weave together the US military logistics and transport agencies and businesses whose managerial ranks are filled with former military officers. However, profiting from the seemingly unlimited outlays of the US military – so careless in its distribution of money, so generous in its rewarding of feckless swindlers – is not limited to US companies. Many a local firm in the Peninsula and the larger Arab world has gone from the shadowlands of obscurity to the sunny uplands of fame and fortune by hocking overpriced contracts to the US. These companies, in turn, hired many subcontractors, spreading the largesse among the local recruitment agencies, construction firms, fuel transport and trading companies, and any number of smaller businesses. But the most lavishly rewarded beneficiaries have been the largest firms with the good fortune to be located in Kuwait, where the US invasion of Iraq in 2003 and the drawdown in 2009 were staged. Among these companies was DHL, which until Desert Shield/Desert Storm had a monopoly contract for delivery of goods and materiel to the US forces overseas. In 1990 and 1991, it had been forced to compete against FedEx, but because of its long-standing presence in Kuwait in 2009, it was better positioned to take advantage of the drawdown contracts. Many other firms, not necessarily known for military work but specialising in logistics, similarly reaped ample recompense from US wars in the region.

Among the logistics and transportation firms most radically transformed because of the work they did for the US military during its 2003 war on Iraq was the company that secured the second-largest Pentagon windfall, Kuwait-based Agility. Its trajectory illustrates the inextricable ties of commerce and war embodied in logistics work. Agility was first established in 1979 as a state-owned firm named Public Warehousing Company, in the business of warehousing and delivery. When Kuwait privatised the firm in 1996, 25 per cent of its shares were bought by Abdulaziz Sultan's National Real Estate Corporation and the firm was placed under the management of Tarek Sultan, Abdulaziz's son. The Sultan family already owned the largest Kuwaiti retailer and was also a major shareholder in several financial businesses in Kuwait. Public Warehousing served the former and was financed by the latter. At that stage, Public Warehousing was also operating in the US Military's Camp Doha near Shuwaikh port, providing food to US soldiers based there. Taking advantage of its extant supply chain, access to both logistics and finance, and cross-ownership of food retail, the business sought a bigger share of US military logistics contracts in Kuwait.[87] From the late 1990s onwards, the company has frequently hired retired US military officers who worked in the US Army or Navy's logistics and supply commands to run its Defense and Government Services.[88] This strategy has proven fruitful.

While Agility's revenue had been US$154 million just before the US invasion of Iraq, in 2008 its annual revenue had shot up to US$6.3 *billion*. It had been so successful in cornering the market on provision of goods and logistical services to the US military that when in 2005 it looked for a US$500 million loan to underwrite a mergers and acquisition deal, the loan syndicate was oversubscribed and the loan amount bumped up by 10 per cent. The firms in the consortium that lent to the firm soon to be renamed Agility included Bank of America, Bank of Ireland, HSBC, BNP Paribas (of Brazil), and various Kuwaiti and Gulf banks. By 2010, Agility had received more than US$8 billion in contracts from the US military, second only to KBR Halliburton's US$39 billion.[89] Agility had also become the largest logistics firm in the Middle East and was operating in a number of Gulf ports, including Dammam and Jeddah. Most strikingly, in 2004, the Kuwaiti government had given it a twenty-five-year build-operate-transfer concession to run the state's entire customs business at all ports of entry.[90] Agility had served as a conduit for an old Kuwaiti merchant family to expand its reach beyond Kuwait itself and into the lucrative military and government services market.

Today, Agility operates in 120 nations. Its work draws on its Kuwaiti experiences: specialised work for chemical and gas industries, transportation management, and border control. Like many other logistics businesses operating in Africa and Asia, it has a logistics-security division that provides armed protection for land and maritime transport. Agility has relayed its logistical expertise, warehousing, and retail trade into the military-logistics business and back into civilian logistics.[91] Access to capital and, perhaps even more importantly, to powerful connections has been crucial for a Kuwait-based company to reach the same zeniths of rent-extraction as its US-based counterparts.

US military personnel have a long tradition of circulating between government and business. Just after the drawdown from Iraq, prodigious numbers of spies and soldiers set up consulting firms shilling their expertise in 'frontier contexts' to their former employers and others in governments and militaries.[92] The most shameless of these carpetbaggers is Erik Prince, the heir to an automotive-parts company, who transformed his inheritance and his military connections from his Navy SEAL days into successive private military companies. The first of these was the notorious Blackwater. At some stage while operating these firms of mercenaries, Prince was also a CIA agent, apparently running spy networks overseas.[93]

When in 2010 Blackwater's legal problems started mounting, the company was renamed (twice!) and sold on. Prince himself cleaned up millions and was invited to the UAE by Mohammed bin Zayed al-Nahyan, the crown prince of Abu Dhabi and the man in charge of the Emirate's security apparatuses. There he formed Reflex Responses, which immediately received a US$529 million contract to train South African and Colombian mercenaries to help 'with intelligence gathering, security, counterterrorism and suppression of any revolts' in the emirate. Thereafter, he acted as a UAE military envoy in forming – along with South African mercenaries – the Puntland Maritime Police Force, which policed maritime trade routes in the Gulf of Aden.[94] Providing anti-piracy security at sea, however, did not fulfil Prince's gargantuan ambitions.

Prince next moved from providing security for transport, to furnishing logistics as well as insurance and other services, in this case for Chinese mining and energy firms in East Africa. His vehicle was Frontier Services Group, founded in 2012. The firm is listed in Hong Kong (though Erik Prince continues to live in Abu Dhabi), and its main investors are a Hong Kong–based tycoon and the Citic Group, a Chinese state-owned investment company.[95] Prince has planned a multi-billion-dollar 'austere logistics' company involved in paramilitary and para-intelligence work in places where Chinese investments require armed protection. Eventually the firm intends to expand into trucking and maritime logistics.[96] Frontier Services Group is reported to have interests in Pakistan, where China is involved in the construction of the port of Gwadar, and in Democratic Republic of the Congo, Guinea, and South Sudan.[97] Prince has offered to become the viceroy of Afghanistan, prevent illegal fishing in

Mozambique, control Libyan borders using mercenaries, and militarily manage migrant movements across the Mediterranean.[98] The logic of military logistics is the kernel of all these imperial ventures.

It is something of a cliché that amateurs talk strategy while professionals do logistics. The fungibility of commercial and military transport – and especially maritime shipping – and commercial logistics' borrowings from the military are well-trodden terrains of study.[99] On battlefields around the world, when the fighting recedes, the material and places of war-making are expediently transformed into sites of logistics and commerce. Military airfields become airports; landing sites for warships become ports; the detention centre at Camp Bucca in Iraq becomes Basra Logistics City; and the bases at Subic Bay and Clark in the Philippines become air-sea hubs.[100] But just as easily as military bases become emporia of trade, they can be reconverted into military outposts.[101] Quartermasters of capital are so often indistinguishable from the masters of trade.

Epilogue

Unwarranted optimism is the magical ingredient in capital accumulation, no less in the business of commercial shipping and maritime transport: optimism about ever-expanding markets, forever-abundant cheap finance, algorithmic models that predict a sunny future and turn masses of shapeless data into clear marketing and business plans, integrative softwares that resolve all value-chain friction, cascading automations that sanitise ports and ships and other places and peoples. Reading the PR releases of shipping firms and the trade journals that serve the business, one gets a sense that all is well and all manner of things is well. Yet viewed through the prism of war and politics, maritime transport tells us a different story.

In the time that it took to write and revise this book, no more than eighteen months altogether, the face of maritime transportation in the Arabian Peninsula has changed. Many of the fast-growing ports with grandiose claims about their location in the world of commerce have slowed down – dropping dozens, sometimes scores, of places in global rankings. Plans for fantastical logistical and economic cities have proliferated even as they seem less feasible than ever. Despite President Trump unashamedly courting every two-bit tyrant and autocrat on the Arabian Peninsula, many – the sadistic and infantile crown prince of Saudi Arabia Muhammad bin Salman foremost among them – have turned to China for investment opportunities, trade agreements, and hydrocarbon deals. This, at the very moment when the Chinese economy seems to be slowing down or at least transforming in complex ways, not least because of the possibilities of looming trade wars. At the same time, China seems to be consolidating its hold over ports in the Indian Ocean, acquiring some as debt repayment and others in deals with amenable political leaders. Wars waged by some Peninsula countries work to the detriment of their neighbours and enemies, but also of themselves: Abu Dhabi's spartan posture can and does hurt Jabal Ali, whose transhipment business to Qatar and Iran has abated with the increasing belligerence of Saudi Arabia and Abu Dhabi towards those two countries. In the Red Sea, from one month to the next, competition intensifies over access to deepwater ports and logistics hubs by the regional powers. Companies merge, split up, are devoured by competitors and rivals. Shipping alliances emerge and disintegrate.

But the more recent transformations also belie changes taking place more slowly. The trajectory of Yemeni ports is dramatically at odds with that of other ports in the Arabian Peninsula. Where Jabal Ali, Salalah, Hamad, and Dammam have arisen out of unspoilt coasts to become linchpins in regional and global networks of trade, the ports of Yemen, once thriving, had mixed fortunes in the post-colonial moment but have been catastrophically destroyed in the war waged on the country by Saudi Arabia and the UAE.

An unmistakable strategy of the Saudi-UAE coalition's bombing campaign has been the long-term hobbling of the Yemeni economy. The strategy has translated into total domination of navigable harbours and port structures by the coalition as future strategic bases for commercial and military control. The war has fragmented Yemen into areas controlled by coalition members, their clients, and other local actors. The UAE and its local allies (who have also been at loggerheads with their sponsor) hold the port of Aden as their prize, and have set up a new base in the island of Soqotra across the Gulf of Aden, which the British had found inhospitable as a coaling station nearly 200 years before. In December 2017 Saudi Arabia established a foothold on the coastal ports of the province of Mahra in eastern Yemen and on the border with Oman. The ports of Aden and Hodeidah lie in ruins, with the debris of their gantry cranes haunting the slowly decaying portside berths. Meanwhile, Saudi Arabia and the UAE have been diverting containerised cargo to Jeddah or to Jabal Ali. Even humanitarian cargo is routed to the port of Jizan in Saudi Arabia.[1] As UAE and Saudi Arabia also shift political positions, local alliances and enmities become murkier.[2]

In August 2018, it was reported that a Saudi-based marine construction company, Huta Marine, had been asked to tender a proposal for the construction of an oil-export terminal at the Yemeni port of Al Ghaydah on the Indian Ocean.[3] Al Ghaydah, which is also one of two landing sites for internet cables in Yemen, has a small fishing port, but the city proper sits back from the coast itself, on a river-wadi, blocked at the sea by a sand-bar. Huta Marine is based in Jeddah and has been involved in the construction of King Abdullah Port. Its managing director is a German engineer. The company's chairman and majority shareholder is Saleh bin Laden, one of the scions of the famous, powerful, and wealthy construction family (which, in 2017, had its wings clipped by Muhammad bin Salman).

Even if the trajectory of Al Ghaydah differs from the history of the more prosperous mechanised ports of the Gulf countries, its story is in other ways the story of ports in the global South. The infrastructure there will be built through the imperial ambitions of powerful states seeking conduits for extracting raw commodities and conveying them out to sea. The capital expended to build this infrastructure comes from another country, not Yemen itself, and any profits will be repatriated there. The managerial expertise for building the port will hail from Europe. The workers will likely be local labourers desperate for employment. The materials used to construct this port, the cement and sand and steel, will probably come from afar, plundering distant riverbeds or beaches or quarries.

The port will provide Saudi Arabia with another outlet for its oil, but all that passes through the port will be exported. The highly automated oil terminal will employ few people and will affect the local economy little. The oil terminal faces the Indian Ocean and its exports will be intended for destinations across the seas. The effects of such an economic expansion on Mahra will be the further incorporation of this distant and culturally autonomous province into Yemen proper. Local grandees who agree to such a deal will be bought off and enriched at the cost of the local population. The buyers of the oil, countries of East and Southeast Asia, will benefit from the extracted goods and may even one day intervene (through naval escorts or bases) to protect their interests.

Ports bind together cities across the seas to hinterland economies and social relations. They are conglomerations of people from near and far; in a place like eastern Yemen, which has a long history of transoceanic diasporas, many residents will have networks of trade or kinship or friendship both across the seas and in the mountains that so jaggedly flank the city. Whether a mechanised port modelled on extractive harbours of colonial times will benefit these social relations, solidify and enrich them, allow them to flourish and expand, remains to be seen. The concrete, steel, and stone structures that support shipping depend on laws, insurance, finance, engineering, and everyday practices of counting and accounting and accountability. But they also depend on the thickening of these social relations to survive. The port of Al Ghaydah may be a much later version of the oil terminals of the Gulf: made by oil companies, securitised, distant and automated, and demonic, just as Abdulrahman Munif describes them in *Cities of Salt*. But Al Ghaydah's fate depends not only on economic calculations in far cities across the ocean or on the politics of Mahra and Yemen and the Arabian Peninsula, but also on the people who will build the port, work on it, steam from it, and live and die there, in war and in peace.

Glossary and Abbreviations

AIOC – Anglo-Iranian Oil Company (previously Anglo-Persian Oil Company; later British Petroleum)
AIS – Automatic Identification System
able seaman – an experienced seafarer
APOC – Anglo-Persian Oil Company (later Anglo-Iranian Oil Company; later still, British Petroleum)
Aramco – Arab American Oil Company (originally CASOC; later Saudi Arabian Oil Company)
BAPCO – Bahrain Petroleum Company
ballast – weight carried by empty ships to keep them balanced
Baltic Dry Index – pricing index for bulk freight; based in London
beam – width of a ship at its widest point
bill of lading – ship's documentations acknowledging shipment and receipt of named cargoes
bulk good – solid or liquid goods not carried in containers; the five main dry bulk cargoes are coal, grain, bauxite, iron ore, and phosphate rock
bunker – ships' fuel (coal or petroleum)
cabotage – transportation of goods or cargo between two locations in one country by a carrier from another country
CASOC – California Arabian Standard Oil Company (later Aramco)
CENTCOM – US Central Command; a Department of Defense geographic area covering the Arab *Mashriq*, Egypt, Iran, Pakistan, Afghanistan, and Central Asia
chartering – when a shipowner leases out their ship to a charterer for a single trip or a contracted length of time
China Containerised Freight Index – an index of containerised freight rates
container – a standardised metal box (20, 40 or 45 feet long) used for transportation of cargo

continental shelf – the shallower part of submerged land flanking the coast
dhow – a generic name for a broad range of different ships used in the Indian Ocean and the Arabian Peninsula. Dhows were originally sailing boats, but are now motorised
draught – the vertical distance between the waterline and the bottom of the ship's hull
entrepôt shipping – shipping from a given point of origin to a final destination through a third port known as a transhipment or entrepôt port
exclusive economic zone – a marine zone designated by the United Nations Convention on the Law of the Sea as the area whose natural resources can be exploited by a specific neighbouring country
feeders – medium-sized freighters used to tranship good from a hub port to a different port
FEU – Forty-foot Equivalent Unit (a standardised container size)
flags of convenience – or 'open registries', a maritime registration mechanism in which a given country allows ships from other countries to register under its rules. Usually associated with laxer tax, labour, and environmental laws
forward contracts – a contract between a buyer and a seller to purchase a commodity at a predetermined price at a given future date
freeboard – the distance between the surface of the sea and lowest open deck
freight forwarders – a person or company that ships cargoes on behalf of other companies or persons
freight futures – a financial derivative that speculates on the future price of freights
freight options – a financial derivative in which a buyer has the right to buy or sell a freight rate at a specified price on a specified future date
gantry crane – a giant crane whose arm straddles container ships and moves the containers from atop
GCC – Gulf Cooperation Council (members: Bahrain, Kuwait, Oman, Qatar, Saudi Arabia, United Arab Emirates)
HARPEX – a freight index devised by ship brokers, Harper Petersen & Co
hawala – an informal system of money transfer used in the Middle East and South Asia

hubs – ports which by virtue of location or facilities become the central operating port for a given region or company
ITF – the OECD's International Transport Forum
ITF – International Transport-Workers' Federation
lascar – a seafarer of South Asian (and also Arab or East African or Chinese) origin
LNG – liquified natural gas
MARPOL – the International Convention for the Prevention of Pollution from Ships
Mashriq – the Arab East, or the Levant
master – ship's captain
Nakba – the Catastrophe; the expulsion of Palestinians from their country Palestine, which became Israel in 1948
nakhoda – a sea captain (in Arabic and Persian)
P&I Club – Protection and Indemnity Club; a marine mutual insurance company
P&O – Peninsular and Oriental Shipping Company
Port State Control – a regime of inspections whose inspectors investigate a visiting ship's compliance with international maritime conventions
Rapid Deployment Joint Task Force (RDJTF) – the predecessor to CENTCOM
reefers – refrigerated containers
rhumb lines – an imaginary line on a map which crosses all meridians at the same angle
ro/ro – roll-on/roll-off ships used for transportation of wheeled vehicles
sabkha – salt flats
seabed – the ocean floor
serang – the head of a crew of lascars; can also be a recruiter or boson
Shanghai Containerised Freight Index – an index of containerised freight rates
ship brokers – a representative of a ship's owner who works with charterers to arrange cargo or vessel charters
shipping agents – an agent responsible for handling of cargo on behalf of a shipping company
shipping derivatives – financial instruments that are based on speculation on freight prices (includes freight futures and freight options)

skiff – a small coastal boat; many skiffs are today motorised and very fast
SOLAS – the International Convention for the Safety of Life at Sea
spot pricing – current market price for a commodity
STCW – the International Convention on Standards of Training, Certification and Watchkeeping for Seafarers
TAPLine – Trans-Arabian Pipeline; Aramco's pipeline from Saudi Arabia to the Mediterranean coast
territorial waters – a twelve-nautical-mile belt of coastal waters extending from the baseline of a coastal state, as defined by the United Nations Convention on the Law of the Sea
TEU – Twenty-Foot Equivalent Unit (a standardised container size). Containers can also be forty or forty-five feet long and most are; but ship and port capacities are measured in TEUs
time charters – chartering a vessel for a specified time
tramp shipping – ships that operate on the spot market without a set schedule or route or destination
transhipments – the shipment of goods to an intermediate port and from there to another destination
ULCC – Ultra-Large Crude Carrier
UNCLOS – United Nations Convention on the Law of the Sea
UNCTAD – United Nations Conference on Trade and Development
VLCC – Very Large Crude Carrier
World Container Index – Drewry's containerised freight index

Bibliography

Media (Online and Print) and Trade Journals

8 Days (Singapore)
Aden (Yemen)
Akhbar Dubay (UAE)
Al Ahram (Egypt)
Al Araby al Jadid (UK)
Al Bayan (UAE)
Al Bayan magazine (Lebanon)
Al Hayat (London)
Al Ittihad (UAE)
Al Madina (Saudi Arabia)
Al Mustaqbal (Iraq)
Al Sharq al-Awsat (London)
Al Siyasa (Kuwait)
Al Thawra (Syria)
Arab News (UAE)
Asia Times (Hong Kong)
Bloomberg (USA)
Business Monitor Online (UK)
CorpWatch (USA)
Courthouse News Service (USA)
Defense News (USA)
Financial Times (UK)
Guardian (UK)
Gulf Mirror (UAE)
Gulf News (UAE)
ICIS Chemical Business (UK)
IHS Fairplay (UK)
Independent (UK)

International Railway Journal (USA)
Jane's (UK)
Journal of Commerce (USA)
Khaleej Time (UAE)
Loadstar (UK)
Marine Money International (USA)
Maritime Executive (USA)
Maritime Herald (Bulgaria)
Middle East Logistics (UAE)
Military Times (USA)
National (UAE)
New York Times (USA)
Port of Aden Annual (Yemen)
Railway Gazette (USA)
Reuters (UK)
South China Morning Post (China)
Wall Street Journal (USA)
Washington Post (USA)
World Maritime News (Netherlands)

Court Cases

'In the Matter of an Arbitration between Petroleum Development (Trucial Coast) Ltd. and the Sheikh of Abu Dhabi', *The International and Comparative Law Quarterly* 1(2): 247–61.

'Petroleum Development (Qatar) Ltd. v. Ruler of Qatar; Lord Radcliffe, Third Arbitrator; April 1950', *Cambridge Law Reports*: 161–4.

'Ruler of Qatar v. International Marine Oil Company, Ltd.; Arbitral Award of June 1953; Sir Alfred Bucknill (Referee)', *Cambridge Law Reports*: 534–47.

Published Sources

AbdulRahman, Abdullah. 2013. *Al-Imarat fi Dhakira Abna'uha: Al Hayat al-Iqtisadiyya* (*The Emirates in its Children's Memory: Economic Life*). Dar al-Kotob al-Wataniyya.

Abdo, Ass'ad S. 1986. 'The Ideal-Typical Sequence Model: Its Applicability to the Development of Transport in Saudi Arabia, the Sudan and other Middle Eastern Countries', *GeoJournal* 13(2): 173–81.

Abdo, Muhammad Fawzi. 1988. *The Urbanisation of Kuwait since 1950: Planning, Progress and Issues*. Unpublished doctoral dissertation, University of Durham.

Adi, Hakim. 2010. 'The Comintern and Black Workers in Britain and France 1919–37', *Immigrants & Minorities* 28(2–3): 224–45.

Ahmad, S. Maqbul. 1989. *Arabic Classical Accounts of India and China*. Indian Institute of Advanced Study.

Ahuja, Ravi. 2006. 'Mobility and Containment: The Voyages of South Asian Seamen, c.1900–1960', *International Review of Social History* 51: 111–41.

Ahuja, Ravi. 2012. 'Capital at Sea, Shaitan Below Decks? A Note on Global Narratives, Narrow Spaces, and the Limits of Experience', *History of the Present* 2(1): 78–85.

Akif, Syed Abu Ahmad. 2011. *Passionate Passages: Journeys to the Land of Desire. An Anthology of Four Classical Travelogues of the Hajj and the Hejaz (1786–1966 CE)*. Tahira and Kashfi Memorial Society.

Al-ʿAkri, ʿAbd al-Nabi. 2015. *Dhakira al-Watan wa al-Manfa* (*Memories of Home and Exile*). Dar Fardis.

Alawi, Amir Ahmad. 2009. *Journey to the Holy Land*. Translated and with an introduction by Mushirul Hasan and Rakhshanda Jalil. Oxford University Press.

Albaharna, Husain M. 1968. *The Legal Status of Arabian Gulf States: A Study of Their Treaty Relations and International Problems*. Manchester University Press.

Alexander, Lewis M (ed.). 1973. *The Law of the Sea: Needs and Interest of Developing Countries*. University of Rhode Island, Kingston.

Alizadeh, Amir and Nikos Nomikos. 2009. *Shipping Derivatives and Risk Management*. Palgrave Macmillan.

AlShehabi, Omar Hesham. 2014. 'Radical Transformations and Radical Contestations: Bahrain's Spatial-Demographic Revolution', *Middle East Critique* 23(1): 29–51.

AlShehabi, Omar Hesham and Saleh Suroor. 2016. 'Unpacking "Accumulation by Dispossession", "Fictitious Commodification", and "Fictitious Capital Formation": Tracing the Dynamics of Bahrain's Land Reclamation', *Antipode* 48(4): 835–56.

Amin, Sayed Hassan. 1986. *Marine Pollution in International and Middle Eastern Law*. Royston Limited.

Appel, Hannah. 2015. 'Offshore Work: Infrastructure and Hydrocarbon Capitalism in Equatorial Guinea' in Hannah Appel et al., (eds), *Subterranean Estates: Life Worlds of Oil and Gas*. Cornell University Press.

Asfour, M.M. 1963. 'The Ports and Trade of the Red Sea Basin'. Unpublished doctoral thesis, Durham University.

Aslanian, Sebouh, 2011. *From the Indian Ocean to the Mediterranean: The Global Trade Networks of Armenian Merchants from New Julfa*. University of California Press.

Al-Awwami, Sayyid Ali Baqir. 2011. *Al-Haraka al-Wataniyya al-Sa'udiyya 1953–1973* (*National Movement in Saudi Arabia 1953–1973*). Two volumes. Riyad al-Rayyis.

ARAMCO World. 1962. 'Giant of the Sea', 13(10): 3–6.

Balachandran, Gopalan. 2003. 'Circulation through Seafaring: Indian Seamen, 1890–1945' in Claude Markovits, Jacques Pouchepadass, Sanjay Subrahmanyam (eds), *Society and Circulation: Mobile People and Itinerant Cultures in South Asia 1750–1950*. Anthem Press.

Balachandran, Gopalan. 2012. *Globalizing Labour? Indian Seafarers and World Shipping, c. 1870–1945*. Oxford University Press.

Baldry, John. 1982. 'Al-Hudaydah and the Powers During the Sa'udi-Yemeni War of 1934', *Arabian Studies VI*: 7–34.

Baltimore, Paul Reed. 2014. *From the Camel to the Cadillac: Automobility, Consumption, and the U.S.-Saudi Special Relationship*. Unpublished doctoral dissertation, University of California Santa Barbara.

Barak, On. 2015. 'Outsourcing: Energy and Empire in the Age of Coal, 1820–1911', *International Journal of Middle East Studies* 47(3): 425–45.

Barth, Hans-Jörg and Nuzrat Yar Khan. 2008. 'Biogeophysical setting of the Gulf' in Abuzinada, Abdulaziz H. et al., 2008. *Protecting the Gulf's Marine Ecosystems from Pollution*. Birkhäuser.

Barty-King, Hugh. 1994. *The Baltic Exchange, 1744–1994: Baltic Coffee House to Baltic Exchange*. Quiller Press.

Bastashevski, Mari. 2016. 'The Perfect Con', *e-flux* 75. www.e-flux.com.

Belgrave, Charles. 1960. *Personal Column*. Hutchinson.

Beling, Willard A. 1961. *Pan-Arabism and Labor*. Harvard University Press.

Benton, Lauren. 2010. *A Search for Sovereignty: Law and Geography in European Empires, 1400–1900*. Cambridge University Press.

Bernes, Jasper. 2013. 'Logistics, Counterlogistics and the Communist Prospect', *Endnotes* 3.

Bezabe, Samson. 2015. *Subjects of Empires/Citizens of States: Yemenis in Djibouti and Ethiopia*. AUC Press.

Bilder, Richard B. 1970. 'East-West Trade Boycotts: A Study in Private, Labor Union, State, and Local Interference with Foreign Policy', *University of Pennsylvania Law Review* 118(6): 841–938.

BIMCO (Baltic and International Maritime Council) and ICS (International Chamber of Shipping). 2015. *International Chamber of Shipping Manpower Report: The Global Supply and Demand for Seafarers*. www.ics-shipping.org.

Bin Sulayem, Sultan. 1995. 'Jabal Ali Free Zone in Dubai' in Richard Bolin (ed.), *Mainline Free Zones: Mediterranean, Gulf, Indian Subcontinent*. Flagstaff Institute.

Bishara, Fahad Ahmad. 2017. *A Sea of Debt: Law and Economic Life in the Western Indian Ocean, 1780–1950*. Cambridge University Press.

Bishara, Fahad Ahmad. 2018. '"No country but the ocean": Reading International Law from the Deck of an Indian Ocean Dhow, ca. 1900', *Comparative Studies in Society and History* 60(2): 338–66.

Bishop, R Doak, 1997. *International Arbitration of Petroleum Disputes: The Development of a 'Lex Petrolea'*. Centre for Energy, Petroleum and Mineral Law and Policy.

Bliddal, Henrik. 2011. *Reforming Military Command Arrangements: The Case of the Rapid Deployment Joint Task Force*. US Army War College's Strategic Studies Institute.

Blum, Andrew. 2012. *Tubes: Behind the Scenes at the Internet*. Viking Books.

Bolin, Richard (ed.). 1995. *Mainline Free Zones: Mediterranean, Gulf, Indian Subcontinent*. Flagstaff Institute.

Bolin, Richard (ed.). 1999. *The Changing World of Free Zones*. Flagstaff Institute.

Boodrookas, Alex. 2018. 'Crackdowns and Coalitions in Kuwait', *Middle East Report Online* (18 June 2018).

Borscheid, Peter. 2012. 'Introduction' in Peter Borscheid and Niels Viggo Haueter (eds), *World Insurance: The Evolution of a Global Risk Network*. Oxford University Press.

Bose, Sugata. 2006. *A Hundred Horizons: The Indian Ocean in the Age of Global Empire*. Harvard University Press.

BP Shipping Ltd. 2015. *Riding the Waves: BP Shipping, 1915–2015; A Century of Maritime Achievement and Service*. BP Shipping.

Brand, Laurie A. 1994. 'Economics and Shifting Alliances: Jordan's Relations with Syria and Iraq, 1975–81', *International Journal of Middle East Studies* 26(3): 393–413.

Braudel, Fernand. 1986. *Civilization & Capitalism, 15th-18th Century, Volume 2: The Wheels of Commerce*. Trans. Siân Reynolds. Phoenix Press.

Brown, Lt Col Ronald J. 1998. *U.S. Marines in the Persian Gulf, 1990–1991: With Marine Forces Afloat in Desert Shield and Desert Storm*. History and Museums Divisions Headquarters, US Marine Corps.

Bsheer, Rosie. 2018. 'A Counter-Revolutionary State: Popular Movements and the Making of Saudi Arabia', *Past and Present* 238(1): 233–77.

Buckley, Michelle. 2014. 'Construction Work, "Bachelor" Builders and the Intersectional Politics of Urbanisation in Dubai' in Abdulhadi Khalaf et al., (eds), *Transit States: Labour, Migration and Citizenship in the Gulf*. Pluto Press.

Burt, John A. 2014. 'The environmental costs of coastal urbanization in the Arabian Gulf', *City* 18(6): 760–70.

Burt, John A., et al., 2015. 'An assessment of Qatar's coral communities in a regional context', *Marine Pollution Bulletin* 105: 473–9.

Cable, Vincent and Ann Weston. 1979. *South Asia's Exports to the EEC: Obstacles and Opportunities*. Overseas Development Institute.

Carafano, James Jay, Richard Weitz, and Martin Andersen. 2009. 'Maritime Security: Fighting Piracy in the Gulf of Aden and Beyond'. Heritage Foundation Special Report SR-59.

Carey, Jane Perry Clark. 1974. 'Iran and Control of Its Oil Resources', *Political Science Quarterly* 89(1): 147–74.

Carlisle, Rodney. 1982. *Sovereignty for Sale: The origins and evolution of the Panamanian and Liberian flags of convenience*. US Naval Institute Press.

Carlisle, Rodney. 2017. *Rough Waters: Sovereignty and the American Merchant Flag*. US Naval Institute Press.

Chadda, Maya. 1986. *Paradox of Power: The United States in Southwest Asia, 1973–1984*. ABC-CLIO.

Central Intelligence Agency, 'Soviet Global Military Reach', National Intelligence Estimate 11-6-84/S (13 September 1984).

Chalcraft, John. 2011. 'Migration and Popular Protest in the Arabian Peninsula and the Gulf in the 1950s and 1960s', *International Labor and Working-Class History* 79: 28–47.

Chatterjee, Pratap. 2009. *Halliburton's Army: How a Well-Connected Texas Oil Company Revolutionized the Way America Makes War*. Nation Books.

Chaudhuri, K.N. 1985. *Trade and Civilization in the Indian Ocean: An Economic History from the Rise of Islam to 1750*. Cambridge University Press.

Chin, Warren. 2005. 'Operations in a war zone: The Royal Navy in the Persian Gulf in the 1980s' in Ian Speller (ed.), *The Royal Navy and Maritime Power in the Twentieth Century*. Frank Cass Publishers.

Chorin, Ethan Daniel. 2000. *Clausewitz Meets the Sea in Yemen*. Unpublished doctoral dissertation, University of California Berkeley.

Chua, Charmaine. 2014. 'Logistics, Capitalist Circulations, Chokepoints' on *The Disorder of Things* blog: thedisorderofthings.com.

Chua, Charmaine. 2017. '"Sunny Island Set in the Sea": Singapore's Land Reclamation as Colonial Project' in Deborah Cowen, Alexis Mitchell, Emily Paradis, and Brett Story (eds), *Infrastructures of Citizenship: Digital Life in the Global City*. McGill-Queens University Press.

Citino, Nathan. 2000. 'Defending the "postwar petroleum order": The US, Britain and the 1954 Saudi–Onassis Tanker deal', *Diplomacy & Statecraft* 11(2): 137–60.

Cohen, Stephen. 2005. 'Boom Boxes: Shipping Containers and Terrorists'. Berkeley Roundtable on the International Economy, research paper no. 7.

Cole, Juan Ricardo. 1992. *Colonialism and Revolution in the Middle East*. Princeton University Press.

Cole, Peter. 2013. 'No Justice, No Ships Get Loaded: Political Boycotts on the San Francisco Bay and Durban Waterfronts', *International Review of Social History* 58: 185–217.

Comaroff, Joshua. 2014. 'Built on Sand: Singapore and the New State of Risk', *Harvard Design Magazine* No. 39 (Fall/Winter 2014).

Cooley, Alexander. 2008. *Base Politics: Democratic Change and the US Military Overseas*. Cornell University Press.

Cordesman, Anthony H., Robert Shelala, and Omar Mohamed. 2014. *The Gulf Military Balance. Volume III: The Gulf and the Arabian Peninsula*. Rowman and Littlefield.

Cowen, Deborah. 2014. *The Deadly Life of Logistics: Mapping Violence in Global Trade*. University of Minnesota Press.

Crystal, Jill. 1995. *Oil and Politics in the Gulf: Rulers and Merchants in Kuwait and Qatar*. Cambridge University Press.

Curzon of Kedleston, Marquess. 1923. *Tales of Travel*. Hodder and Stoughton.

Daniels, John. 1971. *Kuwait Journey*. White Crescent Press Ltd.

Davidson, Christopher. 2008. *Dubai: The Vulnerability of Success*. Hurst & Co.

Davies, Andrew. 2013. 'From "Landsman" to "Seaman"? Colonial discipline, organisation and resistance in the Royal Indian Navy, 1946', *Social & Cultural Geography* 14(8): 868–87

Degenerate Communism. 2015. 'Choke Points: Mapping an Anticapitalist Counterlogistics in California' in *Short Circuit: A Counterlogistics Reader*. No New Ideas Press.

Demir, Soliman. 1979. *Arab Development Funds in the Middle East*. Pergamon Press.

Department of Defense. 2000. *World Port Studies*. Ports for National Defense Program.

Dietrich, Christopher R.W. 2017. *Oil Revolution: Anticolonial Elites, Sovereign Rights, and the Economic Culture of Decolonization*. Cambridge University Press.

Disney, Nigel. 1977. 'South Korean Workers in the Middle East', *MERIP Reports* 61: 22–24+26.

Dolzer, Rudolf and Christoph Shreuer. 2012. *Principles of International Investment Law*. Oxford University Press.

Eiland, Howard and Michael W. Jennings. 2014. *Walter Benjamin: A Critical Life*. Harvard University Press.

Emery, K.O. 1967. 'Geological Aspects of Sea-Floor Sovereignty' in Alexander, Lewis M (ed.) *The Law of the Sea: Offshore Boundaries and Zones*. Ohio State University Press.

Ewald, Janet. 2000. 'Crossers of the Sea: Slaves, Freedmen, and other Migrants in the Northwestern Indian Ocean, c. 1750–1914', *The American Historical Review* 105(1): 69–91.

Facey, William and Gillian Grant. 1996. *The Emirates by the First Photographers*. Stacey International.

Facey, Roy. 2008. 'Pollution from sea based sources' in Abuzinada, Abdulaziz H. et al., 2008. *Protecting the Gulf's Marine Ecosystems from Pollution*. Birkhäuser.

Fajardo, Kale Bantigue. 2011. *Filipino Crosscurrents: Oceanographies of Seafaring, Masculinities and Globalization*. Minnesota University Press.

Fakhro, Elham. 2013. 'Land Reclamation in the Arabian Gulf: Security, Environment, and Legal Issues', *Journal of Arabian Studies* 3(1): 36–52.

Al-Fahim, Mohammed A.J. 1995. *From Rags to Riches: A Story of Abu Dhabi*. The London Centre of Arab Studies.

Farnie, D.A. 1969. *East and West of Suez: The Suez Canal in History*. Clarendon Press.

Fattah, Hala. 1997. *The Politics of Regional Trade in Iraq, Arabia and the Gulf 1745–1900*. State University of New York.

Field, Michael. 1985. *The Merchants: The Big Business Families of Saudi Arabia and the Gulf*. The Overlook Press.

Finnie, David H. 1958. *Desert Enterprise: The Middle East Oil Industry and Its Local Environment*. Harvard University Press.

Finnie, David H. 1992. *Shifting Lines in the Sand: Kuwait's Elusive Frontier with Iraq*. I.B. Tauris.

Fletcher, Max E. 1958. 'The Suez Canal and World Shipping, 1869–1914', the *Journal of Economic History* 18(4): 556–73.

Footman, David. 1986. *Antonin Besse of Aden: The Founder of St Antony's College Oxford*. Macmillan Press.

Forty, Adrian. 2012. *Concrete and Culture*. Reaktion Books.

Foucault, Michel. 1986. 'Of Other Spaces', Trans. Jay Miskowiec, *Diacritics* 16(1): 22–7.

Fox-Hodess, Katy. 2017. '(Re-)Locating the Local and National in the Global: Multi-Scalar Political Alignment in Transnational

European Dockworker Union Campaigns', *The British Journal of Industrial Relations* 55(3): 626–47.

Fraser, Henry S. 1926. 'Sketch of the History of International Arbitration', *Cornell Law Review* 11(2): 179–208.

Fuccaro, Nelida. 2009. *Histories of City and State in the Persian Gulf*. Cambridge University Press.

Al-Gain, Mujahid A. and Joseph A. D'Emidio. 1994. 'Saudi Arabia's Industrial Complexes', *The Military Engineer* 562: 74–5.

El Gammal, Farouk M. and El-Sayed El-Bushra. 1986. 'Geographic Analysis of Manufacturing Industry in Saudi Arabia', *GeoJournal* 13(2): 157–71.

Galpern, Steven G. 2009. *Money, Oil and Empire in the Middle East: Sterling and Postwar Imperialism, 1944–1971*. Cambridge University Press.

Galvani, John, Peter Johnson and Rene Theberge. 1973. 'The October War: Egypt, Syria, Israel', *MERIP Reports* 22: 3–21.

Gardner, Andrew M. 2010. *City of Strangers: Gulf Migration and the Indian Community in Bahrain*. Cornell University Press.

Gavin, R.J. 1975. *Aden Under British Rule 1839–1967*. C. Hurst & Company.

George, Rose. 2013. *Deep Sea and Foreign Going: Inside Shipping, the Invisible Industry that Brings You 90% of Everything*. Portobello Books.

Gerard, David. 2017. *Attack of the 50 Foot Blockchain: Bitcoin, Blockchain, Ethereum & Smart Contracts*. Self-published.

Ghabra, Shafeeq N. 1987. *Palestinians in Kuwait: The Family and the Politics of Survival*. Westview Press.

Al-Ghadban, A.N. and A.R.G. Price. 2002 'Dredging and Infilling' in Khan, N.Y., M. Munawar and A.R.G. Price (eds), 2002. *The Gulf Ecosystem: Health and Sustainability*. Backhuys Publishers.

Ghanem, Shihab M.A., 1989. *Industrialization Problems in the UAE with Particular Reference to the Shortage of Indigenous Skilled Manpower*. Unpublished doctoral thesis, University of Wales.

Ghanem, Shihab M.A. 1992. *Industrialization in the United Arab Emirates*. Avebury.

Ghazali, Salah Muhammad Issa. 2007. *Al Jama'at Al Siyasiyya Al Kuwaitiyya fi Qarn 1910–2007* (*Political Organisations in Kuwait 1910–2007*). Self-published.

Gill, Sahiba and the Coalition for Fair Labor. 2018. *Forced Labor at NYU Abu Dhabi: Compliance and the Cosmopolitan University*. Coalition for Fair Labor.

Glassman, Jim and Young-Jin Choi. 2014. 'The chaebol and the US military–industrial complex: Cold War geopolitical economy and South Korean Industrialization', *Environment and Planning A* 46: 1160– 1180.

Glick, Leslie Alan. 1980. *Trading with Saudi Arabia: A Guide to Shipping, Trade, Investment, and Tax Laws of Saudi Arabia*. Croom Helm.

Golumbia. David. 2016. *The Politics of Bitcoin: Software as Right-Wing Extremism*. University of Minnesota Press.

Gower, G.L. 1968. 'A History of Dredging', *Dredging: Proceedings of the Symposium Organized by the Institution of Civil Engineers, 18th October 1967*. The Institution of Civil Engineers.

Grathwol, Robert P. and Donita M. Moorhus. 2009. *Bricks, Sand, and Marble: U.S. Army Corps of Engineers Construction in the Mediterranean and Middle East, 1947–1991*. Center of Military History and Corps of Engineers, United States Army.

Gray Mackenzie & Company Limited. 1978. *The Gulf Pattern 1977–1982: trade, ports, economies*. Prepared by Peat, Marwick, Mitchell & Co. Gray Mackenzie & Co Ltd.

Gregson, Nicky. 2017. 'Logistics at Work: Trucks, Containers and the Friction of Circulation in the UK', *Mobilities* 12(3): 343–64.

Greenway, Ambrose. 2009. *Cargo Liners: An Illustrated History*. Seaforth Publishing.

Al-Gurg, Easa Saleh. 1998. *The Wells of Memory: An Autobiography*. John Murray.

Günel, Gökçe. 2016. 'The Infinity of Water: Climate Change Adaptation in the Arabian Peninsula', *Public Culture* 28(2): 291–315.

Al-Hamdi, Sabri Falih. 2014. *Harka Al-Tahdith fi Al-Mamlaka al-Arabiyya Al-Sa'udiyya, 1926–1953* (*Modernisation in the Kingdom of Saudi Arabia, 1926–1953*). Al Dar al-Arabiyya Li l-Ulum Nashirun.

Hanieh, Adam. 2011. *Capitalism and Class in the Gulf Arab States*. Palgrave MacMillan.

Hansen, Bent, and Khairy Tourk. 1974. 'The Suez Canal Project to Accommodate Super-Tankers: An Economic Appraisal', *Journal of Transport Economics and Policy* 8(2): 103–21.

Harlaftis, Gelina, 2014. 'The Onassis Global Shipping Business, 1920s–1950s', *Business History Review* 88: 241–71.

Harlow, Barbara, and Mia Carter. 2003. *Archives of Empire: From the East India Company to the Suez Canal*. Duke University Press.

Headrick, Daniel R. 1990. *The Tentacles of Progress: Technology Transfer in the Age of Imperialism, 1850–1940*. Oxford University Press.

Heard-Bey, Frauke. 1982. *From Trucial States to United Arab Emirates*. Longman.

Heard-Bey, Frauke. 2012. 'United Arab Emirates: Economic boom and insurance' in Peter Borscheid and Niels Viggo Haueter (eds), *World Insurance: The Evolution of a Global Risk Network*. Oxford University Press.

Heibel, Chris. 2012. 'Commercial Sea/Air Multimodal Operations: Support to the Warfighter', *Defense Transportation Journal* (August): 8–10.

Henderson, Edward. 1988. *This Strange Eventful History: Memoirs of Earlier Days in the UAE and Oman*. Quartet Books.

Henriques, Robert. 1960. *Marcus Samuel: First Viscount Bearsted and Founder of the "Shell" Transport and Trading Company, 1853–1927*. Barrie and Rockliff.

Al-Hijji, Ya'qub Yusif. 1993. *Nuwakhuda al-Safar al-Shira'i fi al-Kuwayt* (*The Nakhudas of The Age of Sail in Kuwait*). Rabi'an.

Ho, Engseng. 2004. 'Empire through Diasporic Eyes: A View from the Other Boat', *Comparative Studies of Society and History* 46(2): 210–46.

Ho, Engseng. 2006. *The Graves of Tarim: Genealogy and Mobility across the Indian Ocean*. University of California Press.

Holmes, Amy Austin. 2014. 'The Base that Replaced the British Empire: De-Democratization and the American Navy in Bahrain', *Journal of Arabian Studies* 4(1): 20–37.

Hoskins, Halford Lancaster. 1966. *British Routes to India*. Frank Cass & Co. Ltd.

Hourani, George F. 1995. *Arab Seafaring in the Indian Ocean in Ancient and Early Medieval Times*. Princeton University Press.

Howard, Michael. 1966. 'Britain's Strategic Problem East of Suez', *International Affairs* 42(2): 179–83.

Howarth, David, and Stephen Howarth. 1986. *The Story of P&O: The Peninsular and Oriental Steam Navigation Company*. Weidenfeld and Nicolson.

Hughes, Anne M. 1979. 'The Future of Gulf Ports', *Geography* 64(1): 54–6.

Hussin, Iza. 2014. 'Circulations of Law: Cosmopolitan Elites, Global Repertoires, Local Vernaculars', *Law and History Review* 32(4): 773–95.

IUMI (International Union of Marine Insurance). 2017. 'Global Marine Insurance Report 2017'. IUMI.

Jakobsen, Erik W., Christian Svane Mellbye, M. Shahrin Osman and Eirik H. Dyrstad. 2017. 'The Leading Maritime Capitals of the World 2017'. Menon Economics Publication 28/2017.

James, C.L.R. 1953. *Mariners, Renegades, and Castaways: The story of Herman Melville and the world we live in*. Allison & Busby.

Joesten, Joachim. 1963. *Onassis: A Biography*. Tower Books.

Jones, Geoffrey. 1987. *Banking and Oil: The History of the British Bank of the Middle East*, Vol 2. Cambridge University Press.

Jones, Stephanie. 1989. *Trade and Shipping: Lord Inchcape, 1852–1932*. Manchester University Press.

Jones, Toby Craig. 2017. 'After the Pipelines: Energy and the Flow of War in the Persian Gulf', *South Atlantic Quarterly* 116(2): 417–25.

Joshi, A.N. 1950. *Life and Times of Chevalier Framroze Dinshaw, OBE*. Brihad Gujarat Publication House.

Kanna, Ahmed. 2012. 'A politics of non-recognition? Biopolitics of Arab Gulf worker protests in the year of uprisings', *Interface* 4 (1): 146–64.

Kanoo, Khalid M. 1997. *The House of Kanoo: A Century of an Arabian Family Business*. London Centre of Arab Studies.

Katzman, Kenneth. 2015. *The United Arab Emirates (UAE): Issues for U.S. Policy (14 September 2015)*. Congressional Research Service.

Kéchichian, Joseph A. 2008, 'A Vision of Oman: State of the Sultanate Speeches by Qaboos Bin Said, 1970–2006', *Middle East Policy* 15(3): 112–33.

Kennedy, Paul. 2017. *The Rise and Fall of British Naval Mastery*. Penguin.

Keshavarzian, Arang. 2010. 'Geopolitics and the Genealogy of Free Trade Zones in the Persian Gulf', *Geopolitics* 15(2): 263–89.

Kesterman, Frank. 1975. 'Shipping and Port Operations in the Persian Gulf', *Journal of Maritime Law and Commerce* 7: 315–26.

Kettell, Brian. 1998 'Analysing the Emergence of an Offshore Banking Centre: The Case of Bahrain' in Michael Bowe, Lino Briguglio and James W. Dean (eds), 1998. *Banking and Finance in Islands and Small States*. Pinter.

Khalili, Laleh. 2014. 'Scholar, Pope, Soldier, Spy', *Humanity* 5(3): 417–34.

Khalili, Laleh. 2017. 'Pacifying Urban Insurrections', *Historical Materialism* 25(2): 115–30.

Khalili, Laleh. 2017. 'The infrastructural power of the military: The geoeconomic role of the US Army Corps of Engineers in the Arabian Peninsula', *European Journal of International Relations* 24(4): 911–33.

Khalili, Laleh. 2017. 'The Roads to Power: The Infrastructure of Counterinsurgency', *World Policy Journal* 34(1): 93–9.

Al-Khatib, Ahmad. 2007. *Kuwayt: Min al-Imara ila al-Dawla* (*Kuwait: From Emirate to State*). Markaz Thaqafi al-Arabi.

Kingston, Christopher. 2014. 'Governance and institutional change in marine insurance, 1350–1850', *European Review of Economic History* 18(1): 1–18.

Kingston, Robert C. 1983. 'The U.S. Central Command: Securing the First and Final Battles', *The Military Engineer* 75(490): 490–3.

Klinghoffer, Arthur Jay. 1975. 'Soviet Oil Politics and the Suez Canal', *The World Today* 31(10): 397–405.

Krane, Jim. 2009. *Dubai: The Story of the World's Fastest City*. Atlantic Books.

Lancaster, William and Fidelity Lancaster. 2011. *Honour is in Contentment: Life Before Oil in Ras al-Khaimah (UAE) and Some Neighbouring Regions*. De Gruyter.

Law, John. 1986. 'On the Methods of Long Distance Control: Vessels, Navigation and the Portuguese Route to India' in John Law (ed.), *Power, Action and Belief: A New Sociology of Knowledge*? Routledge.

Lawless, Dick. 1994. 'The role of seamen's agents in the migration for employment of Arab seafarers in the early twentieth century', *Immigrants & Minorities* 13(2): 34–58.

Lawless, Richard. 1994. 'Recruitment and Regulation: Migration for Employment of "Adenese" Seamen in the Late Nineteenth and Early Twentieth Centuries', *New Arabian Studies* 2: 75–100.

Lawless, Richard. 1995. *From Ta'izz to Tyneside: An Arab Community in the North-East of England during the Early Twentieth Century*. University of Exeter Press.

Lefebvre, Jeffrey A. 2003. 'U.S. Military Hegemony in the Arabian/Persian Gulf: How Long Can It Last?', *International Studies Perspectives* 4(2): 186–90.

Leffler, William L., Richard Pattarozzi and Gordon Sterling. 2011. *Deepwater Petroleum Exploration Production: A Nontechnical Guide*. PennWell Corporation.

Levinson, Marc. 2006. *The Box: How the Shipping Container Made the World Smaller and the World Economy Bigger*. Princeton University Press.

Lewis, Bernard. 1969. 'The Great Powers, the Arabs and the Israelis', *Foreign Affairs* 47(4): 642–52.

Limbert, Mandana. 2010. *In the Time of Oil: Piety, Memory, and Social Life in an Omani Town*. Stanford University Press.

Lippman, Thomas. 2008. *Arabian Knight: Colonel Bill Eddy USMC and the Rise of American Power in the Middle East*. Selwa Press.

Lobo-Guerrero, Luis. 2012. 'Lloyd's and the Moral Economy of Insuring against Piracy', *Journal of Cultural Economy* 5(1): 67–83.

Longhurst, Henry. 1959. *Adventure in Oil: The Story of British Petroleum*. Sidgwick and Jackson.

Longva, Anh Nga. 1997. *Walls Built on Sand: Migration, Exclusion and Society in Kuwait*. Westview Press.

Lutz, Catherine (ed.). 2009. *The Bases of Empire: The Global Struggle against US Military Posts*. Pluto Press.

Lutz, Catherine. 2001. *Homefront: A Military City and the American Twentieth Century*. Beacon Press.

Luxemburg, Rosa. 2003. *The Accumulation of Capital*. Trans. Agnes Schwarzchild. Routledge.

MacKenzie, Donald. 2003. 'An Equation and its Worlds: Bricolage, Exemplars, Disunity and Performativity in Financial Economics', *Social Studies of Science* 33(6): 831–68.

MacKenzie, Donald. 2006. *An Engine, Not a Camera: How Financial Models Shape Markets*. MIT Press.

MacKenzie, Donald and Yuval Millo. 2003. 'Constructing a Market, Performing Theory: The Historical Sociology of a Financial Derivatives Exchange', *American Journal of Sociology* 109(1): 107–45.

MacLean, Matthew, 2017. *Spatial Transformations and the Emergence of the 'National': Infrastructures and the Formation of the United Arab Emirates, 1950–1980*. Unpublished doctoral dissertation, New York University.

Mahan, Alfred T. 1902. 'Persian Gulf and International Relations', *Retrospect and Prospect: Studies in International Relations, Naval and Political*. Little, Brown, and Company.

Makki, Yusif. 2012. 'Hizb al-Ba'th al-ʿArabi al-Ishtiraki fi al-ʿArabiyya al-Sa'udiyya' (The Arab Socialist Ba'ath Party of Saudi Arabia) in Muhammad Jamal Barut (ed.), *Al-Ahzab wa al-Harakat wa al-Tanzimat al-Qawmiyya fi al-Watan al-ʿArabi* (Pan-Arab Parties, Movements and Organisations in the Arab World). Markaz Dirasat al-Wahda al-ʿArabiyya.

El-Mallakh, Ragei. 1979. *Qatar: Development of an Oil Economy*. Routledge Library Editions.

Malallah, Khalid Yasin. 2012. *Al-Tarikh al-Bahri li A'ila Mal-Allah* (*The Seafaring History of the Mal-Allah Family*). Maktaba al-Amiriyya.

Mann, F.A. 1984. 'The *Aminoil* Arbitration', *British Yearbook of International Law* 54(1): 213–21.

Markkula, Johanna. 2013. '"Any port in a storm": responding to crisis in the world of shipping', *Social Anthropology* 19(3): 297–304.

Markovits, Claude. 2000. *The Global World of Indian Merchants, 1750–1947: Traders of Sind from Bukhara to Panama*. Cambridge University Press.

Mathew, Johan. 2016. *Margins of the Market: Trafficking and Capitalism across the Arabian Sea*. University of California Press.

Mathew, Johan. 2019. 'On Principals and Agency: Reassembling Trust in Indian Ocean Commerce', *Comparative Studies in Society and History* 61(2): 242–68.

Matthiesen, Toby. 2013. *Sectarian Gulf: Bahrain, Saudi Arabia, and the Arab Spring That Wasn't*. Stanford University Press.

Matthiesen, Toby. 2014. 'Migration, Minorities, and Radical Networks: Labour Movements and Opposition Groups in Saudi

Arabia, 1950–1975', *International Review of Social History* 59: 473–504.

Matthiesen, Toby. 2014. *The Other Saudis: Shiism, Dissent and Sectarianism*. Cambridge University Press.

McCartney, Laton. 1988. *Friends in High Places: The Bechtel Story, the Most Secret Corporation and How It Engineered the World*. Simon and Shuster.

McKinsey & Company, Inc. for the British Transport Docks Board. 1967. *Containerization: The Key to Low-Cost Transport*. British Transport Docks Board.

Menarchik, Douglas. 1993. *Powerlift – Getting to Desert Storm – Strategic Transportation and Strategy in the New World Order*. Praeger.

Merk, Olaf, Bénédicte Busquet and Raimonds Aronietis, 2015. *The Impact of Mega-ships: Case-Specific Policy Analysis*. OECD, International Transport Forum.

Meyer-Reumann Legal Consultancy. 2003. 'Background and Business Opportunities in the Free Trade Zone in Yemen', *Arab Law Quarterly* 18(3/4): 401–8.

Miller, Michael B. 2006. 'Pilgrims' Progress: The Business of the Hajj', *Past and Present* 191: 189–228.

Mitchell, Timothy. 2011. *Carbon Democracy: Political Power in the Age of Oil*. Verso.

Mofid, Kamran. 1990. 'Economic Reconstruction of Iraq: Financing the Peace', *Third World Quarterly* 12(1): 48–61.

Moon, Chung-In. 1986. 'Korean Contractors in Saudi Arabia: Their Rise and Fall', *Middle East Journal* 40(4): 614–33.

Moore, Pete W. 2004. *Doing Business in the Middle East: Politics and Economic Crisis in Jordan and Kuwait*. Cambridge University Press.

Moubarak, Walid. 1987. 'The Kuwait Fund in the Context of Arab and Third World Politics', *Middle East Journal* 41(4): 538–52.

Mudayris, Falah Abdallah. 2004. *al-Ḥarakat wa-al-jamaʿat al-siyasiyya fi al-Baḥrayn, 1938–2002 (Political movements and organisations in Bahrain, 1938–2002)*. Dar al Kunuz al-Dabiyya.

Mudayris, Falah Abdallah. 2008. *Tatawwur al-ʿalaqat al-Kuwaytiyya al-Filastiniyya wa-athar al-ihtilal al-ʿIraqi fiha, 1921–2007 (Development of Kuwaiti-Palestinian Relations and the Effect of the Iraqi Occupation, 1921–2007)*. Dar al Qurtas lil Nashr.

Muller, M. 1985. 'Strike of crew members supported by ITF held unlawful by Dutch Court applying Philippine law', *Journal of Maritime Law and Commerce* 16(3): 423–6.

Al-Mumayyiz, Amin. 1963. *Al-Mamlaka al-ʿArabiyya al-Saʿudiyya kama ʿAraftuha (The Kingdom of Saudi Arabia as I knew It)*. Dar al-Kutub.

Munif, Abdelrahman. 1984. *Cities of Salt*. Trans. Peter Theroux. Random House.

Munro, J. Forbes. 1987. 'Shipping Subsidies and Railway Guarantees: William Mackinnon, Eastern Africa and the Indian Ocean, 1860–93', *The Journal of African History* 28(2): 209–30.

Munro, J. Forbes. 2003. *Maritime Enterprise and Empire: Sir William Mackinnon and His Business Network, 1823–93*. Boydell Press.

Al-Najdi, Ahmad b Majid. 1971. *Arab Navigation in the Indian Ocean Before the Coming of the Portuguese; being a translation of Kitāb al-Fawāʾid fī uṣūl al-baḥr waʾl-qawāʾid of Aḥmad b. Mājid al-Najdī*. Ed. G.R. Tibbetts. The Royal Asiatic Society of Great Britain and Ireland.

Al-Nakib, Farah. 2016. *Kuwait Transformed: A History of Oil and Urban Life*. Stanford University Press.

National Commission on the BP Deepwater Horizon Oil Spill and Offshore Drilling (Deepwater Horizon Commission). 2010. 'Staff Working Paper No. 1: A Brief History of Offshore Oil Drilling'.

Navias, Martin S. and E.R. Hooton. 1996. *Tanker Wars: The Assault on Merchant Shipping During the Iran-Iraq Crisis, 1980–1988*. I.B.Tauris.

Neblett, William. 1967 'The 1958 Conference on the Law of the Sea: What Was Accomplished' in Lewis M. Alexander (ed.) *The Law of the Sea: Offshore Boundaries and Zones*. Ohio State University Press.

Neveling, Patrick. 2015. 'Export Processing Zones, Special Economic Zones and the Long March of Capitalist Development Policies During the Cold War' in Leslie James and Elisabeth Leake (eds), *Decolonization and the Cold War*. Bloomsbury.

Nizan, Paul. 1987. *Aden Arabie*. Trans Joan Pinkham. Columbia University Press.

North, Douglass. 1958. 'Ocean Freight Rates and Economic Development 1750–1913', *The Journal of Economic History* 18(4): 537–55.

Noussia, Kyriaki. 2010. *Confidentiality in International Commercial Arbitration: A Comparative Analysis of the Position under English, US, German and French Law*. Springer Verlag.

O'Brien, Patrick. 1997. 'Intercontinental Trade and the Development of the Third World since the Industrial Revolution', *Journal of World History* 8(1): 75–133.

Ogle, Vanessa. 2017. 'Archipelago Capitalism: Tax Havens, Offshore Money, and the State, 1950s–1970s', *The American Historical Review* 122(5): 1431–1458.

Olivet, Cecilia and Pia Eberhardt. 2014. *Profiting from Crisis: How corporations and lawyers are scavenging profits from Europe's crisis countries*. Transnational Institute.

OPEC. 2015. *World Oil Outlook*. Vienna: Organisation of Petroleum Exporting Companies.

Ornestein, Dara. 2011. 'Foreign Trade Zones and the Cultural Logic of Frictionless Production', *Radical History Review* 109: 36–61.

Owen, David. 2017. 'The World Is Running Out of Sand: It's one of our most widely used natural resources, but it's scarcer than you think', *the New Yorker* 29 May 2017.

Owtram, Francis Carey. 1999. *Oman and the West: State Formation in Oman since 1920*. Unpublished doctoral dissertation, LSE.

Padmalal, D. and K. Maya. 2014. *Sand Mining: Environmental Impacts and Selected Case Studies*. Springer.

Page, Stephen. 1985. *The Soviet Union and the Yemens. Influence on Asymmetrical Relationships*. Praeger.

Palan, Ronen. 2003. *The Offshore World: Sovereign Markets, Virtual Places, and Nomad Millionaires*. Cornell University Press.

Pampanini, Andrea H. 1997. *Cities from the Arabian Desert: The Building of Jubail and Yanbu in Saudi Arabia*. Praeger.

Pelham, Nicolas. 2018. 'The Precarious Rise of the Gulf Despots', *The London Review of Books* 40(4): 21–4.

Petouris, Thanos. 2018. 'The Aden Port Strikes of 1948: Antecedents of Trades Unionism in a British Colony'. Unpublished paper presented at the workshop on Maritime Transportation in the Middle East, SOAS University of London.

Philby, H. St. J.B. 1958. 'The Hijaz Railway', *The Geographical Journal* 124(4): 588–9.

Pilbeam, Pamela. 2014. *Saint-Simonians in Nineteenth-Century France: From Free Love to Algeria*. Palgrave Macmillan.

Pilkey, Orrin H. and J. Andrew G. Cooper. 2014. *The Last Beach*. Duke University Press.

Plonski, Sharri. 2018. 'Settler Colonial Infrastructures: The View from Haifa Port'. Unpublished paper presented at the workshop on Maritime Transportation in the Middle East, SOAS University of London.

Poisson, Richard David. 1982. 'Seafarers and International Shipping Standards'. Unpublished Masters Dissertation, University of Rhode Island.

Polmar, Norman and Michael White. 2010. *Project Azorian: The CIA and the Raising of the K-129*. Naval Institute Press.

Porras, Ileana M. 2006. 'Constructing International Law in the East Indian Seas: Property, Soverignty, Commerce and War in Hugo Grotius De lure Praedae – The Law of Prize and Booty, or "On How to Distinguish Merchants from Pirates"', *Brooklyn Journal of International Law* 31(3): 741–804.

Porter, Theodore M. 1995. *Trust in Numbers: The Pursuit of Objectivity in Science and Public Life*. Princeton University Press.

Prange, Sebastian R. 2011. 'A Trade of No Dishonor: Piracy, Commerce, and Community in the Western Indian Ocean, Twelfth to Sixteenth Century', *The American Historical Review* 115(5): 1269–1293.

Prange, Sebastian R. 2013. 'The Contested Sea: Regimes of Maritime Violence in the Pre-Modern Indian Ocean', *Journal of Early Modem History* 17: 9–33.

Prescott, J.R.V. 1975. *The Political Geography of the Oceans*. David and Charles.

Qasrawi, Sophia. 2004. *Foreign Direct Investment in the UAE: Determinants and Recommendations*. The Emirates Center for Strategic Studies and Research.

Ralph, Michael. 2012. '"Life . . . in the midst of death": Notes on the relationship between slave insurance, life insurance and disability', *Disability Studies Quarterly* 32(2).

Ramos, Stephen. 2010. *Dubai Amplified: The Engineering of a Port Geography*. Ashgate Publishing.

Al-Rasheed, Madawi. 2010. *A History of Saudi Arabia*. Cambridge University Press (Second edition).

Rawls, Lucia Wren. 1987. *The role of Aramco in Saudi Arabian development: A case study of dependent development*. Unpublished doctoral dissertation, University of South Carolina.

Raza, Ali and Benjamin Zachariah. 2012. 'To Take Arms Across a Sea of Trouble: The "Lascar System", Politics, and Agency in the 1920s', *Itinerario* 36(3): 19–38.

Rediker, Marcus. 2014. *Outlaws of the Atlantic: Sailors, Pirates, and Motley Crews in the Age of Sail*. Beacon Press.

Rihani, Ameen. 1930. *Around the Coasts of Arabia*. Constable & Co Ltd.

Ritchie, G.S. 1967. *The Admiralty Chart: British Naval Hydrography in the Nineteenth Century*. Hollis and Carter.

Rodney, Walter. 1982. *How Europe Underdeveloped Africa*. Howard University Press.

Roh, Saeyeon. 2012. *The Pre-Positioning of Humanitarian Aid: The Warehouse Location Problem*. Unpublished doctoral dissertation, Cardiff University.

Ronaldshay, Earl of. 1928. *The Life of Lord Curzon: Being the Authorized Biography of George Nathaniel, Marquess Curzon of Kedelston, K.G.* Ernest Benn Ltd.

Rossi, Gifford S. 1995. *An Arabian Adventure: A Dream Achieved*. Kegan Paul International.

Rossiter, Ned. 2015. 'Coded Vanilla: Logistical Media and the Determination of Action', *South Atlantic Quarterly* 114(1): 135–52.

Royall, John. 1999. 'Marketing Your Zone: How to Reach Your Potential Users' in Richard Bolin (ed.), *The Changing World of Free Zones*. Flagstaff Institute.

Ruprecht, Anita. 2007. 'Excessive Memories: Slavery, Insurance and Resistance', *History Workshop Journal* 64(1): 6–28.

Al-Sa'id, Raf'at. 1976. *Tarikh al-Munadhamat al-Yasariyya al-Masriyya 1940–1950* (*History of Leftist Egyptian Organisations, 1940–1950*). Dar al-Thaqafa al-Jadid.

Sanger, Richard H. 1954. *The Arabian Peninsula*. Cornell University Press.

Sasikumar, S.K. and Philip Martin. 2017. 'New Era in India – Gulf Labour Migration', *Labour & Development* 24(1): 1–13.

Seccombe, Ian J. 1986. '"A disgrace to American enterprise": Italian labour and the Arabian American oil company in Saudi Arabia, 1944–54', *Immigrants & Minorities* 5(3): 233–57.

Seccombe, Ian and Richard Lawless. 1987. *Work Camps and Company Towns: Settlement Patterns and the Gulf Oil Industry*. Centre for Middle Eastern and Islamic Studies Occasional Papers Series no. 36, Durham University.

Seddon, Mohammad Siddique. 2014. *The Last of the Lascars: Yemeni Muslims in Britain 1836–2012*. Kube Academic.

Sekula, Allan. 2018[1995]. *Fish Story*. Mack Books (re-press).

Schwebel, Judge Stephen M. 2010. 'The kingdom of Saudi Arabia and Aramco arbitrate the Onassis agreement', *World Energy Law and Business* 3(3): 245–56.

Schwebel, Stephen M. 2011. *Justice in International Law*. Cambridge University Press.

Shallat, Todd. 1994. *Structures in the Stream: Water, Science, and the Rise of the US Army Corps of Engineers*. University of Texas Press.

Shaykh Ya'qub, Ishaq. 2011. *Wujuh fi Masabih al-Dhakira* (*Faces in the Illumination of Memory*) vol IV. Dar al Farabi.

Sheppard, Charles, et al. 1992. *Marine Ecology of the Arabian Region: Patterns and Processes in Extreme Tropical Environments*. Academic Press.

Sheppard, Charles, et al. 2010. 'The Gulf: a young sea in decline', *Marine Pollution Bulletin* 60(1): 13–38.

Sherwood, Marika. 1991. 'Race, nationality and employment among Lascar seamen, 1660 to 1945', *Journal of Ethnic and Migration Studies* 17(2): 229–44.

Sibilia, Elizabeth. 2018. 'Oceanic accumulation: Geographies of speculation, overproduction, and crisis in the global shipping economy', *Environment and Planning A: Economy and Space* 51(2): 467–86.

Al-Shinnawi, Abdulaziz Muhammad. 2010. *Al Sakhra fi Hafr Qanat Suis* (Forced Labour in the Digging of the Suez Canal). Hay'at al-Masriyya al-Ammah lil-Kitab.

Shorrock, William I. 1970. 'The Origin of the French Mandate in Syria and Lebanon: The Railroad Question, 1901–1914', *International Journal of Middle East Studies* 1(2): 133–53.

Simpson, Edward. 2006. *Muslim Society and the Western Indian Ocean: The seafarers of Kachchh*. Routledge.

Al-Sirafi, Atiya. 1997. *Lamahat min Tarikhuna Al-Ummali wa al-Niqabi* (Profiles in the History of Workers and Unions). Markaz Ibn Khaldun.

Slight, John. 2015. *The British Empire and the Hajj, 1865–1956*. Harvard University Press.

Slot, B.J. 2009. 'French Relations with the Independent Shaikhdoms of the Lower Gulf', *Liwa: Journal of the National Centre for Documentation & Research* 1(2): 10–21.

Smith, Pamela Ann. 1984. *Palestine and the Palestinians, 1876–1983*. Croom Helm.

Snipes, Captain Michael R. 1988. 'Re-Flagged Kuwaiti Tankers: The Ultimate Flag of Convenience for an Overall Policy of Neutrality'. Unpublished thesis presented to The Judge Advocate General's School, United States Army.

Sobel, Dava. 1995. *Longitude: The True Story of a Lone Genius Who Solved the Greatest Scientific Problem of His Time*. Fourth Estate.

Stanley-Price, Nicholas. 2012. *Imperial Outpost in the Gulf: The Airfield at Sharjah (UAE), 1932–1952*. Book Guild Publishing.

Stark, Freya. 1990[1961]. *Dust in the Lion's Paw: An Autobiography 1939–1946*. Arrow Books.

Starosielski, Nicole. 2015. *The Undersea Network*. Duke University Press.

Stegner, Wallace. 1971. *Discovery!: The Search for Arabian Oil*. Selwa Press.

Steinberg, Philip E. 2009. 'Sovereignty, Territory, and the Mapping of Mobility: A View from the Outside', *Annals of the Association of American Geographers* 99(3): 467–95.

Stern, Philip J. 2011. *The Company-State: Corporate Sovereignty and the Early Modern Foundations of the British Empire in India*: Oxford University Press.

Stopford, Martin. 1997. *Maritime Economics*. Routledge.

Stork, Joe and Jim Paul. 1983. 'Arms Sales and the Militarization of the Middle East', *MERIP Reports* 112: 5–15.

Stork, Joe and Martha Wenger. 1991. 'The US in the Persian Gulf: From Rapid Deployment to Massive Deployment', *Middle East Report* 168: 22–6.

Stratton, Morton B. 1944. 'British Railways and Motor Roads in the Middle East – 1918–1930', *Economic Geography* 20(2): 116–29.

Stratton, Morton B. 1944. 'British Railways and Motor Roads in the Middle East, 1930–1940', *Economic Geography* 20(3): 189–203.

Tackney, Cathy. 1972. 'Dealing Arms in the Middle East. Part I: History and Strategic Considerations', *MERIP Reports* 8: 3–14.

Takriti, Abdel Razzaq. 2013. *Monsoon Revolution: Republicans, Sultans, and Empires in Oman 1965–1976*. Oxford University Press.

Taryal, M.S. and Chowdhury, M.K. 1987. 'Variability of Cement Strength in Saudi Arabia' in Emery Farkas and Pail Klieger (eds), *Uniformity of Cement Strength, ASTM STP 961*. American Society for Testing and Materials.

Tétreault, Mary Ann. 1995. *The Kuwait Petroleum Corporation and the Economics of the New World Order*. Quorum Books.

Thoman, Richard S. 1956. *Free Ports and Foreign Trade Zones*. Cornell Maritime Press.

Thuong, Le T and Lisa Elvey. 1985. 'The End of the Supertanker Era', *Transportation Journal* 25(2): 4–17.

Toscano, Alberto. 2011. 'Logistics and Opposition', *Mute* 3(2).

Toscano, Alberto. 2014. 'Lineaments of the Logistical State', *ViewPoint* 4.

Twitchell, K.S. with the collaboration of Edward J. Jurji. 1953. *Saudi Arabia: With an Account of the Development of Its Natural Resources*. Princeton University Press.

Ulrichsen, Kristian Coates. 2016. *The Gulf States in International Political Economy*. Palgrave.

UNCTAD. 2017. *Review of Maritime Transport 2017*. UNCTAD.

Al-Uways, Muhammad Sultan. 2014. *Khawr Dubay: Hikaya fi Dhakirati (Dubai Creek: Stories from Memory)*. Dar al-Arabiyya.

van Creveld, Martin. 1977. *Supplying War: Logistics from Wallenstein to Patton*. Cambridge University Press.

van der Linden, Marcel. 2010. 'Re-constructing the origins of modern labor management', *Labor History* 51(4): 509–22.

Varner, Roy and Wayne Collier. 1978. *A Matter of Risk: The Incredible Story of the CIA's Hughes Glomar Explorer Mission to Raise a Russian Submarine*. Random House.

Villiers, Alan. 1966. *Sons of Sinbad: Sailing with the Arabs in their Dhows*. Hodder & Stoughton Ltd.

Vine, David. 2009. *Island of Shame: The Secret History of the US Military Base on Diego Garcia*. Princeton University Press.

Vitalis, Robert. 2006. *America's Kingdom: Mythmaking on the Saudi Oil Frontier*. Stanford University Press.

Walker, A.R. 1989. 'Recessional and Gulf War Impacts on Port Development and Shipping in the Gulf States in the 1980's', *GeoJournal* 18(3): 273–84.

Watt, D.C. 1962. 'Labor Relations and Trades Unionism in Aden, 1952–1960', *Middle East Journal* 16(4): 443–56

Welland, Michael. 2009. *Sand: A Journey Through Science and the Imagination*. Oxford University Press.

Westlake, John. 1907. 'Muscat Dhows', *Law Quarterly Review* 23: 83–87.

Wilson, Rodney. 1983. *Banking and Finance in the Arab Middle East*. Macmillan Publishers.

Zahlan, A.B. 1984. *The Arab Construction Industry*. Croom Helm.

Zahlan, A.B. 1991. *Acquiring Technological Capacity: A Study of Arab Consulting and Contracting Firms*. Macmillan.

Zainal, Khadija, Hashim al-Sayed, and Ismail Al-Madany. 2008 'Coastal pollution in Bahrain and its management' in Abuzinada, Abdulaziz H. et al., (eds), *Protecting the Gulf's Marine Ecosystems from Pollution*. Birkhäuser.

Zarach, Stephanie. 2017. *Trading History: The Baltic Exchange Since the 18th Century*. The Baltic Exchange.

Ziadah, Rafeef. 2018. 'Constructing a logistics space: Perspectives from the Gulf Cooperation Council', *Environment and Planning D: Society and Space* 36(4): 666–82.

Ziadah, Rafeef. 2019. 'Circulating Power: Humanitarian Logistics, Militarism, and the United Arab Emirates', *Antipode* 51(5): 1684–1702.

Notes

Introduction

1. UNCTAD, *Review of Maritime Transport* 2017; U.S. Energy Information Administration, *World Oil Transit Chokepoints* 2017.
2. Munif, *Cities of Salt*, 192.
3. From Saif al-Rahbi, 'Distant Waters'.
4. Pearson, *Indian Ocean*, 5.
5. Davis, *City of Quartz*, v.

1 – Route-Making

1. Roslan Khasawneh, 'Contaminated Marine Fuels Clog Ship Engines in Singapore Hub – Surveyor', *Reuters* (27 July 2018).
2. OPEC, *World Oil Outlook 2015*, 127.
3. Steinberg, 'Sovereignty, Territory'.
4. Braudel, *Wheels of Commerce*, 121.
5. Chaudhuri, *Trade and Civilisation*, 69.
6. Ahmad, *Arab Classical Accounts*, 38.
7. Al-Najdi, *Arabic Navigation*, 77.
8. Braudel's account of the circuit of travel undertaken by an Armenian merchant is detailed and fascinating (*Wheels of Commerce*, 145–72). Also see Aslanian, *Armenian Merchants*, Goswami, *Globalization*; Ho, *Tarim*; Markovits, *Traders of Sind* inter alia. However, Mathew, 'Principal', argues that trade networks were not necessarily based on kinship, but required habits of practice, legal frameworks, and regimes of rule for their survival.
9. Braudel, *Wheels of Commerce*, 141–2.

10. Chaudhuri, *Trade and Civilisation*, 83; Braudel, *Wheels of Commerce*, 121.
11. Prange, 'Contested Sea'; 'Trade of No Dishonor'; Bishara, *Sea of Debt*.
12. Benton, *Sovereignty*; Bose, *A Hundred Horizons*; Ewald, 'Crossers of the Sea'; Law, 'Long-Distance Control'; Stern, *The Company-State,* among many hundreds (if not thousands) of other writings.
13. Ritchie, *Admiralty Chart*; Sobel, *Longitude*.
14. Hoskins, *Routes*, 87.
15. Hoskins, *Routes*, 140–1.
16. Farnie, *Suez*, 13.
17. Quoted in Hoskins, *Routes*, 198–9.
18. Fletcher, 'Suez Canal', 556.
19. Barak, 'Outsourcing'; Mitchell, *Carbon Democracy*.
20. Headrick, *Tentacles*, 44.
21. Walt Whitman, 'Passage to India'.
22. Rihani, *Coasts of Arabia*, 310–11.
23. Farnie, *Suez*, 160.
24. Farnie, *Suez*, 160.
25. Headrick, *Tentacles*, 100; Hoskins, *Routes*, 373–82.
26. Starosielski, *Undersea Networks*.
27. See the interactive maps at submarinecablemap.com.
28. Blum, *Tubes*, 197.
29. Braudel, *Wheels of Commerce*, 127. Also see Slight, *Hajj*; and Bose, *A Hundred Horizons*, 193–232. Pearson (*Pilgrimage*, 130–84) disputes the significance of the hajj.
30. Miller, 'Business of Hajj', 201.
31. Miller, 'Business of Hajj', 204.
32. Akif, *Passionate Passages*, 58.
33. Hasan and Jalil, 'Introduction', in Alawi, *Journey*, 22.
34. Akif, *Passionate Passages*, 203.
35. Slight, *Hajj*, 314.
36. Al-Shinnawi, *Sakhra*; Al-Sirafi, *Lamahat*, 54–67.
37. Harlow and Carter, *Archives of Empire*, 555–71.
38. Headrick, *Tentacles*, 40. The transit of warships through the canal was eventually regulated by the Convention of Constantinople, signed on 29 October 1888. The Convention allowed passage of warships of all nations through the canal, but restricted the time they could spend at neutral ports for fuelling or victualling. Farnie, *Suez*, 337.

39. Luxemburg, *Accumulation*, 410. Also see Cole, *Colonialism*, 55.
40. Coastal and local trade in the Indian Ocean continued to use sail for more than a century later, however.
41. O'Brien, 'Intercontinental Trade', 84.
42. Henriques, *Marcus Samuel*, 79.
43. On other causes of this displacement see Mitchell, *Carbon Democracy*.
44. Asfour, 'Ports', 144–52.
45. BP Shipping, *Riding the Wave*, 64.
46. Thuong and Elvey, 'Supertanker Era', 7.
47. Frank Kane, 'New Suez Canal Declared Open in Spectacular Ceremony on Edge of Sinai Desert', *National* (6 August 2015).
48. Mike Wackett, 'CMA CGM Hopes New Mega-Boxship Bow Design Will Be on the Nose for Economy', *Loadstar* (1 August 2018); Costas Paris, 'Maersk Tankers Turns to Wind Power to Cut Soaring Fuel Costs', *Wall Street Journal* (30 August 2018).
49. Svilen Petrov, 'Maersk Line Restarts Shipping of Containers to Qatar Through Port of Salalah in Oman', *Maritime Herald* (10 June 2017).
50. Most petroleum and chemical loading terminals are managed by the producers, while the ownership and management structures for bulk or ro/ro (wheeled vehicle) terminals tend to be heterogeneous.
51. Marie Bordet, 'Saadé, confidences d'un tycoon des mers', *Le Point* (6 June 2013); Robert Wright, 'Making Waves in the Mediterranean', *Financial Times* (3 June 2008).
52. United Arab Shipping Company has now merged with the German Hapag-Lloyd. I discuss UASC in Chapter 5.
53. Lloyd's List, 'Top 10 Box Port Operators 2018', *Lloyd's List Maritime Intelligence* (12 December 2018).
54. O'Brien, 'Intercontinental Trade', 79.
55. North, 'Ocean Freight Rates', 544–6.
56. North, 'Ocean Freight Rates', 538.
57. Mathew, *Margins of the Market*, 47.
58. Mathew, *Margins of the Market*, 49.
59. Rihani, *Coasts of Arabia*, 242. Emphasis added.
60. Lancaster and Lancaster, *Life Before Oil*, 49.

61. Lancaster and Lancaster, *Life Before Oil*, 45; Simpson, *Seafarers of Kachchh*.
62. The repeal was passed in September 2006, effective October 2008. For the text of the 1986 regulation, see ec.europa.eu.
63. The 2008 crash saw the Baltic Dry Index plummet from an all-time high of 11,793 points in May 2008 to 663 in December. See Basil Karatzas, 'Baltic Dry Index Has Been Flirting with All Time Lows – Isn't That Good News?' *gCaptain* (17 April 2015).
64. Chaudhuri, *Trade and Civilisation*, 198.
65. MacKenzie and Millo, 'Constructing', 110–11.
66. Alizadeh and Nomikos, *Shipping Derivatives*, 14.
67. 'SGX plans to marry the UK exchange's domination in compiling the Baltic Dry Index, which charts the cost of transporting commodities such as iron ore and grain in bulk, to develop Asian benchmarks for pricing', according to Phillip Stafford, 'SGX Plans to Use Baltic Exchange as Beachhead into Europe', *Financial Times* (15 March 2017).
68. The panellists (or chosen shipbrokers that report on prices) for all the indices that the Baltic Exchange tracks are listed on the Exchange website at balticexchange.com.
69. Alizadeh and Nomikos, *Shipping Derivatives*, 108; Barty-King, *Baltic Exchange*, 82; Zarach, *Trading History*, 103.
70. Zarach, *Trading History*, 105.
71. MacKenzie, 'An Equation', 841–2.
72. MacKenzie, *An Engine*, 133.
73. Clarksons Research also publishes the ClarkSea Index (based on average index of earnings for new ships for various ship sizes) for all ships, including bulk carriers, VLCCs and ULCCs, and container ships.
74. On CCFI, see en.sse.net.cn.
75. Peter Yang, 'The History of the Shanghai Containerized Freight Index (SCFI)', *Flexport* (13 March 2016).

2 – Harbour-Making

1. Foreign Minister Landsdowne's sneering description of Curzon's trip. Finnie, *Lines in the Sand*, 25.
2. 'Landing at Koweit'. Photographer: Unknown [21r] (1/1), British

Library: Visual Arts, Photo 49/1/22, in Qatar Digital Library, qdl.qa.

3. Ronaldshay, *Curzon*, 314.
4. Curzon, *Tales of Travel*, 248–9.
5. Ronaldshay, *Curzon*, 317.
6. Belgrave, *Personal Column*, 16–17.
7. 'With the Viceroy in the Persian Gulf', *Times* (28 December 1903).
8. Munif, *Cities of Salt*, 198–9.
9. *ARAMCO world*, 'Giant of the Sea', 4. By contrast, the world's largest ULCC, *Seawise Giant*, built in the 1970s, was 458 metres long and when fully laden, had a draught approaching 25 metres. It was capable of carrying 564,763 deadweight tonnes of oil, or more than 4 million barrels of oil.
10. Vitalis, *America's Kingdom*, 61.
11. Stegner, *Discovery!*, 152
12. Aramco Annual Report 1946, Mulligan Papers, Box 3, Folder 43; Georgetown University Archives.
13. The information in this paragraph comes from Aramco Annual Report for 1952 through 1974; Mulligan Papers, Box 3, Folder 43; Georgetown University Archives.
14. Aramco Annual Report 1976; Mulligan Papers, Box 3, Folder 43; Georgetown University Archives.
15. Facey and Grant, *Emirates*.
16. See oral histories recounted in AbdulRahman, *Al-Imarat*, about pearling, fishing, and other pre-oil economic activities.
17. Ramos, *Dubai Amplified*, 58; Heard-Bey, *Trucial States*, 189–91.
18. Memo from Political Resident Bushire to Secretary of State for India (16 February 1938) in 'Confidential 86/7 – ix B.52. P.C.L. TRUCIAL COAST'; India Office Records IOR/R/15/1/679, British Library.
19. Sir William Halcrow and Partners, 'Dubai Harbour: Report on Proposed Improvements' (January 1955); FO 371/114696, UK National Archives.
20. Halcrow and Partners, 'Dubai Harbour: Report on Proposed Improvements'.
21. Halcrow and Partners, 'Dubai Harbour: Report on Proposed Improvements'.
22. Halcrow and Partners, 'Dubai Harbour: Report on Proposed

Improvements'. The same factors were listed in Halcrow's Sharjah report in more or less the same order, but with further emphasis on the shortage of suitable construction material.

23. W.H. Adams, 'Minutes of Discussion Regarding Halcrow's Survey of Dubai and Sharjah Creeks' (28 January 1955); FO 371/114696, UK National Archives.
24. Wilson, *Rashid's Legacy*, 96; 133.
25. Davidson, *Dubai*, 86.
26. Heard-Bey, *Trucial States*, 261.
27. Krane, *Dubai*, 72.
28. Ramos, *Dubai Amplified*, 72–3.
29. Ramos, *Dubai Amplified*, 109.
30. Levinson, *The Box*.
31. Dubai Ports International was formed in 1999 initially to manage a port in Jeddah, Saudi Arabia.
32. In 2016, Jabal Ali was the ninth largest container port in the world by volume and the only port in the top 10 not located in East or Southeast Asia. The only other Middle Eastern ports in the top 50 were Sharjah's Khor Fakkan at 39, and Jeddah at 40. 'Top 50 Container Ports in 2016: Shanghai Tightens Grip on Crown', *Journal of Commerce Online* (10 August 2017). Salalah in Oman and Bandar Abbas in Iran which had been on the list two years before are no longer in the top 50.
33. Lloyd's List. '100 Ports 2018', lloydslist.maritimeintelligence.informa.com; Journal of Commerce, 'Top 50 Global Containers Ports 2018', joc.com. The two news sources have slightly different systems of ranking especially at the lower reaches, but their output volumes match.
34. Ghanem, *Industrialization*, 54.
35. MacLean, *Spatial Transformations*, 237–8.
36. MacLean, *Spatial Transformations*, 237–8.
37. Sekula, *Fish Story*, 12.
38. Gavin, *Aden*, 29.
39. Footman, *Besse*, 3.
40. Rihani, *Coasts of Arabia*, 313.
41. Ma'alla, where the customhouse was located was described by Ameen Rihani, who visited the city in the early 1920s, as a 'Somali village'. Rihani, *Coasts of Arabia*, 316.

42. Rihani, *Coasts of Arabia*, 311.
43. Barak, 'Outsourcing', 433.
44. Bose, *Hundred Horizons*, 75.
45. Joshi, *Dinshaw*, 53
46. Joshi, *Dinshaw*, 110.
47. Nizan, *Aden Arabie*, 96.
48. Sanger, *Arabian Peninsula*, 204.
49. Halliday, *Arabia*, 159.
50. 'Aden Port Development: Notes of a Meeting Held at Britannic House, 8th May, 1951, 2.45 pm.' ARC7189. Aden, Anglo-Iranian Oil Co Limited, BP Archives, Warwick.
51. *Port of Aden Annual* 1956–1957, 36.
52. Gavin, *Aden*, 327.
53. Halliday, *Arabia*, 241.
54. WorldBank, 'Report and Recommendation of the President of Executive Directors on a Proposed Credit to the People's Democratic Republic of Yemen for an Aden Port Rehabilitation Project'; Report No. P-1667a-YDR (11 August 1975).
55. 'DP World Eyes Yemeni Port Projects', *Port Technology* (19 October 2015).
56. Quoted in Eiland and Jennings, *Benjamin*, 241.
57. This is not only the solid waste and sewage produced by thousands of passengers the cruise-ship ferries to sea, but also the engine effluents – liquid and gas. An undercover investigation showed that the air pollution on the deck of such a ship was worse than at the centre of a city. Will Coldwell, 'Air on board cruise ships "is twice as bad as at Piccadilly Circus"', *Guardian* (3 July 2017).
58. Singapore, Fujairah, Rotterdam, Hong Kong, and Antwerp are the biggest bunkering ports in the world, in that order.
59. U.S. Energy Information Administration, *World Oil Transit Chokepoints* 2017.
60. Facey, 'Pollution', 174.
61. Facey, 'Pollution', 166–78.
62. Amin, *Marine Pollution*.
63. Facey, 'Pollution', 175n18.
64. In an eponymous article about desalination plants in the Gulf, Gökçe Günel calls this the assumption of 'infinity of water'.

65. An OECD report on the impact of megaships estimated that a 19,000 TEU ship (i.e., a ship carrying 19,000 twenty-foot containers) has a draught of sixteen metres and to accommodate it nearly 20 million cubic metres of soil needs to be dredged. Merk et al., *Mega-ships*, 96–7.
66. Sheppard et al., 'The Gulf'.
67. Sheppard et al., *Marine Ecology*, 296.
68. On the Netherlands see van den Ven, *Manmade Lowlands*; on Singapore, Chua, '"Sunny Island"'.
69. Gower, 'Dredging'.
70. Lancaster and Lancaster, *Life before Oil*, 69.
71. Sheppard et al., *Marine Ecology*, 42; Burt et al., 'Coral Communities'; Barth and Khan, 'The Gulf'; Burt, 'Coastal Urbanization'; Al-Ghadban and Price, 'Dredging', 215.
72. Barth and Khan, 'The Gulf'; Zainal et al., 'Coastal Pollution', 151; Al-Ghadban and Price, 'Dredging', 210.
73. Fakhro, 'Land Reclamation'.
74. Cynthia O'Murchu and Simeon Kerr, 'Disputed Land Development Boosts Wealth of Bahrain Royals', *Financial Times* (10 December 2014).
75. See AlShehabi, 'Radical Transformations'; AlShehabi and Suroor, 'Unpacking'.
76. United Nations Environment Programme (UNEP), 2014, 'Sand, Rarer than One Thinks'.
77. In their monograph advocating for the conservation of beaches and prevention of sand-mining in beaches, Pilkey and Cooper write, 'No data from widespread deserts are available to support this concern, and since desert sand comes from many sources, it is likely that at least some of it is suitable for concrete. Finding a desert-sand source for construction will likely require prospecting to find properly shaped grains. We believe that the alleged unsuitability of desert sand may be an urban legend.' Pilkey and Cooper, *Last Beach*, 34.
78. Welland, *Sand*, 244–5.
79. Padmalal and Maya, *Sand Mining*, 32–50.
80. Pilkey and Cooper, *Last Beach*, 33–4.
81. Owen, 'Sand'; Comaroff, 'Sand'; Vince Beiser, 'The World's Disappearing Sand', *New York Times* (23 June 2016).
82. MacLean, *Spatial Transformations*.

83. Interview with Captain Prasad M. Tendulkar (founder and managing director of Seacrest Marine Services), Mumbai, 5 November 2016.
84. Forty, *Concrete*, 70.
85. Arabian Cement Company incorporated in 1955, but there is some dispute as to whether production began then or later. See Taryal and Chowdhury, 'Cement', 80; El Gammal and El-Bushra, 'Manufacturing Industry', 159.
86. Qatar National Cement Factory. El-Mallakh, *Qatar*; Crystal, *Oil and Politics*, 158.
87. Kuwait Cement Company. kuwaitcement.com.
88. Yemen Bajil Cement factory was built with a loan from the USSR. yemenweb.com.
89. Union Cement Company. Ghanem, *Industrialization*, 54.
90. Oman Cement. oxfordbusinessgroup.com. An earlier date of 1973 has also been claimed. See Kéchichian, 'A Vision of Oman', 118.
91. Bahrain Falcon Cement Factory. falcon-cement.com.

3 – Palimpsests of Law and Corporate Sovereigns

1. Harlaftis, 'Onassis'; Evans, *Ari*; Lilly, *Fabulous Greeks*.
2. Lilly, *Fabulous Greeks*, 112.
3. 'Correspondence and Newspaper Clipping Relating to an Oil Agreement with the Saudi Government'; 5/3/13/4 Aristotle Onassis; St John Philby Papers, Middle East Archives; St Antony's College, Oxford.
4. Harlaftis, 'Onassis', 265.
5. Lippmann, *Arabian Knight*, 271–2.
6. Joesten, *Onassis*, 177.
7. Joesten, *Onassis*, 180.
8. Evans, *Ari*, 133.
9. Citino, 'Saudi–Onassis', 147.
10. Citino, 'Saudi–Onassis', 149.
11. Lilly, *Fabulous Greeks*, 131–33.
12. Harlaftis, 'Onassis', 267.
13. Lippmann, *Arabian Knight*, 271–2.
14. 'No. 219 Statement of Policy by the National Security Council; NSC5428' (23 July 1954), Foreign Relations of the

United States 1952–1954, The Near and Middle East, Volume IX, Part 1, Document 219.

15. 'No. 219 Statement of Policy by the National Security Council; NSC5428' (23 July 1954), Foreign Relations of the United States 1952–1954, The Near and Middle East, Volume IX, Part 1, Document 219, fn 5.
16. 'The Ambassador in Saudi Arabia (Wadsworth) to the Department of State' (4 November 1954), Foreign Relations of the United States, 1952–1954, The Near and Middle East, Volume IX, Part 1, Document No. 372.
17. 'The Secretary of State to the Embassy in Saudi Arabia' (27 December 1954), Foreign Relations of the United States, 1952–1954, The Near and Middle East, Volume IX, Part 1, Document No. 380.
18. Citino, 'Saudi–Onassis', 152.
19. 'Memorandum of a Conversation, Department of State, Washington, February 9, 1955', Foreign Relations of the United States, 1955–1957, Near East: Jordan-Yemen, Volume XIII, Document No. 164.
20. Schwebel, 'Onassis', 4.
21. Schwebel, 'Onassis', 6.
22. Schwebel, 'Onassis', 10.
23. Schwebel, 'Onassis', 11.
24. Schwebel, 'Onassis', 12.
25. Fraser, 'Arbitration', 199.
26. Bishop, *Lex Petrolea*, 23; Mann, '*Aminoil*', 217.
27. Dietrich, *Oil Revolution*, 113.
28. Noussia, *Confidentiality*.
29. Schwebel, *Justice*, 140.
30. Dolzer and Shreuer, *Principles*, 9.
31. Olivet and Eberhardt, *Crisis*; Claire Provost and Matt Kennard, 'The Obscure Legal System that Lets Corporations Sue Countries', *Guardian* (10 June 2015); 'The Arbitration Game: Governments Are Souring on Treaties to Protect Foreign Investors', *Economist* (11 October 2014). It is worth noting that some countries, Brazil among them, have refused to sign any agreements that have an investor-state dispute-settlement provision.
32. Asa Fitch, 'Djibouti Files Arbitration Against DP World Over Alleged Corruption in Port Deal', *Wall Street Journal* (9 July

2014); 'Yemen's Aden port to cancel DP World deal-official', *Reuters* (26 August 2012).

33. Simeon Kerr and Michael Peel, 'DP World Faces Loss of Yemen Port Deal', *Financial Times* (17 September 2012).
34. Brian O'Neill, 'Aden's Port in the Storm', Carnegie Endowment for International Peace blog (6 September 2012).
35. 'GAR 100; 10th Edition: Quinn Emanuel Urquhart & Sullivan' at *Global Arbitration Review* (6 March 2017), globalarbitrationreview.com; also see Quinn Emanuel Business Litigation Report 2012, jdsupra.com.
36. Simeon Kerr and John Aglionby, 'DP World accuses Djibouti of illegally seizing container terminal', *Financial Times* (23 February 2018).
37. 'Dubai State-Controlled Port Company Defeats Effort by Djibouti to Nix Concession Due to Alleged Corruption', *Investment Arbitration Reporter* (21 February 2017).
38. 'Djibouti Ordered to Pay DP World $530M in Port Dispute', *Maritime Executive* (5 April 2019).
39. Patrick McGeehan, 'Work at Terminals Untouched by Firestorm of Security Debate', *New York Times* (23 February 2006); 'The Wrong Way to Guard the Ports', *New York Times* (16 February 2006).
40. 'DP World Forced Sale of US Assets Worth $1bn-Plus', *Financial Times* (12 December 2006).
41. Leffler et al., *Deepwater Petroleum*, 6–7; Deepwater Horizon Commission, 'Staff Working Paper No. 1', 1–2.
42. Prescott, *Oceans*, 144.
43. United States v. California, 332 U.S. 19 (1947). Also see United States v. California, 381 U.S. 139 (1965).
44. '150 – Proclamation 2667 – Policy of the United States with Respect to the Natural Resources of the Subsoil and Sea Bed of the Continental Shelf September 28, 1945', Truman Presidential Library, presidency.ucsb.edu.
45. Asquith of Bishopstone on *Petroleum Development (Trucial Coast) Ltd. and the Sheikh of Abu Dhabi*.
46. 'Aide-Mémoire Regarding Demarcation of Shores and Territorial Waters by Governments of Iran, Saudi Arabia and Iraq and Their Relation to Proclamations to Be Issued by Rulers of Gulf States' (19 May 1949), R/15/5/267, India Office Records, British Library.

47. Albaharna, *Legal Status*, 279.
48. *Petroleum Development (Trucial Coast) Ltd. vs. the Sheikh of Abu Dhabi.*
49. US State Department, 'Maritime Jurisdiction', 135.
50. Neblett, '1958 Conference', 42.
51. *Ruler of Qatar v. International Marine Oil Company, Ltd.*
52. *Ruler of Qatar v. International Marine Oil Company, Ltd.*
53. 'Persian Gulf Concession Being Weighed in Paris', *Washington Post* (28 August 1951).
54. 'Memo from Foreign Office to Bahrain' (1 March 1952); FO 371/98431, UK National Archives.
55. 'Memo from RFG Sarelle to WLF Nuttall, Ministry of Fuel and Power' (11 March 1952); FO 371/98431, UK National Archives.
56. As oilman Edward Henderson wrote about Buraimi in his memoirs, 'I could see this was a struggle in the first place between oil companies, with governments becoming more and more involved.' Henderson, *Strange Eventful History*, 154.
57. 'Memo from British Agent to E.F. Henderson, Petroleum Development (Trucial Coast) Ltd.', (10 January 1950), IOR/R/15/4/9, India Office Records, British Library.
58. See for example, Alan Rush, 'Obituary: Edward Henderson', *The Independent* (4 May 1995).
59. 'Seabed Frontier between Bahrain and Saudi Arabia' (1957); FO 371/126934, UK National Archives.
60. 'Political Agreement between His Majesty's Government in the United Kingdom and the Central Mining and Investment Corporation Limited and the Superior Oil Company Regarding the Oil Concession Agreement with the Sheikh of Qatar' (17 January 1950); FO 371/82084, UK National Archives.
61. Even where the oil companies were not owned by their respective home states, they acted closely in concert with the home state government officials, as was the case with Aramco, for example and the US, until Aramco was purchased by the Saudi government. See Mitchell, *Carbon Democracy* and Vitalis, *America's Kingdom*.
62. *Petroleum Development (Trucial Coast) Ltd. and the Sheikh of Abu Dhabi*. Italics in the original.

63. Bishara, *Sea of Debt*, 9.
64. Bishara, *Sea of Debt*, 13. See also Hussin, 'Circulations of Law'.
65. Keene, *Anarchical Society*, 54–5.
66. Porras, 'Grotius and the Law of Prize'.
67. British legal imperialist Henry Sumner Maine, quoted in Keene, *Anarchical Society*, 77.
68. Bishara, *Sea of Debt*, 17.
69. 'Continental Shelf and Marine Area' IOR/R/15/5/267, Indian Office Records, British Library.
70. Christopher Pinto of Sri Lanka in Alexander, *Developing Countries*, 3–13.
71. Maureen Franssen of the US in Alexander, *Developing Countries*, 14–15. It is worth noting that at the time, the conference was discussing seabed manganese nodules because of the publicity around a seabed mining ship partially owned by the Hughes Corporation, *Glomar Explorer*. In reality, however, *Glomar Explorer*'s manganese mission was a cover for a CIA project to raise a sunken Soviet submarine. See Polmar and White, *Project Azorian*; Varner and Collier, *Glomar Explorer*.
72. Interestingly, it was a US government lawyer who brought up this point. John Laylin in Alexander, *Developing Countries*, 25–8.
73. Zuhair Mikdashi of Lebanon in Alexander, *Developing Countries*, 80.
74. Sergio Thompson-Flores of Brazil in Alexander, *Developing Countries*, 40–2.
75. Emery, 'Geological Aspects', 138.
76. The last census of such zones in 2007 by the International Labour Organisation, counted some 3,500 EPZs (or such zones with similar names), excluding some 5,000 single-factory EPZs in Bangladesh alone. 'How to promote decent work and workers' rights in export processing zones' (20 November 2017), ilo.org.
77. Interestingly, no British home ports were free ports.
78. Thoman, *Free Ports*, 10–11; Ornestein, 'Foreign Trade Zones'.
79. In the Arab world, Beirut and Tripoli had been free ports since 1933. Beirut also revamped its free zone laws in the

early 1970s. 'New Free Zone Regime in the Port of Beirut', *Al Bayan* magazine (December 1972).

80. Fattah, *Regional Trade*, 25; Fuccaro, *City and State*, 57.
81. W.H. Adams, 'Minutes of Discussion Regarding Halcrow's Survey of Dubai and Sharjah Creeks' (28 January 1955); FO 371/114696, UK National Archives.
82. Richard Bolin, in a Q&A session transcribed in Royall, 'Marketing Your Zone', 25.
83. Neveling, 'Export Processing Zones', 68.
84. Neveling, 'Export Processing Zones', 68.
85. 'Free Zones and Their Role in Strengthening Economic Development', *Al Thawra* (24 October 1971).
86. Usama Ghayth, 'A True Evaluation of Infitah Projects', *Al Ahram* (24 September 1976).
87. For more information see sinewswartrade.com.
88. Ong, *Neoliberalism*, 103. Also see Ogle, 'Archipelago'; Palan, *Offshore World*.
89. Moore, *Doing Business*, 96.
90. 'Amendment of the law of Customs, Duties, Taxes and Tariffs and Establishment of Free Zones', *Aden* (9 December 1970); 'Mahmoud Ashish discusses soundness and importance of new economic steps', *Aden* (14 October 1970).
91. Meyer-Reumann Legal Consultancy, 'Yemen Free Zones', 403.
92. Ramos, *Dubai Amplified*, 110.
93. 'Interview: One Billion Dollars to Establish Free Zone in Dubai: Mahdi al Tajir Discusses Free Zone and Employment Policy', *Akhbar Dubay* (17 January 1974).
94. Nazik al-Muhammadi, 'Work Has Started on the World's Biggest Man-Made Port in the Jabal Ali Area', *Al-Ittihad* (23 November 1976).
95. Wilson, *Rashid's Legacy*, 488; Ghanem, *Industrialisation Problems*, 67–8.
96. Keshavarzian, 'Free Trade Zones', 274–75; Catherine Wallis, 'Dubai, Sharjah Comply with Unified Customs Rules', *Gulf Mirror* (15 May 1982).
97. 'Dubai Government Allows the Founding of Global Corporations in Jabal Ali Free Zone', *Al Hayat* (7 October 1992).
98. Keshavarzian, 'Free Trade Zones', 275–6; 'Barter Is Right!', *Khaleej Times* (9 January 1984).

99. 'One Third Damaged Tankers Docked off UAE Coast', *Asharq al-Awsat* (14 November 1984); 'Dispute with Lloyd's Over Insurance Rates', *Al Mustaqbal* (4 August 1984).
100. Cable and Weston, *South Asia's Exports to the EEC*, 10–11.
101. Cable and Weston, *South Asia's Exports to the EEC*, 127–28.
102. Arun Solomon, 'Garment Units Look for Quota-Free Bases', *Gulf News* (1 May 1989).
103. Bin Sulayem, 'Jabal Ali Free Zone', 71.
104. Qasrawi, *Foreign Direct Investment*, 15.
105. Qasrawi, *Foreign Direct Investment*, 49–50. Historically, such requirement for local agents allowed the rulers to protect their allies among the merchants from having to compete with corporate interests from overseas but also by giving them sole rights for importation of goods. Hanieh, *Capitalism and Class*, 75.
106. Ziadah, 'Humanitarian Logistics'; 'Constructing a Logistics Space'; Roh, *Humanitarian Aid*.
107. Qasrawi, *Foreign Direct Investment*, 55.
108. Pampanini, *Jubail and Yanbu*, 13.
109. 'Massive Sums Earmarked for Al Jubail Projects', *Al Madina* (21 August 1975); 'Al Jubail Port to be Expanded', *Al Madina* (28 August 1975).
110. 'Yanbu Given Higher Priority in Light of Gulf Troubles', *8 Days* (21 March 1981).
111. Pampanini, *Jubail and Yanbu*, 21.
112. Al-Gain and D'Emidio, 'Industrial Complexes', 75.
113. Jubail's Commercial Seaport is managed by Sharjah-based Gulftainer, while the King Fahd Industrial Port is operated by Jeddah-based Gulf Stevedoring Contracting Co (which is 51 per cent owned by Gulftainer). Peter Shaw-Smith, 'Gulf Stevedoring Sees Strong Throughput at Saudi Arabia's Jubail Terminal', *IHS Fairplay* (6 February 2018).
114. Pampanini, *Jubail and Yanbu*, 53–9.
115. Walker, 'Gulf War Impacts', 280.
116. EY, 'Economic Cities – Opening Vistas of Growth in the Kingdom of Saudi Arabia', 2015.
117. Khalil Hanware, 'PetroRabigh Exports First Shipment from King Abdullah Port', *Arab News* (6 January 2014).
118. 'King Abdullah Economic City: Brave Ideas, Shaky Sand', Wikileaks Diplomatic Cables (10 December 2007).

119. 'Saudi Arabia Builds City from Scratch', *DW* (10 April 2018).
120. 'New "King Abdullah Economic City" on the Red Sea: The Dubai of the Future or White Elephant?' Wikileaks Diplomatic Cables (23 August 2006).
121. Peter Waldman, 'The $2 Trillion Project to Get Saudi Arabia's Economy Off Oil', *Bloomberg* (21 April 2016).
122. Kingdom of Saudi Arabia, *Vision 2030*, 50.
123. 'Egypt Signs $10bn Deal with Saudi Arabia to Support Neom Project', *Arab News* (6 March 2018).
124. Glen Carey, Vivian Nereim and Christopher Cannon, 'Sun, Sea and Robots: Saudi Arabia's Sci-Fi City in the Desert', *Bloomberg* (26 October 2017).

4 – Roads and Rails Leading Away

1. Rodney, *Underdeveloped*, 209.
2. Harry St John Philby, however, writes that the line between Medina and Amman in Jordan was used in 1924, while the segment between Ma'an and Aqaba in Transjordan was used in the Second World War by the British military. Philby, 'Hijaz Railway', 588.
3. Mahan, 'Persian Gulf', pp. 217–18.
4. Many Saint-Simonians had been inspired by Michel Chevalier's 1832 pamphlet 'The Mediterranean System', which saw steam, rail, and canals in Suez and Panama as modernity and progress. Pilbeam, *Saint-Simonians*, 110–11; 133.
5. Vilma, 'Transport in Levant', 64.
6. Vilma, 'Transport in Levant', 67.
7. Shorrock, 'Railroad Question', 135
8. Such a railroad was not constructed. Iran, however, acquired a railroad during World War II as a logistics line from the Gulf to supply the Soviet Union.
9. Lord Curzon quoted in Stratton, 'British Railways 1918–1930', 117.
10. Wilminton, *Middle East Supply Centre*, 129.
11. Luxemburg, *Accumulation*, 401–402.
12. Letter dated 16 September 1945, McIntosh Papers, Box 3, Folder 35, Georgetown University Archives.
13. Baltimore, *Automobility*, 70.
14. 'Sharqieh Ltd.: Account with Ford Motor Co. (1932–1934)',

Box 32, Folder 2, Philby papers, Middle East Centre Archives, St Antony's College, Oxford; Field, *The Merchants*, 36.

15. Sanger, *Arabian Peninsula*, 12.
16. The statistics include the first and the most recent numbers reported in International Road Federation, *World Road Statistics* 1967–2018.
17. Munif, *Cities of Salt*, 461–2.
18. Aramco Annual Report 1944, Mulligan Papers, Box 3, Folder 43, Georgetown University Archives.
19. Khalili, 'Infrastructural Power'; Grathwol and Moorhus, *US Army Corps of Engineers*.
20. 'The Minister in Saudi Arabia (Eddy) to the Secretary of State' (24 March 1945), Foreign Relations of the United States: Diplomatic Papers, 1945, The Near East and Africa, Volume VIII Document 849.
21. Menoret, *Joyriding in Riyadh*, 7.
22. 'Pinhead Railway from Dammam to Dhahran Planned by Arabian-American Oil Company, 1946–1947' (29 November 1947), R/15/2/475, India Office Records, British Library.
23. Memorandum from Bahrain Residency to Foreign Office and to Jedda (29 December 1946), R/15/2/475, India Office Records, British Library. Also see C.L. Sulzberger, 'US Oil Towns Dot Saudi Arabian Soil', *New York Times* (28 November 1946).
24. Sanger, *Arabian Peninsula*, 39.
25. Gildea had worked for Union Pacific before World War II and during the war had been an operations manager on the Iranian railroad. See James H. Gildea Middle East Railroad Collection, Bernath Mss 219. Department of Special Collections, Davidson Library, University of California, Santa Barbara.
26. 'Trans-Arabian Rail Link Plan Takes New Step', *Washington Post* (21 April 1952); 'Telegram from the Department of State to the Embassy in Saudi Arabia' (5 March 1955); Foreign Relations of the United States, 1955–1957, Near East: Jordan-Yemen, Volume XIII, Document 166.
27. Stanley Swinton, 'U.S. Capital Modernizes Saudi Arabia', *Washington Post* (17 July 1949).
28. Aramco Annual Reports for 1955 and 1959, Mulligan Papers, Box 3, Folder 43, Georgetown University Archives.

29. Rodney, *Underdeveloped*, 209.
30. Rawls, *Aramco*, 175.
31. International Road Federation, *World Road Statistics*, 1953–2016. Though the Federation began collating the statistics in 1953, Saudi Arabia and Kuwait only began reporting their road statistics in 1967. Also see Table 4.1.
32. Abdo, 'Development of Transport', 175.
33. Abdo, *Kuwait*, 159.
34. Abdo, *Kuwait*, 138.
35. Abdo, *Kuwait*, 93. Also see Al-Nakib, *Kuwait*.
36. Fuccaro, *City and State*, 198.
37. Belgrave, *Personal Column*, 85.
38. Henderson, *Strange Eventful History*, 92.
39. 'Muscat Roads' in Crawford Papers, SAD.504/3/159–205; Durham University Archives.
40. Takriti, *Monsoon Revolution*, 45.
41. Takriti, *Monsoon Revolution*, 304.
42. Owtram, *Oman*, 201.
43. Limbert, *Time of Oil*, 36.
44. Christopher Dickey, 'U.S. Firm, Headed by Ex-CIA Man, Provides Oman More than Stability', *Washington Post* (27 April 1986).
45. 'TTI Origins and Early Oman – Political Situation in Oman – Investment in Dhofar' (31 January 1972), Critchfield Papers, Box 13, Folder 3, Georgetown University Archives.
46. 'Memorandum from the President's Assistant for National Security Affairs (Brzezinski) and the Director of the Office of Management and Budget (McIntyre) to President Carter' (1 April 1980), Foreign Relations of the United States, 1977–1980, Volume XVIII, Middle East Region; Arabian Peninsula, Document 68.
47. Grathwol and Moorhus, *US Army Corps of Engineers*, 525.
48. Christopher Cavas, 'Interview: Vice Adm. John Miller', *Defense News* (4 March 2015).
49. Baldry, 'Saudi-Yemeni War of 1934'.
50. Villiers, *Sons of Sinbad*, 50.
51. 'Telegram from the Department of State to the Embassy in Saudi Arabia' (5 December 1957); Foreign Relations of the United States, 1955–1957, Near East: Jordan-Yemen, Volume XIII, Document 435.

52. 'Memorandum from the President's Assistant for National Security Affairs (Kissinger) to President Nixon' (19 December 1969), Foreign Relations of the United States, 1969–1976, Volume XXIV, Middle East Region and Arabian Peninsula, 1969–1972; Jordan, September 1970; Document 177.
53. 'Memorandum from the Assistant Secretary of State for Near Eastern and South Asian Affairs (Sisco) to Secretary of State Rogers' (12 May 1971), Foreign Relations of the United States, 1969–1976, Volume XXIV, Middle East Region and Arabian Peninsula, 1969–1972; Jordan, September 1970; Document 184.
54. International Development Association, 'Report and Recommendation', 6.
55. IDA, 'Report and Recommendation', 5. Kuwait Fund for Arab Economic Development was established in 1961 and until the 1970s provided aid only to Arab states in the shape of loans at concessional rates. On the Fund's aid to both North and South Yemen, see Moubarak, 'Kuwait Fund', 543; Demir, *Arab Development Funds*, 9–19.
56. Slot, 'French Relations', 19.
57. Lancaster and Lancaster, *Life before Oil*, 55–6.
58. Al-Uways, *Khawr Dubay*, 72.
59. Al-Fahim, *Rags to Riches*, 81.
60. MacLean, *Spatial Transformations*, 160.
61. Heard-Bey, *Trucial States*, 330.
62. Heard-Bey, *Trucial States*, 331.
63. 'European and Gulf Experts Discuss Ports', *Al Bayan* (30 November 1991).
64. 'Security Assessment – The Gulf States; United Arab Emirates; Infrastructure', *Jane's Sentinel* (6 August 2015).
65. Ghazanfar Ali Khan, 'New Timeline for 2,177-km GCC Rail Project', *Arab News* (28 February 2016).
66. Paul McLoughlin, 'Gulf States Put Brakes on Joint-GCC Railway Plan', *Al Araby al Jadid* (4 May 2016).
67. 'Haramain High Speed Rail Opening Date in Jeopardy', *Railway Gazette* (2 February 2018).
68. Keith Barrow, 'GCC Railway to Link Four Gulf States by 2021', *International Railway Journal* (13 March 2018).
69. 'UAE to Have Rail Link with Saudi Arabia by End-2021 – Official', *Middle East Logistics* (14 March 2018); 'UAE

Announces Restart of Etihad Rail Scheme after 2 Year Hiatus', *Middle East Logistics* (11 Mar 2018).

5 – 'Mechanic, Merchant, King'

1. The title comes from W.H. Auden's *The Sea and the Mirror*.
2. Alan Cowell and Heather Timmons, 'Britain, the Continent and the Issue of Foreign Ownership', *New York Times* (1 December 2005).
3. Howarth and Howarth, *P&O*.
4. Munro, *Mackinnon*.
5. Joshi, *Dinshaw*, 53; 'Centenary of Cowasjee Dinshaw' in *Port of Aden Annual* 1954–1955, 30–2.
6. Munro, 'Shipping Subsidies', 216.
7. Quoted in Munro, *Mackinnon*, 155.
8. Jones, *Inchcape*.
9. Howarth and Howarth, *P&O*, 149.
10. Howarth and Howarth, *P&O*, 168–81.
11. Munro, *Mackinnon*, 159.
12. Except where indicated, the empirical material in BP shipping's story comes from BP Shipping, *Riding the Wave*.
13. Mitchell, *Carbon Democracy*.
14. Parra, *Oil Politics*, 86.
15. Tétreault, *Kuwait Petroleum Corporation*, 107.
16. 'D.P.C FitzPatrick, 'Conversation with Yusuf al Ghanim, 9th December 1956' in File Number 50, Public Relations Adviser (ARC106932); British Petroleum Archives; Warwick University.
17. Tétreault, *Kuwait Petroleum Corporation*, 107–10.
18. Walker, 'Gulf War Impacts', 279; Tétreault, *Kuwait Petroleum Corporation*, 131–2.
19. UNCTAD, *2016 Review of Maritime Transport*, 7.
20. Glick, *Trading with Saudi Arabia*, 6.
21. 'Hapag-Lloyd, UASC shipping merger weathers Qatar row: source' in *Reuters* (9 June 2017).
22. 'Typescript Trek Notes on the Persian Gulf' (March 1959); Crawford Papers SAD.504/3/240; Durham University Archives.
23. Memo from D.A. Roberts to S. Weir, 'Dubai Deepwater

Harbour' (11 August 1967); FO 1016/839, UK National Archives.

24. Zahlan, *Arab Construction Industry*, 73.
25. Zahlan, *Arab Construction Industry*, 107.
26. Zahlan, *Arab Construction Industry*, 28.
27. Zahlan, *Arab Consulting and Contracting Firms*, 194.
28. Glassman and Choi, 'The Chaebol'; Moon, 'Korean Contractors'; Khalili, 'Infrastructural Power'.
29. Zahlan, *Arab Consulting and Contracting Firms*, 134–5; 'Lists of British firms, Omani and other foreign businesses operating in Oman' (1 October 1973); Hawley Papers HAW 15/7/48–85; Durham University Archives.
30. Zahlan, *Arab Consulting and Contracting Firms*, 138–43; *Bulletin: Quarterly Magazine of Consolidated Construction Company* 115 (3Q 2015); 'CAP to Run the Port for Duqm for the Next 28 Years', *World Maritime News* (21 March 2014).
31. 'Typescript trek notes on the Persian Gulf' (March 1959); Crawford Papers SAD.504/3/228; Durham University Archives.
32. Al-Gurg, *Wells of Memory*, 110.
33. Michael Prest, 'Drydock prospects improve with management bid', *MEED* (22 July 1977).
34. Kanoo, *The House of Kanoo*, 122.
35. Al-Fahim, *Rags to Riches*, 75.
36. Smith, *Palestine and Palestinians*, 138.
37. Unless otherwise specified, the story of Gray Mackenzie is drawn from 'Charles Noble, Gray Mackenzie and Company, Ltd'; an official history (1973); Correspondence and notes concerning the history of the company and of its associates and subsidiaries, 1953–77 (MS27734A); Gray Mackenzie and Company Ltd. (CLC/B/123); Inchcape Group collection; London Metropolitan Archives.
38. 'Memo to FAK Harrison, Commonwealth Relations Officer, Downing Street' (8 March 1948), in 'Trade: Reports on Persian Gulf Market and trading possibilities', IOR/L/PS/12/3797, India Office Records, British Library.
39. Field, *The Merchants*, 285.
40. Stark, *Dust in the Lion's Paw*, 14.
41. Footman, *Besse*, 214–34.

42. Field, *The Merchants*, 314–20.
43. Field, *The Merchants*, 244–5.
44. Douwe Miedema, Shurna Robbins, Sarah White, 'Special Report: In $22 Billion Saudi Family Feud, Who Knew What?' *Reuters* (10 June 2011); Frank Kane, 'Saudi Arabia's Multibillion Corporate Collapse: Al-Gosaibi Exec on His Role in 8-Year Saga', *Arab News* (2 July 2017).
45. Sanger, *Arabian Peninsula*, 7; 10.
46. Field, *The Merchants*, 35.
47. Kanoo, *House of Kanoo*, 32–3; 'Conveyance of Mails at Bahrain' (12 August 1945); Indian Office Records IOR/R/15/2/1412; British Library, London; 'Shipping agents for foreign steamship companies' (28 February 1936), Indian Office Records, IOR/R/15/2/1383; British Library, London.
48. Kanoo, *House of Kanoo*, 171.
49. Field, *The Merchants*, 282–3.
50. Field, *The Merchants*, 285.
51. Kanoo, *House of Kanoo*, 229.
52. Kanoo, *House of Kanoo*, 228.
53. 'Typescript Trek Notes on Bahrain, Kuwait and Qatar' (31 May 1955); Crawford Papers SAD.504/3/112–57; Durham University Archives.
54. Field, *The Merchants*, 254–5.
55. al-Mumayyiz, *Al-Mamlaka*, 517–19.
56. 'Biographical Sketch of Abdullah ibn Darwish' (16 July 1962); William Mulligan Papers, Box 3, Folder 14; Georgetown Archives.
57. Kingston, 'Marine insurance'; Ralph, 'Slave insurance'; Ruprecht, 'Slavery and insurance'.
58. Al-Hijji, *Nuwakhuda*, 381–95.
59. Harlaftis, 'Onassis', 256; Stopford, *Maritime Economics*, 197–8.
60. Stopford, *Maritime Economics*, 199; Sibilia, 'Oceanic Accumulation'.
61. 'Shipping Portfolio League Table 2014', *Marine Money International* 2015.
62. Wilson, *Banking and Finance*, 3–13.
63. 'Possible Modification of the Political Agreement or Exclusion of the Shaikhs' Co-operation Thereafter';

Attachment to memo to the Political Resident in Bushire from Political Agent in Bahrain (27 June 1938), in 'Confidential 86/7 – ix B.52. P.C.L. TRUCIAL COAST' IOR/R/15/1/679, India Office Records, British Library.
64. Wilson, *Banking and Finance*, 48; Jones, *Banking and Oil*, 17.
65. Jones, *Banking and Oil*, 137–44; also see Malallah, *Al-Tarikh al Bahri*, 279–85; AbdulRahman, *Al-Imarat*, 243–45.
66. Jones, *Banking and Oil*, 156.
67. Jones, *Banking and Oil*, 160–8.
68. Kettell, 'Offshore Banking in Bahrain', 135.
69. Borscheid, 'Introduction', 5–7.
70. Kanoo, *House of Kanoo*; Twitchell, *Saudi Arabia*, 193–4.
71. Kanoo, *House of Kanoo*, 231.
72. IUMI, '2017 Statistical Report'.
73. Jakobsen et al., 'Maritime Capitals 2017'.
74. Lobo-Guerrero, 'Lloyd's and the Moral Economy'.
75. Al-Gurg, Wells of Memory, 80.
76. Wilson, *Rashid's Legacy*, 131.
77. Barney Gimbel, 'Searching for the Next Dubai' in *Fortune Magazine* (22 February 2008).
78. Field, *The Merchants*, 259.
79. Ghabra, *Palestinians in Kuwait*, 41.
80. Al-Gurg, *Wells of Memory*, 91.
81. Belgrave, *Personal Column*.
82. Simeon Kerr, 'Obituary: William Duff (1922–2014),' *Financial Times* (28 February 2014).
83. Galpern, *Money, Oil and Empire*, 208–9.
84. Vitalis, *America's Kingdom*; Khalili, 'Infrastructural Power'.
85. Kanoo, *House of Kanoo*, 152
86. Rossi, *Arabian Adventure*.
87. Cowen, *Deadly Life of Logistics*, 20.
88. Cohen, 'Boom Boxes'; also see Lawrence Wein, 'A Threat in Every Port', *New York Times* (14 June 2009).
89. Carafano et al., 'Maritime Security', 4.
90. Gregson, 'Logistics at Work', 344.
91. Rossiter, 'Coded Vanilla', 135; Cowen, *Deadly Life of Logistics*, 41.
92. Gerard, *50 Foot Blockchain*; Golumbia, *Politics of Bitcoin*.

93. Eric Johnson, 'Hurdles Make Blockchain Slow Burn for Container Shipping', *Journal of Commerce* (31 July 2018).

6 – Landside Labour

1. The account that will follow comes from C.L. Tucker to E.H.O. Elkington, 'Report on strike of AIOC workers, Aden, November 16th/December 11th, 1948' (10 January 1949); ARC7189, Aden, The Anglo-Iranian Oil Co Limited, BP Archives, Warwick. If other sources are used, they are footnoted. Also see Petouris, 'Aden Port Strikes of 1948'.
2. The same BP report enumerates the number of employees as follows: Port Trust (500 employees); Cory Bros (250); Cowasjee Dinshaw and Bros (600 in cargo and shipping section); Antoine Besse (1000); Luke Thomas (250); Caltex bunkering (200); P&O (30 employed in bunkering). AIOC itself employed 434 skilled and unskilled workers, many on the ports or in bunkering.
3. 'Memo from Errock in Kuwait to Earl Home at the Foreign Office' (3 July 1963); LAB 13/1597; UK National Archives.
4. 'Memo from Errock in Kuwait to Earl Home at the Foreign Office' (3 July 1963); LAB 13/1597; UK National Archives.
5. Nizan, *Aden Arabie*, 94–5.
6. Kanoo, *House of Kanoo*, 123–4.
7. R.S. Porter, 'Report of Census of Labour in Bahrain, 1956' (April 1957); LAB 13/1240; UK National Archives.
8. Kesterman, 'Ports in the Middle East', 317–18.
9. On subcontracting as a mode of discipline, see Appel, 'Offshore Work', 264.
10. 'Port of Kuwait; First Report on Organisation and Port Operations by G.T. Johnson' (19 November 1953); FO 371/104376; UK National Archives.
11. Rodney, *How Europe Underdeveloped Africa*, 209.
12. Cowen, *Deadly Life of Logistics*; Levinson, *The Box*.
13. Vitalis's *America's Kingdom* is the scholarly exposition of the internationalisation of the Jim Crow regime.
14. 'Letter from Don Hawley to Parents' (17 August 1958); Hawley papers HAW9/8/20–21; Durham University Archives.

15. Seccombe and Lawless, *Work Camps*; Seccombe, 'Italian Labour'; Vitalis, *America's Kingdom*.
16. Buckley, "Bachelor' Builders'; Gardner, *City of Strangers*; Gill, *Forced Labor*.
17. Van der Linden, 'Origins of Labor Management'.
18. Villiers, *Sons of Sinbad*, 283–4.
19. Daniels, *Kuwait Journey*, 22–3.
20. AbdulRahman, *Al-Imarat*, 248; 257.
21. Finnie, *Desert Enterprise*, 107–108.
22. Lancaster and Lancaster, *Life Before Oil*, 76. See also Abd al-Rahman, *Al-Imarat*, 33.
23. Finnie, *Desert Enterprise*, 93.
24. Kanoo, *House of Kanoo*, 133.
25. 'Monthly Report Kuwait Oil Company' (May 1947); RG 84; Box 10; Call number 845–63.6; 'Saudi Arabia, US Consulate, Dhahran', Economic Reports of US State Department; US National Archives.
26. On protests by local Saudis, see Shaykh Ya'qub, *Wujuh*, 12–43.
27. Mudayris, *Tatwwur*, 16–21; Al-Ghazali, *Al Jama'at*, 439–41.
28. Aramco Annual Reports 1948 and 1949, Mulligan Papers, Box 3, Folder 44, Georgetown University Archives. Aramco Annual Report 1950, Mulligan Papers, Box 3, Folder 45, Georgetown University Archives.
29. Al-Hamdi, *Harka al-Tahdith*, 119.
30. Aramco Annual Reports 1951 and 1953, Mulligan Papers, Box 3, Folder 43, Georgetown University Archives, 39.
31. Finnie, *Desert Enterprise*, 94.
32. Ghabra, *Palestinians in Kuwait*, 67–8.
33. Longhurst, *Adventures in Oil*, 220–2.
34. Smith, *Palestine and Palestinians*, 173.
35. Smith, *Palestine and Palestinians*, 115.
36. Mudayris, *Al-Harakat*, 18–19.
37. Beling, *Pan-Arabism and Labor*, 68.
38. 'Labour Situation in Abu Dhabi. Labatt Visit, 12–14 January 1969' (14 February 1969); RG 59; Box 1289 'Trucial States'; US Department of State Economic Reports; US National Archives.
39. 'Labour Situation in Abu Dhabi. Labatt Visit, 12–14 January 1969' (14 February 1969); RG 59; Box 1289 'Trucial States'; US Department of State Economic Reports; US National

Archives. Also see similar sentiments being fanned by the Kuwaiti state in Crystal, *Oil and Politics*, 1968.

40. See, for example, 'Aramco Labour' (1945–48); India Office Records IOR/R/15/2/885; British Library.
41. Longva, *Walls Built on Sand*, 106–7; Gardner, *City of Strangers*, 58–64; Vitalis, *America's Kingdom*, 272; Hanieh, *Capitalism and Class*, 61.
42. R.L. Morris, 'Dubai Ref 5/29/A' (20 December 1968); LAB 13/2165; UK National Archives.
43. R.L. Morris, 'Dubai Ref 5/29/A' (20 December 1968); LAB 13/2165; UK National Archives.
44. Grathwol and Moorhus, *Bricks, Sand and Marble*, 532–3.
45. Sasikumar and Martin, 'India–Gulf Labour Migration', 2–3.
46. Maria Botros, 'Meet the UAE's First Female Crane Operator, Aisha al Marzouqi', *Gulf News* (27 January 2015).
47. 'Jebel Ali Container Terminal 3 Inaugurated (UAE)', *World Maritime News* (28 January 2014).
48. 'Equipment Operator (Gantry Crane) (Saudi Female Only); Hutchison Ports Dammam' (9 May 2018); Website of Naukrigulf.com.
49. But also see Awwami, *Al-Haaka Al-Wataniyya*, Vo. 1, 77–276, for a comprehensive account of the strikes of 1953 and 1956 by a political sympathiser.
50. See Awwami, *Al Haraka al Wataniyya*; Al-Ghazali, *Al Jama'at*, 445–55; Mudayris, *Al Harakat*, 37–73.
51. Al-Rasheed, *Saudi Arabia*, 94. It is however important to note a dissent from this view. Yusif Makki argues that it was only after labour leaders were detained and imprisoned from 1956 onwards in 'Ubayd prison in Al-Ahsa' that their political education and attachment to the Ba'th party began. Makki, 'Hizb al-Ba'th', 293. Makki also dates strikes against *mat'am abu rub'* to the early 1960s. 'Hizb al-Ba'th', 295.
52. 'Fortnightly Review of Economic Development in Aden Colony, Aden Protectorate and Yemen for the Period November 16–30, 1958' (4 December 1958); Department of State–Aden; RG 59; Box 4523; Call number 846c.00/2–458; Economic Reports of the State Department; US National Archives.
53. Al-Khatib, *Kuwayt*, 173–5; Vitalis, *America's Kingdom*.
54. Finnie, *Desert Enterprise*, 102.

55. Beling, *Pan-Arabism and Labor*. 67.
56. Al-ʿAkri, *Dhakira*, 16.
57. Al-Ghazali, *Al Jamaʻat*, 450.
58. Footman, *Besse*, 191.
59. 'Annual Economic Review of Aden, 1955/1956' (9 May 1956); Department of State-Aden; RG59; Box 4523; Call number 846.00/3–156; Economic Reports of the State Department; US National Archives.
60. 'Social and Labour Developments in Qatar' (26 June 1965); LAB 13/2164; UK National Archives.
61. R.L. Morris, 'Persian Gulf Sheikhdoms' (13 June 1965); LAB 13/2165; UK National Archives.
62. Makki, 'Hizb al-Baʻth', 300.
63. C.J. Treadwell, 'Labour Troubles on Das Island' (20 April 1970); LAB 13/2165; UK National Archives.
64. See Bsheer, 'A Counter-Revolutionary State' for an extensive exposition of the nationalist, communist and other left forces in Saudi in those decades. Chalcraft, 'Migration and Popular Protest' and Matthiesen, 'Migration, Minorities' show the extent to which both foreign workers and nationals who had travelled to radical centres in the Arab world acted as messengers of revolt in the Arabian Peninsula. Al Ghazali, *Al Jama'at*, 453–5 analyses how circulation *within* the Peninsula itself was crucial for the formation of political movements.
65 'Aramco Labour' (1945–1948); India Office Records IOR/R/15/2/885; British Library.
66. Mudayris, *Al-Harakat*, 46; 49.
67. Daniels, *Kuwait Journey*, 57.
68. R.L. Morris, 'Persian Gulf Sheikhdoms' (13 June 1965); LAB 13/2165; UK National Archives.
69. Matthiesen, *The Other Saudis*; *Sectarian Gulf*.
70. R.L. Morris, 'Social and Labour Development in Abu Dhabi' (3 July 1965); LAB 13/2165; UK National Archives. Also see Al-Fahim, *Rags to Riches*, 115.
71. Bonnie Barron, 'Legal Blow for Families of Slain Nepali Laborers', *Courthouse News Service* (27 August 2013).
72. Watt, 'Labor Relations', 445.
73. 'State of Qatar: Report on Labour, Industrial and Social Development' (6 December 1968); LAB 13/2164; UK National Archives.

74. 'Fortnightly Review of Economic Development in Aden Colony, Aden Protectorate and Yemen for the Period August 16–31, 1958' (5 September 1958); Department of State-Aden; RG 59; Box 4523; Call number 846c.00/2–458; Economic Reports of the State Department; US National Archives.
75. 'Note of a discussion on Arab labour affairs at the US Embassy in Beirut' (9 December 1968); LAB 13/2165; UK National Archives.
76. 'From British Embassy in Beirut' (8 February 1969); LAB 13/2141; UK National Archives.
77. Boodrookas, 'Crackdowns and Coalitions'.
78. 'Note of a discussion on Arab labour affairs at the US Embassy in Beirut' (9 December 1968); LAB 13/2165; UK National Archives.
79. 'Port of Salalah Holds Union Elections' in *Times of Oman* (23 February 2013).
80. Sunil Vaidiya, 'PDO Employees Demand Dismissal of Trade Union; Seek Recognition of New Union to Serve Employees' Interests', *Gulf News* (8 June 2011).
81. B.C. Nelson, 'Aramco Employee Relations – Past, Present, Future' (N.D. but likely 1968), US Army Corps of Engineers, 77–92–02 Box 1 of 35; US National Archives.
82. 'State of Qatar: Report on Labour, Industrial and Social Developments' (6 December 1968); LAB 13/2164. UK National Archives. Incidentally, non-nationals were recruited for this job because they 'were prepared to live on dhows' rather than in proper housing.
83. 'Labour Problems in Bahrein and the Southern Gulf, Report of Visit to Bahrein 13–17 October 1966'; LAB 13/2163; UK National Archives.
84. Awwami's account of the 1953 and 1956 strikes has extraordinarily rich detail about the coercive force of the Saudi state. Awwami, *Al-Haaka Al-Wataniyya*, Vol 1, 77–276.
85. Ahmad al-Wasil, 2012. 'Al-Shuyui' al-atiq Ishaq al-Shaykh Yaqub' ('The Staunch Communist Ishaq Shaykh Yaqub') in *Jadaliyya*, jadaliyya.com; also see Vitalis, *America's Kingdom*, 154; Chalcraft, 'Migration and Popular Protest', 31–2.
86. 'Telegraph to Secretary of State' (19 January 1959);

Department of State-Aden; RG 59; Box 4523; Call number 846c.062/1–1559; Economic Reports of the State Department; US National Archives.

87. Telegram from Doha to Foreign Office (21 November 1961); LAB 13/1509; UK National Archives.
88. See the debates in Toscano, 'Lineaments'; 'Logistics and Opposition'; Bernes, 'Counterlogistics'; Degenerate Communism, 'Chokepoints'; Chua, 'Logistics' and of course, Cowen, *Deadly Life of Logistics*.
89. Cole, 'No Justice, No Ships'; Chua; 'Logistics'.
90. Bastashevski, 'Perfect Con'.
91. See press releases by Unite: 'London Gateway Port Poses Threat to Workers' Conditions' (12 February 2013); and 'Gateway Campaign Goes International' (13 November 2013) both at unitetheunion.org.
92. Fox-Hodess, 'Dock Worker Union Campaigns'.
93. Werner Bamberger, 'Zionist Tie Denied in Ship Picketing' in *New York Times* (21 April 1960).
94. Bilder, 'Trade Boycotts', 880–81fn184.
95. 'Second Federal Judge Refuses to Ban Picketing of Egyptian Ship' in *Jewish Telegraphic Agency* (20 April 1960).
96. 'Arabs Halt Picketing', *New York Times* (7 May 1960).
97. Bilder, 'Trade Boycotts', 879fn180; 'Arab Unions Vote U.S. Ship Boycott', *New York Times* (23 April 1960).

7 – Shipboard Work

1. James, *Mariners*, 26.
2. Foucault, 'Of Other Spaces', 27.
3. Rediker, *Outlaws*, 13.
4. McPhee, *Looking for a Ship*, 93.
5. Quoted in Sekula, *Fish Story*, 121.
6. McPhee, *Looking for a Ship*, 125.
7. Markkula, 'Any Port in a Storm'.
8. Fajardo, *Filipino Crosscurrents*.
9. Cited in Sherwood, 'Lascar Seamen', 229.
10. Balachandran, 'Circulation', 95.
11. Villiers, *Sons of Sinbad*, 297.
12. Sherwood, 'Lascar Seamen', 230–1.

13. Lawless, *From Ta'izz to Tyneside*, 74–153; Seddon, *Last of the Lascars*, 84–115, 156–79 ; Sherwood, 'Lascar Seamen'.
14. Sherwood, 'Lascar Seamen', 233.
15. Sherwood, 'Lascar Seamen', 241.
16. The longstanding connections are still present: Messageries Maritimes merged with Compagnie Générale Transatlantique to form Compagnie Générale Maritime in the 1970s, which was in turn acquired by Compagnie Maritime d'Affrètement (CMA) in 1996 to become CMA CGM.
17. Lawless, '"Adenese" Seamen', 78.
18. Lawless, 'Seamen's Agents', 42.
19. Lawless, 'Seamen's Agents', 35; '"Adenese" Seamen', 77. Also Seddon, *The Last of the Lascars*.
20. Ahuja, 'Mobility and Containment', 111.
21. Ahuja, 'South Asian Seamen', 119.
22. C.L. Tucker to E.H.O. Elkington, 'Report on strike of AIOC workers, Aden, November 16th/December 11th, 1948' (10 January 1949); ARC7189, Aden, The Anglo-Iranian Oil Co Limited, BP Archives, Warwick.
23. Ho, 'View from the Other Boat'; Bezabe, *Subjects of Empire*.
24. Villiers, *Sons of Sinbad*, 64–5.
25. Ahuja, 'South Asian Seamen', 125.
26. Raza and Zachariah, 'To Take Arms', 19.
27. Lawless, 'Seamen's Agents', 47.
28. Lawless, '"Adenese" Seamen', 92; 'Rules for Joint Supply Registration and Engagement of Somali and Arab Seamen' (17 July 1930) in File, 'Race Relations; Agreements with Shipping Companies' Document 175A/Box 154; the archives of National Union of Seamen, Warwick University Archives.
29. Quoted in Adi, 'The Comintern', 237.
30. Davies, 'From "Landsman" to "Seaman"', 876.
31. BP Shipping, *Riding the Waves*, 92–107.
32. Lilly, *Fabulous Greeks*, 63–4.
33. Longurst, *Adventures in Oil*, 239.
34. McKinsey, *Containerization*.
35. George Horne, 'The Tanker: Queen of the Seas' in *New York Times* (23 September 1956).
36. Bishara, 'No Country but the Ocean', 345

37. Mathew, *Margins of the Market*, 50–1.
38. Quoted in Carlisle, *Rough Waters*, 83. Also see Bishara, 'No Country but the Ocean'; Westlake, 'Muscat Dhows'.
39. Carlisle, *Rough Waters*, 87–115.
40. Carlisle, *Sovereignty for Sale*, 10–11.
41. Carlisle, *Sovereignty for Sale*, 118.
42. Quoted in Carlisle, *Sovereignty for Sale*, 113.
43. UNCTAD, *Maritime Review*, 21; BIMCO & ICS, *Manpower Report*.
44. William Depasupil, 'Filipino Seafarers Top Choice' in *Manila Times* (30 April 2016); Fajardo, *Filipino Crosscurrents*.
45. See George, *Deep Sea*, 119–38.
46. Strike Club Marine Delay Insurance brochure, thestrikeclub.com.
47. Greenway, *Cargo Liners*, 125.
48. Included in Seaman Church Institute Human Rights Project report, Appendix A, in Poisson, 'Seafarers', 10.
49. Muller, 'Strike of Crew Members'.
50. Greenway, *Cargo Liners*, 125.

8 – The Bounties of War

1. BP Shipping, *Riding the Wave*, 60.
2. Richard F Hunt, 'Capetown Gains from Suez Crisis', *New York Times* (3 February 1957).
3. Kathleen McLaughlin, 'Closing of Suez Reshaping Trade: Despite Similarities to 1956, New Patterns Developing', *New York Times* (20 August 1967).
4. Thomas Ronan, 'British Tea Habit Is Costlier One', *New York Times* (1 January 1957).
5. 'Emigration Wave Rises in Britain: Moves to Canada, Australia and New Zealand Laid to Economic Fears at Home', *New York Times* (7 December 1956).
6. 'US Asks for Release of Reserve Ships', *New York Times* (11 December 1956).
7. Tétreault discusses how the Kuwaiti government encouraged private investment in the KOTC, but does not mention the effect of the closure of Suez on the decision-making process that led to the firm's establishment. See Tétreault, *Kuwait Petroleum Corporation*, 108.

8. Hansen and Khairy, 'Suez', 103. 'Big Tonnage Rise in Tankers Seen', *New York Times* (10 August 1957).
9. 'Britain Prepares for Big Tankers', *New York Times* (9 June 1957).
10. Kenneth Love, 'British Study Shift of Base on Cyprus to Kenya or Aden', *New York Times* (23 June 1957).
11. Sylvan Fox, 'The Suez Canal: Not Indispensable but Often a Vital Timesaver', *New York Times* (7 June 1967).
12. Fox, 'The Suez Canal'.
13. Werner Banberger, 'Pressures Keep Cargo Rates High', *New York Times* (23 July 1967).
14. Carey, 'Iran', 147.
15. Kathleen McLaughlin, 'Closing of Suez Reshaping Trade: Despite Similarities to 1956, New Patterns Developing', *New York Times* (20 August 1967).
16. Wilcke, 'World's Commerce Learns to Bypass Suez Canal', *New York Times* (6 November 1967).
17. Wilcke, 'World's Commerce Learns to Bypass Suez Canal'.
18. Klinghoffer, 'Soviet Oil Politics'.
19. Farnsworth, Clyde H., 'Busy Europe and Mideast Ports Cast Doubts on Oil Cut's Effects', *New York Times* (22 December 1973).
20. Tétreault, *Kuwait Petroleum Corporation*, 51–2.
21. Lewis, 'The Great Powers', 645. Emphasis added.
22. Farnsworth, Clyde H., 'Busy Europe and Mideast Ports Cast Doubts on Oil Cut's Effects', *New York Times* (22 December 1973).
23. *L'Orient Le Jour,* 22 and 25 October 1973 quoted in Galvani et al., 'October War'.
24. Salih al-Salih, 'No long delays at present for ships waiting outside port', *Al Siyasa* (21 November 1973).
25. John Kifner, 'Life among the ruins in Beirut', *New York Times Magazine* (6 December 1981).
26. Joseph Fitchett, 'Fighting Dims Beirut's Regional Role', *Washington Post* (25 November 1975).
27. Marvine Howe, 'Beirut Showing Signs of Recovery from Wounds of War', *New York Times* (26 May 1977).
28. Wilson, *Banking and Finance*, 99–100; Brand, 'Shifting Alliances', 408.
29. Joseph Fitchett, 'Oil Boom Times Over, Abu Dhabi Is

Undergoing Slump', *Washington Post* (30 October 1977); Wilson, *Banking and Finance*, 120.
30. George H. Cord, 'Persian Gulf's Would-Be Wall Street', *New York Times* (4 June 1978).
31. Brand, 'Shifting Alliances', 408.
32. 'Huge Belfast Shipyard May Shut', *New York Times* (8 November 1975).
33. Terry Robards, 'The Oil Powers Assemble a Fleet', *New York Times* (23 March 1975).
34. Walker, 'Gulf War Impacts'.
35. Walker, 'Gulf War Impacts', 276.
36. Walker, 'Gulf War Impacts', 278.
37. Navias and Hooton, *Tanker Wars*, 66.
38. Mofid, 'Financing the Peace', 52.
39. Navias and Hooton, *Tanker Wars*, 74–5, 83.
40. Chin, *Royal Navy*, 187.
41. Navias and Hooton, *Tanker Wars*, 139.
42. Navias and Hooton, *Tanker Wars*, 144.
43. Ulrichsen, *Gulf States*, 188.
44. Navias and Hooton, *Tanker Wars*, 183.
45. Jones, 'After the Pipelines'.
46. US Supreme Court, *Benito Estenger*, No. 192. 176 U.S. 568.
47. Mount, 'Prize Cases', 329.
48. Snipes, 'Re-flagged Kuwaiti Tankers', 29–30.
49. Snipes, 'Re-flagged Kuwaiti Tankers', 26.
50. Pratap Chatterjee, 'Dubai Does Brisk War Business', *CorpWatch* (24 February 2006).
51. Menarchik, *Powerlift*, 150.
52. Brown, *U.S. Marines in the Persian Gulf*, 55.
53. Kanoo, *The House of Kanoo*, 249–50. Kanoo also served the British and French sea-lift during Desert Shield.
54. Pampanini, *Jubail and Yanbu*, 99.
55. Pampanini, *Jubail and Yanbu*, 100.
56. Matina Stevis-Gridneff, 'Global Powers Race for Position in Horn of Africa', *Wall Street Journal* (1 June 2018).
57. Mahan, 'Persian Gulf', 224–5.
58. Mahan, 'Persian Gulf', 237.
59. Howard, 'East of Suez', 180.
60. Page, *Soviet Union and the Yemens*, 29.
61. Page, *Soviet Union and the Yemens*, 64.

62. Tackney, 'Dealing Arms', 8.
63. Vine, *Island of Shame*, 78.
64. CIA, 'Soviet Military Reach', 17.
65. Chadda, *Paradox of Power*, 76.
66. Stork and Paul, 'Arms Sales', 8.
67. Bliddal, *RDJTF*, 1.
68. Bliddal, *RDJTF*, 37.
69. Menarchik, *Powerlift*, 7; Chadda, *Paradox of Power*, 143.
70. Kingston, 'U.S. Central Command'.
71. Stork and Wenger, 'U.S. in the Persian Gulf'. Incidentally, Ras al Mish'ab had been the landing point for the material Aramco needed to build the TAPLine some thirty years before.
72. Kingston, 'U.S. Central Command'.
73. Khalili, 'Infrastructural Power'.
74. Lefebvre, 'U.S. Military Hegemony'.
75. Menarchik, *Powerlift*, 175.
76. Department of Defense, 'Base Structure Report', 84.
77. Department of Defense, 'Base Structure Report', 68.
78. Department of Defense, 'Base Structure Report', 70.
79. Katzman, *UAE*, 17; Nick Webster, 'US Aircraft Carrier Takes a Break in Dubai from Anti-Terror operations', *National* (4 March 2018).
80. Heibel, 'Support to the Warfighter', 8–9.
81. On opposition to US bases see Vine, *Island of Shame*; Cooley, *Base Politics*; Lutz, *Bases of Empire*, and especially Holmes, 'American Navy in Bahrain'.
82. Cordesman et al., *The Gulf*, 36.
83. Holmes, 'American Navy in Bahrain'.
84. McCartney, *Bechtel*, 113–25.
85. Henderson, *Strange Eventful History*.
86. Chatterjee, *Halliburton's Army*.
87. Elaine Burridge, 'PWC Logistics Evolves into Agility', *ICIS Chemical Business* (20 November 2006); Mike Scott, 'Company Staff Earn Bonus in Disaster Relief', *Financial Times* (13 October 2006).
88. Pratap Chatterjee, 'Agility Fraud Claim Points to Shell Game', *Asia Times* (4 February 2010); Walter Pincus, 'Agency Extends Contract for Firm that Hired Its Former Director', *Washington Post* (5 January 2011).

89. Kathleen Miller, 'U.S. Seeks to Debar Federal Contractors', *Washington Post* (26 December 2011); 'Agility Results Show Effect of US Indictment', *Business Monitor Online* (19 August 2011).
90. 'Kuwait Investing in Freight Transport Growth', *Business Monitor Online* (8 March 2013); 'Agility Looks to Arab Spring States', *Business Monitor Online* (12 September 2012).
91. Cowen, *Deadly Life of Logistics*.
92. Khalili, 'Pacifying Urban Insurrections'; 'Scholar, Pope, Soldier, Spy'.
93. David Feitch, 'Erik Prince: Out of Blackwater and Into China', *Wall Street Journal* (24 January 2014).
94. Mark Mazzetti and Eric Schmitt, 'Private Army Formed to Fight Somali Pirates Leaves Troubled Legacy', *New York Times* (4 October 2012).
95. Don Weinland and Charles Clover, 'Citic Boosts Stake in Erik Prince's Security Group Frontier', *Financial Times* (5 March 2018).
96. Paul Davies, 'Prince of Logistics: Ex-Blackwater Chief Looks to China-Africa', *Financial Times* (14 January 2014).
97. George Chen, 'Into Africa: Ex-Navy SEAL Sets Trail for Investors', *South China Morning Post* (19 November 2012).
98. Erik Prince, 'A Public-Private Partnership Will Solve Europe's Migrant Crisis', *Financial Times* (3 January 2017); Matthew Cole and Jeremy Scahill, 'Erik Prince in the Hot Seat', *Intercept* (24 March 2016); Joseph Cotterill, 'Mozambique's Prosecutor Opens Case into $2bn Hidden Loans Scandal', *Financial Times* (29 January 2018).
99. Kennedy, *The Rise and Fall of the Great Powers*; van Creveld, *Supplying War*.
100. Cowen, *Deadly Life of Logistics*, 163–70.
101. Andrew Tilghman, 'The U.S. Military Is Moving into These 5 Bases in the Philippines', *Military Times* (21 March 2016).

Epilogue

1. Scott Paul, '"If the World Knows, They'll Stop the War": Reflections from Southern Yemen', *justsecurity.org* (14 May 2018).

2. Andrew England and Simeon Kerr, 'UAE attacks on Yemen reveal fractures in Saudi-led coalition', *Financial Times* (29 August 2019).
3. 'Saudi Arabia "to Build Oil Port" in Yemen's al-Mahra: Sources', *Al Jazeera* (20 August 2018).

Index

Note on alphabetisation

Arab names beginning with al- are alphabetised under the first letter of the main name; e.g. al-Khobar appears under K.

Royal or princely Arab families are alphabetised under their family name; e.g. the Al Saud, Abdulaziz is alphabetised under S. 'Al' here indicates 'house of'.

Ship names are italicised and alphabetised under vessel names rather than maritime prefixes such as *MV* (merchant vessel), *HMS* (His/Her Majesty's Ship) *RIMS* (Royal Indian Marine Ship), *SS* (steamship), etc.; e.g. *MV Umm Casbah* is alphabetised under U.